THE CLOTHING TRADE IN PROVINCIAL
ENGLAND, 1800–1850

Perspectives in Economic and Social History

Series Editors: *Andrew August*
                                   Robert E. Wright

Titles in this Series

Forthcoming Titles

Welfare and Old Age in Europe and North America: The Development of
Social Insurance
Bernard Harris (ed.)

Financing India's Imperial Railways, 1875–1914
Stuart Sweeney

THE CLOTHING TRADE IN PROVINCIAL ENGLAND, 1800–1850

BY

Alison Toplis

Routledge
Taylor & Francis Group

LONDON AND NEW YORK

First published 2011 by Pickering & Chatto (Publishers) Limited

Published 2016 by Routledge
2 Park Square, Milton Park, Abingdon, Oxfordshire OX14 4RN
711 Third Avenue, New York, NY 10017, USA

First issued in paperback 2015

Routledge is an imprint of the Taylor & Francis Group, an informa business

BRITISH LIBRARY CATALOGUING IN PUBLICATION DATA

Toplis, Alison.
The clothing trade in provincial England, 1800–1850. – (Perspectives in economic and social history)
1. Clothing trade – England – History – 19th century. 2. Clothing trade – England – History – 19th century – Sources.
I. Title II. Series
338.4'7687'0942'09034-dc22

ISBN-13: 978-1-138-66444-9 (pbk)
ISBN-13: 978-1-8489-3116-9 (hbk)

Typeset by Pickering & Chatto (Publishers) Limited

CONTENTS

In memory of my father, Ian Toplis

ACKNOWLEDGEMENTS

This book has had a long genesis, ultimately a seed sewn when I undertook my MA in the History of Dress at the Courtauld Institute of Art many years ago. My thanks to Aileen Ribeiro for her guidance there and for consistently giving me working dress topics to research, engaging my interest in an area which I hope has finally borne fruit. My current research derives from my PhD thesis undertaken at the University of Wolverhampton.

I would like to thank the staff of Worcester Record Office, Hereford Record Office, Worcester Family History Centre, Hereford Local Studies Library, Hereford Museum, Malvern Library, University of Wolverhampton Learning Centre and Colwall Library for their help; specifically, Althea Mackenzie and Catherine Willson at Hereford Museum for their expertise and time; Daire Carr, my editor at Pickering and Chatto; and the University of Wolverhampton for their financial support during the writing of my thesis and now as an honorary research fellow.

I am grateful for the permission to reproduce illustrations for this book from Worcestershire Record Office, Herefordshire Heritage Services, Malcolm Dyer on behalf of The Dyer Collection, Chepstow Museum and Worcester City Council.

I thank the Pasold Research Fund, firstly for giving me a grant to help research part of chapter 3 at the National Archives and secondly, for allowing me to reproduce parts of chapter 1 and chapter 2 which have appeared in *Textile History*, 40:2 (2009), as the article 'The Manufacture and Provision of Rural Garments, 1800-1850: a Case Study of Herefordshire and Worcestershire'.

I owe a huge debt of gratitude to the supervisory team for my thesis who set me off on this journey, Margaret Ponsonby, Malcolm Wanklyn and especially Laura Ugolini, without whom this would not have been possible, and who has given me a measure of the standard I would like to one day reach. John Benson, Steve King, Ian Mitchell and John Styles have also added much to this work with their insightful comments and criticisms. Also, I am extremely grateful to Rebecca Arnold for her inspiration and intellectual support and the two anonymous reviewers who made me think hard once more about what I wanted to write.

The support and encouragement of my family has been unconditional, John, Isobel and specifically Milly, whose life has been bounded by this research.

All mistakes are entirely my own.

LIST OF FIGURES

INTRODUCTION

In 1835, the editor of the *Hereford Journal* received a letter railing against the spending habits of female servants, particularly their clothing purchases, and the downward spiral of moral decline that this led them into:

> All articles of consumption among female servants in particular are nearly fifty per cent cheaper than during the war ... [and there is an] extraordinary highness of wages [for female servants] ... there are few tradesmen or farmers' daughters having no other dependance [*sic*] who think they can afford to put upon their backs clothing to the same amount as an ordinary servant can ... the consequence is that servants are now *eaten out with pride* ... besides, the vanity of mind induced by dress, produces that *fickleness of disposition*[1]

The writer's particular grievance seems to be the (in his or her opinion) excessive wages paid to servants. However, the comments echoed much criticism of how working people, especially servants, had dressed above their social station since the seventeenth century.[2] The fact they were expressed once more in a provincial newspaper shows that such views were still current in the 1830s. However, the debate had shifted slightly. As well as criticizing the blurring of social divisions, the letter pointed out the irresponsible behaviour of the servants and the effect this had on those around them. The letter-writer went on to criticize the Poor Law, suggesting that it offered too much support to the rest of the family, leaving female servants to spend money on their own clothes and enjoy life, instead of looking after their aged parents.[3] The focus was on individual consumption of goods, such as clothing, to cultivate sociability outside the home, so neglecting the long-term needs of the whole household.[4] On the other hand, an absence of consumption of clothing was also seen as a difficult:

> Of all the cities in England I travelled through, Hereford seemed the poorest of all. The labourers were ... coarsely clad, and existed in dwellings no better than hovels[5]

Here the problem was blamed on the custom of paying part of the men's wages in cider, leaving no money over to spend on clothing or household goods. Coloured by the author's allegiance to the Temperance Movement, the poor appearance of the labourers shocked the author, as well as their lack of means to better themselves. Thus either too much or too little consumption of clothing presented a dilemma for those who sought to remark on the appearance of working-class people. Evidently, such commentators desired a middle way: a respectable, decent appearance for all.

This book will investigate how provincial working-class consumers were supplied with their clothing. It will question whether different supply networks led to a distinct way of dressing for various sections of the working-class population. The availability and nature of retail networks for the working-class consumer will be examined, as will the extent to which they catered exclusively, or even predominantly, for people living in towns. By considering urban, rural and industrial areas, a more accurate analysis of patterns of clothing acquisition across varied geographic regions will be gained. The type of clothing offered for sale to working-class consumers in retail outlets and by itinerant sellers will be discussed. With the end of the French Wars in 1815, there was over-production in the textile industries, meaning that the price fell and more textiles – and therefore clothing – were available at a cheaper price. This book will discuss if this was reflected in the retail development of shops selling working-class clothing, in particular, ready-made clothing. The complexity of supply networks will be considered and how much scope there was for individuals to decide what type of clothing they might purchase and from which network.[6] The significance of clothing provision via the Old Poor Law and charities in comparison to retailing will then be examined, as will the nature of garments obtained from different sources.

The importance of clothing to the working-class consumer will also be addressed, focussing especially on the extent to which they changed their clothing in accordance with fashion. The acquisition of decent and respectable clothing, as seemingly desired by social commentators, will be discussed in the context of working-class fashions. By examining a wide range of sub divisions in the working-class population, including both young and old, the 'poor' and those with employment and apprenticeships, male and female, rural and urban, a more nuanced approach into how people acquired and regarded their clothing will be achieved. The research is based on the analysis of a wide range of sources derived from different locations, and takes into account economic and social position, geography and stage in the life-cycle, shedding new light onto this neglected area of consumer and retailing history.

The Working-Class Consumer

The definition of the 'working class' is a 'most contested category', and any attempt to use it as a framework for discussion is fraught with complexities and pitfalls.[7] Penelope Corfield details descriptions used by eighteenth-century commentators, which tried to define both an economic role as well as collective status, including: 'lower class', 'working people', 'labouring class' and 'working class', which was in use by the early nineteenth century.[8] Anna Clark sees the first half of the nineteenth century as a period of profound change in the way that society was classified. She argues that it was not until the 1830s and the important political changes of the decade, for example the Reform Act, that 'middle class' developed as a definition, contrasted with the negative connotations of 'working class', disenfranchised from the political process.[9]

This book does not seek to resolve the debate about class definition, but uses 'working-class' pragmatically, as a descriptive term for the majority of the population, at some estimates numbering around 86 per cent of the total.[10] In the geographical area covered by this book, lower middle-class occupations such as farmers, millers, clergy, doctors and lawyers, were often the local elite. They hired servants and workers and acted as overseers, forming arguably a binary class system rather than the three-tier system commonly recognized, but still one in which 'working-class' makes descriptive sense.[11]

The two main areas for the study of consumption have been the early modern period with the 'birth' of the consumer society in the seventeenth and eighteenth centuries, and the rise of mass consumption in the late nineteenth and early twentieth centuries.[12] Certainly by the late nineteenth century, class, and the complexity of strata within a particular class, were to a degree determined by material wealth and the type of consumerism it was therefore possible to engage with.[13] Indeed, historians have recently argued that the 'consumer society' has now superseded class-bound society, the act of consumption defining social standing.[14] This book will not enter the debate surrounding consumerism and the consumer society, but will instead focus on what working-class people could buy and why they might acquire clothes in various ways.

Retailing Clothing 1800–50

In terms of retailing history, the first half of the nineteenth century has received less attention than either the long eighteenth century or the post-1850 period.[15] The majority of research into clothes retailing in particular, has centred on urban areas, starting from the second half of the nineteenth century. Those who have considered the eighteenth and early nineteenth centuries have examined higher status shops that sold apparel to the upper and middle classes or focused on shops in the main streets of fashionable provincial towns.[16] Retail historians used to assume that there was little retailing of new clothing for the working-class consumer before the late nineteenth century.[17]

The work of Beverly Lemire and John Styles has been invaluable in changing perceptions about non-elite dress in the eighteenth century. Both have published seminal work linking the rise of consumerism in the lower classes to the availability of new textile products, namely the rise of the Manchester cotton industry, allied to a strong second-hand market in clothing.[18] They have also studied the distribution of ready-made clothing and the way it was sold in large cities.[19] However, little work has been carried out on retailing lower-status clothing to the working-class consumer, especially in rural and semi-rural settings.[20] Indeed, knowledge about daily practices of buying and selling in general, is still superficial.[21] There is also an assumption that consumers in rural areas did not have access to slop shops and pawnshops, there being a strong divide between the metropolis along with northern industrial cities, and other areas, in the way low-status clothing was acquired.[22] For Styles, only large towns could provide a level of demand necessary to justify carrying large stocks of ready-made clothing, either new or second-hand. In the late eighteenth century, he sees clothes dealers as 'overwhelmingly urban'.[23] This book will consider the situation during the first half of the nineteenth century within the regional context of Herefordshire and Worcestershire, by comparing rural and urban areas.

In 1970, David Alexander suggested that there was a rapid expansion in the numbers of shops in the period immediately prior to 1850.[24] However, more recently, researchers have questioned Alexander's claims, contending that there were steadily increasing numbers of shops over a much longer period. Shops gradually adopted competitive devices such as window dressing, advertising and price display and became the predominant means by which durable goods were sold to the public.[25] Nancy Cox's survey of retailing in the eighteenth century up until 1820 has firmly established the origins of many of these 'nineteenth century' retailing practices in the previous century.[26] Researchers have also now recognized that 'modern' developments in shops and retailing, such as 'ready money', the use of sales and the exchange of unsatisfactory goods, were in existence by the eighteenth century.[27] How far this retail modernity reached, outside larger towns and cities, is a matter of debate. Advertisements, for example, were usually formulaic notices suitable for polite society and new 'novel' goods were available only from traditional and established shops for instance, grocers and drapers. Jon Stobart has pointed out that the early nineteenth century saw a considerable growth in the numbers of shops and also in retail innovations, particularly in the drapery sector.[28] This book will investigate if these innovations were present in a provincial context and the effect that they had on the clothing available for purchase by low-status consumers.[29]

The study of ready-made clothing is one of the most important ways of looking at retail change for the working-class population during this era.[30] The ready-made clothing seller was essentially a middleman, much like drapers and grocers, although some also manufactured garments. Indeed, until the mid-eighteenth century, those supplying ready-made outerwear were sometimes called shopkeeping tailors, along with the descriptive 'salesmen tailors', in contrast to the 'craft' tailors. Their enthusiastic selling techniques and Sunday opening in the city of London were noted by contemporaries in the late sixteenth and seventeenth centuries.[31] By the seventeenth century, salesmen were also associated with the second-hand clothing trade, making identification of new ready-made clothing more difficult.[32] Boundaries between the first and second-hand clothes markets retailed through shops were thus blurred and flexible. Professional nomenclature was used loosely, with new and old displayed together. Where clothes came from, neither identified as new or second-hand, was possibly not as important to a buyer as the price, quality and look of a specific garment that they wanted to purchase.[33] Whereas historians have examined the development of the ready-made clothing trade in terms of the expansion of the mass market, and ultimately mass manufacture by the later nineteenth century, it was also of fundamental importance in the development of clothes retailing. The availability of ready-made clothing allowed non-specialists, general traders, to sell clothing. How successful these sales were and where ready-made clothing sellers were located will be discussed in Chapter 1. The main themes and debates between historians surrounding ready-made clothing in the period before 1850 will be set out in the following section in order to analyse how the provincial trade fits into this framework.

The Manufacture of Ready-Made Clothing Pre-1850

Ready-made clothing has long been associated with low-status clothing. There has been an extensive debate between historians about when ready-made clothing originated and it now seems certain that some ready-made garments were manufactured centuries before the era of factory production and machine-made clothing in the second half of the nineteenth century.

Accounts of ready-made clothing have been found from at least as early as the sixteenth century.[34] Nevertheless, care should be taken in defining what is meant by 'ready-made' clothing. Accessories such as hats, stockings and gloves were usually ready-made by at least the seventeenth century, but there is less evidence for the larger items of clothing such as gowns or coats.[35] Continental Europe often had strict guild controls on manufacturing ready-made clothing. In 1535, in Nuremberg, Germany, tailors were prohibited from making up new clothing to have in stock, suggesting that some had already tried to produce ready-made clothing.[36] As Harald Deceulaer has found in Antwerp and the Southern Low Countries, there was already a buoyant ready-made clothes trade there during the seventeenth century. Where guild control was flexible, as in Antwerp, commercial freedom allowed entrepreneur tailors to produce ready-made clothing for their stocks.[37] Guild control in England was less effective by the seventeenth century, although the ready-made clothing trade still came into conflict with the Tailors' Guild and continued to do so until the nineteenth century, as will be discussed in Chapter 2.[38]

Certainly, where clothing was given or purchased for a number of people at the same time, charity clothing and military and naval clothing being the most obvious examples, making up those garments before purchase appears to have been common since at least the sixteenth century.[39] As noted by Janet Arnold, this type of ready-made clothing manufacture entailed little financial risk as the contract was already negotiated and in the case of liveries or charity clothing, they were paid for, for example, by the monarch or nobleman who had ordered them, albeit perhaps with a delay.[40]

From the late sixteenth century onwards, the idea of uniform for soldiers, and the standardization of that uniform, was taken up by European armies.[41] Wars then presented huge opportunities for nascent clothing manufacturers as thousands of garments were required which could not be supplied through existing stocks. Rules on materials and shapes, along with details negotiated in the contract, provided a minimum standard of quality, standardized items and competitive prices.[42] For instance, the ready-made trade received a boost with orders for military uniforms during the English Civil War of the mid-seventeenth century and again with the Nine Years War and War of the Spanish Succession in the 1690s and 1700s.[43] During the same period, ready-made clothing was increasingly required for colonial settlement and also the navy.[44] The clothing required for seamen is the origin of 'slop' clothing, 'slop' eventually becoming a term meaning a cheap, ready-made garment. The 'ratings', ordinary sailors, did not have an official uniform until 1857. Ready-made clothes were bought before departure and some were kept on board in the slop chest to be purchased under supervision of the purser during the voyage.[45] Despite a reputation for poor quality, Amy Miller has detailed how slops were checked before they were accepted on a ship, and bales that contained slops of an inferior quality were rejected and ultimately suppliers' contracts revoked.[46] Thus the manufacturers who took on such contracts had to oversee a complex process of production, distribution and ultimately payment.

By the late seventeenth century, as Lemire has detailed in her groundbreaking work about the cotton industry, large quantities of ready-made shirts of various qualities, were being imported into England by the East India Company.[47] From the second half of the seventeenth century, references in advertising to ready-made staples became common: coats (petticoats), banyans (a loose gown), cardinals (red cloaks). These were purchased by all social classes from 'warehouses', a new type of shop where stock was sold relatively cheaply for cash, giving the retailer a quick turnover. For example, Samuel Pepys notes purchasing a banyan, a loose fitting informal Indian morning gown, in his diaries.[48] As Aileen

Ribeiro has pointed out, the concentration on everyday ready-made clothing has led historians to overlook the fact that specialist garments, for example, legal and livery robes, clerical dress, theatrical and masque costumes, as well as leather breeches, were also ready-made.[49] Tailors and drapers were thus making up clothing speculatively, putting money into a garment which they made, or got made up, in the hope that they would be able to sell it to a customer at some point in the future.[50] Although large contracts for organizations such as the army and navy continued, there was also the recognition that there was a wider market for sales to the general public. Indeed, Lemire suggests that it was government self-interest, as the largest single customer for ready-made clothing for the army and navy, which meant they did not back the tailors' campaign against ready-made clothes makers in 1702, leaving such retailers to flourish during the eighteenth century.[51]

Cloaks, shirts and petticoats were not fitted or could be gathered in by the wearer to fit the body. They could be made in a size to fit all and therefore represented the lowest risk to make up to sell as ready-made. They would be likely to find a willing purchaser as sizing and fitting could be accomplished by the buyers themselves. When sizing was introduced into the ready-made trade for garments which did need a better fit and how standardized this was, is a matter of debate.[52] For naval clothing, Miller found evidence in the Admiralty records during the second half of the eighteenth century of slop clothing being issued in sizes 36, 38 and 40, an average chest measurement in inches.[53] A civilian numerical sizing system, from 1 (small) to 10 (large), seems to have been developed for men's clothing in the slop shops of London from the 1740s, obtaining some sort of uniformity within the capital by the 1780s.[54] However, the idea that ready-made clothes rarely fitted was maintained into the nineteenth century, showing that such standardization was probably not always accurate or indeed put into practice.[55]

By the late eighteenth century, as Giorgio Riello has noted in his study of footwear, the ready-made markets, along with the second-hand trade, were not only integral elements of industrial change, but also important factors affecting the development of the British economy, including the way goods were retailed and distributed.[56] The repeal of the old Elizabethan apprenticeship statutes in 1814 made it possible to become a tailor without serving an apprenticeship. James Schmiechen sees the break-up of the London Tailors' Union in 1834, after an unsuccessful strike, as leading the way to piecework, homework and increasingly female labour in the capital. Some contemporary commentators saw two distinct trades: the honourable traditional tailor and the dishonourable sweated, piecework slop trade.[57] Schmiechen traces the growth in the ready-made clothing trade from the 1840s onwards, the changes in the trade aided by a doubling in working-class incomes in the second half of the century which allowed more expenditure on clothing, principally of a ready-made variety.[58] As discussed, and as highlighted by Lemire in particular, such patterns of female labour were already prevalent during the eighteenth century, with the ready-made clothing trade already firmly established by the turn of the nineteenth century.[59]

In the French and American ready-made markets, the focus was principally on male garments, perhaps as an off-shoot of military contracts. The female ready-made clothing market was still under-developed, with most garments still made by local dressmakers or at home.[60] In England, it is interesting that the references to women's ready-made dresses often come from the late eighteenth and early nineteenth centuries, when the simple neo-classical ideal dominated. These dresses, when filtered down the social scale away from court and society fashion, were simpler to make and often fitted through drawstrings at the waist and bust and through ties to the internal lining.[61] Such styles would be easier to sell ready-made and Lemire has found examples of a substantial business in dress manufacture emanating from Manchester from the late 1760s.[62] By the second quarter of the nineteenth century, this simplicity had been lost and references to ready-made dresses become rarer.[63]

Ready-made clothing in England between 1830 and 1850 generated much negative commentary.[64] Henry Mayhew interviewed second-hand sellers who criticized the quality of clothes sold as slops and likewise Charles Kingsley in 'Cheap Clothes and Nasty'. Albert Smith wrote *The Natural History of the Gent* as a satirical account of working-class oneupmanship played out through the clothing of the new 'cheap' tailors.[65] Much of this commentary was linked to a new awareness about the sweated trades and the harsh conditions of the workers who made the clothing, in particular, unskilled women who laboured on minute sub-divisions of the work.[66] Thomas Hood's poem 'Song of the Shirt', first published in 1843, exemplified this new worry about the exploitation of workers. Although the outworkers, the seamstresses, who laboured to provide ready-made clothing for poor wages within their own homes had been a continuous, often hidden, trade since the second half of the seventeenth century, by the 1840s their plight was being highlighted by commentators.[67] The problem of the so-called 'dishonourables' was emphasized, with claims that they brought the whole tailoring trade into disrepute and were in stark contrast to the traditional craft tailor.[68] The focus was often on only one sector of the market, the slop trade with poor-quality clothing frequently made with 'shoddy', a material manufactured from reconstituted old rags. The benefits that such new clothing brought to the working classes were not seen to justify the exploitation of a section of that society to provide cheap clothing. Only a few commentators such as Francis Place, from working-class origins himself and who had started his own career making ready-made leather breeches, noted the improvement in cleanliness and hygiene that wearing cotton clothing had brought to working people. In 1828, he observed that the old clothes trade was 'greatly diminished' as people no longer liked wearing second-hand garments.[69] It was not until the second half of the nineteenth century that ready-made clothing came to reflect respectability and affluence for the working-class people in the eyes of English commentators.[70]

Andrew Godley sees the ready-made clothing industry in Britain as the most sophisticated clothing sector in the world, even before garment production was mechanized with the advent of the sewing machine from the 1865 onwards.[71] This book will trace this vibrant and expanding business during the first half of the nineteenth century, and examine how its multifarious strands supplied the varied needs of the working-class consumer.

Regional Studies

A regional approach is taken in this book, concentrating on an area that encompasses varied geographical locations, but is clearly defined by timescale and the limits of that geography. This allows the habits of and influences on the whole strata of the working-class population to be examined with greater precision than a more general survey, including both urban and rural populations.[72] The need for micro-analysis of particular areas and comparison within and outside these boundaries has recently been recognized by historians, both of retailing and of rural history.[73] The local environment impacted significantly on the experience ordinary people had in their daily life. It is therefore essential to understand local circumstances before evidence can be placed in a wider social and cultural context. And these local circumstances can be very place-specific even within a small geographical boundary.[74]

This book will focus on Herefordshire and Worcestershire, the 'near west' as they have been termed.[75] The counties present an intriguing mix of rural, urban and industrial landscapes, old established cathedral cities of Hereford and Worcester, along with new developing industrial settlements such as Dudley, a close proximity to Birmingham,[76] yet with access to the major port centres in the north-west and Bristol. In particular, the available source material on which this study is based is varied, ranging from existing costume in museum collections, poor law records, a depth of newspaper provision with up to four competing titles, a rarity for a provincial area by this period, as well as trade directories and archive documents.[77]

In her study of the clothing trades, Christina Fowler examined a compact area within a county boundary. If primary evidence is restricted to specific areas, she argues, it can reveal a more cohesive and united picture than finding evidence to suit an argument from random surviving nationwide sources. The resulting model, she proposes, is much more likely to produce conclusions that are surprisingly different and challenge currently dominant narratives.[78] Styles drew specifically on his research into non-elite clothing in the north of England for his publication, *The Dress of the People*. He states:

> Examining regional variations in the supply of a basic commodity like clothing can help us avoid excessive concern with the extraordinary and the unusual, and arrive at a more balanced assessment of the relationship between the consumer and the market.[79]

County boundaries are, of course, somewhat arbitrary when studying retailing. Consumers do not determine which shop they will use by which county it is in but by a host of other factors, including geographical proximity, access, type and price of stock. Indeed, there were businesses in towns such as Ludlow and Hay-on-Wye, just over the border from Herefordshire, and likewise Alcester for Worcestershire, which it seems probable were also used by consumers who were customers of the retailers examined in this book but beyond the county borders of this study.[80] A regional study does need a boundary and county boundaries, although not perfect, are one way of defining such research and enable evidence to be sorted and analysed in detail.

The Study of Clothing

This book is focused on the retailing of clothing. Within the category of clothing, it will concentrate on the garments themselves, rather than accessories such as shoes, hats and gloves. This is pragmatic decision, partly driven by the need to organize evidence and partly by the fact that shoes and gloves in particular, were seen as a separate trade with little cross-over with those who made clothes. Milliners are perhaps more problematic, with, for instance, variations in the classification of milliners in trade directories. Some directories, such as *Bentley's Directory*, list them as a separate trade; others list them together with dressmakers. Where distinguishable, in smaller towns and villages women were often listed with both occupations and likewise in the newly industrial areas, such as Dudley. In more traditional market towns, Pershore and Upton-upon-Severn for example, the two roles were separated, at least in the pages of a directory.[81] Certainly, headwear was an important part of an outfit for both men and women and helped to identify status and occupation. However, the hatting trades demand a fuller study than the attention that they receive in this research. This focus on the specific, as with Riello's work on shoes, counters the macro-scale analysis of consumption which risk leading to simplistic and generalized assumptions about demand and the relationship between goods and people.[82]

This research is placed within the current call for a 'new interdisciplinary approach' between object-based curatorial research and academic discourses.[83] Objects and artefacts should also be used actively as evidence rather than passively as illustrations, this book examining surviving examples of 'best' dress in Chapter 6 within their local context. [84] Their investigation can shed light on variations and differences not readily visible through other sources.[85] Empirical knowledge of object-based dress history must underlie the discussion of clothing in other contexts; in this research, retailing.[86] However, dress historians should acknowledge that knowing how and where textiles and clothing were acquired is essential to understanding the clothing that people wore as a result.[87]

The first three chapters of the book will therefore investigate the 'formal', supposedly regulated networks of supply from which the working-class consumer, male and female, could purchase clothing. Chapter 1 will investigate the location of shops and types of clothing retailers across all areas of Worcestershire and Herefordshire, including urban and rural districts. Chapter 2 will trace the development of particular retailers in Worcester and Hereford before considering the role of advertising. Hawkers and pedlars, travelling drapers and markets, and their contribution to clothes retailing, will be examined in Chapter 3. The following two chapters of the book will focus on informal networks of supply, and will explore the 'makeshift' economy in relation to clothing, examining how clothing was obtained without recourse to cash. Chapter 4 will briefly discuss networks of illicit clothing exchange before turning to investigate clothing given out as part of parish relief. Charity clothing and clothing societies will be considered in Chapter 5. The interaction between the formal and informal networks of acquisition will be investigated, questioning how much fluidity there was between the two systems. Who actually acquired clothing through these different methods will be investigated, taking into account issues such as economic necessity, practicality, desire for novelty and decency.

The final chapter will then turn the attention from issues of supply to consumer attitudes towards clothing. Working-class attitudes to fashion and emulation will be investigated. Differentiation between genders and age groups will also be examined. Conclusions can then be drawn about the variety of supply networks which served working-class consumers, their comparative importance, and how they were integrated with each other, as well as the importance of fashion in influencing the choice of clothing for such consumers. As observed in the letter quoted at the beginning of this chapter, female servants were noted as practised consumers of clothing. This book will investigate where their clothing came from and how it might have been obtained.

1 CLOTHING SHOPS AND WORKING-CLASS CONSUMERS

This chapter will systematically investigate what working-class clothing was available for purchase in the towns and villages of provincial England. The best approach would appear to be a detailed regional study of the type offered here. Results can be analysed and contextualized with other similar surveys, for example, John Styles in the north of England and Christina Fowler in the south of England.[1] This chapter will therefore examine the development of clothing shops that were used by working-class consumers in Herefordshire and Worcestershire during the first half of the nineteenth century. It will begin with a brief examination of the history of shopping, within the social and economic context of the two counties. This will be followed by an investigation into the distribution of working-class clothing retailers in Worcestershire and Herefordshire. The development of clothing shops in the towns and rural hinterland of the two counties will be analysed on the basis of evidence from the trade directories. It will also discuss what types of goods were stocked and whether shops catered for specific types of working-class consumer. Finally, the question of how frequently such consumers entered and used shops will be addressed. Any differences in clothing provision between genders and across geographical areas will also be considered.

Worcester

The quantity and quality of shops by the late eighteenth century reflected Worcester's reputation during the previous hundred years as a place of 'refined gentility'.[2] It was seen as one of the premier cities of provincial England, with elegant new buildings and a circle of intellectuals and thinkers.[3] The *Worcester Journal* was one of the first English provincial newspapers to be established in 1709.[4] The Three Choirs Music Festival, founded in 1715, also provided a focus for local society. The importance of the river Severn, then known as 'the greatest highway in the world', gave the city easy access to coal and a wide range of imported luxury goods such as wine and groceries.[5] In the centre of a rich agricultural area, Worcester supplied other parts of England with wheat, hops, fruit and vegetables. It was also a centre for glove manufacturing and from the second half of the eighteenth century, porcelain. Several shops in the early nineteenth century, through their billheads and advertisements, claimed eighteenth-century origins of which to be proud. Richard Sanders, for example, maintained that his clothing warehouse in Lich Street had been established in 1712.[6] The culture of shopping would seem to have been 'old established', to use the terminology from the advertisements. Worcester was a well-developed retail and service centre, better supplied with shops than larger cities such as York and Nottingham in the same period.[7]

However, by the first half of the nineteenth century, Worcester was beginning to experience some long-term economic problems. In retailing terms, the close proximity to and growing pre-eminence of Birmingham began to have a more telling effect. From the census records in 1801, Birmingham was the fourth largest urban area in England with a population of 69,000.[8] In addition, the railway caused great controversy in Worcester and this had still not been resolved by 1850. The Birmingham to Gloucester railway, the first across the county, missed out Worcester. As T. C. Turberville recognized in 1852: 'Worcester [was] ... almost shut out from this advantage, now so indispensable to prosperity'.[9] People living in the county who perhaps previously would have used the facilities of Worcester increasingly went to Birmingham instead. Of course, a direct link may not have helped Worcester's cause anyway, as the inhabitants of the city would then be able to choose to shop directly in the larger retail centre, Birmingham.

The level of the River Severn, the traditional transport route, had also fallen so that the stretch above Worcester was less easily navigable. A campaign in Gloucester stopped any improvements to the river and prevented Worcester from becoming pre-eminent again.[10] Coupled with this was the disastrous decline in the glove trade in the second quarter of the nineteenth century. Before serious stagnation set in during the 1830s, it was claimed that 8,000 people were employed in the glove trade alone, around a third of the population of Worcester.[11] Joseph Bentley, author of a local contemporary commercial directory, linked the decline in the glove trade to a change in fashion from the kid gloves that Worcester manufactured, to lighter gloves made from silk, cotton and lace. The female workers in the city were also resistant to the introduction of improvements to the manufacturing process, which in 1807, resulted in work being put out to Evesham. By 1841, the best work was sent to Torrington in Devon, missing out Worcestershire altogether. Furthermore, the price of Worcester gloves was two or three times that of the French imports, making them economically unattractive, not helped by the reduction of import duty in 1825.[12]

The population of the city had also nearly trebled in fifty years, from 11,131 in 1801 to 27,528 in 1851.[13] Beyond the main streets, Worcester was a medieval city with narrow streets and lanes and poor housing. By the nineteenth century, much of this had deteriorated to slum conditions. As Tuberville stated whilst claiming the need for a Public Health Act: 'Its fair exterior and the outward cleanliness of its principal streets, are but the deceitful masks of hidden insalubrities'.[14] He claimed that there was not sufficient drainage and that Worcester had more open cesspits than any other town of equal size in the kingdom. Despite outbreaks of cholera in 1832 and 1849, by the time that Turberville's history was published in 1852, nothing had yet been done to remedy the situation.[15]

The general status of Worcester as an important place of trade had thus declined considerably by the mid-nineteenth century. From the second quarter of the nineteenth century, fashionable society moved to the new spa resort town of Malvern, seven miles away. Retailers who catered for their needs soon followed. For example, Mrs Hood, a Worcester dressmaker and milliner, opened showrooms near the Abbey in Malvern in the 1830s.[16] George Warwick, a Worcester draper, entered into a partnership with a draper in Malvern before moving there as a sole trader in 1835.[17] As a consequence of this migration of elite society, Worcester's property prices slumped.[18]

The deterioration in Worcester's retailing status was perhaps reflected in a plea by the Chamber of Commerce in the 1840s, in which they implored the county gentry to support their local city rather than shop in London. The Chamber of Commerce found in their investigation that ease of travel meant the nobility and gentry could easily purchase goods in London that they had previously gone to Worcester to buy. Local taxation was also high and a country gentleman claimed that goods from Worcester were inferior and 'dear' (i.e. expensive). The meeting decided that goods ought to be made cheaper without the stigma of being 'cheap', something easier said than carried out.[19] Contemporary diaries of country gentry in the area seem to justify the fears of the Chamber of Commerce. In 1831, Elizabeth Barrett Browning, who was brought up at Hope End near Ledbury, ordered her books from Worcester but received stockings and silk from London.[20] Similarly, Henrietta Halliwell-Phillipps lived at Middle Hill, Broadway and sent to Worcester for household business but bought all her clothes in London.[21] Indeed, by the late 1830s, advertisements for 'cheap linen drapery' were frequent in the *Worcester Journal*, with drapers Sidney & Dickinson claiming that 'selling off' had been practised more in Worcester than anywhere else for the last two years.[22] At the same time, drapers Hill and Turley of the Cross were advertising stock of bankrupts that they had bought to sell on, from as far afield as Liverpool and Nottingham.[23] As early as 1816, William Miles, a Worcester draper, was offering his goods on 'Todd's low plan', named after Todd & Morrison, London drapers who made their fortune by selling quickly in quantity but for small profits, including bankrupts' stock.[24] The inferior goods noted by the Chamber of Commerce, were much in evidence.

Despite these social and economic problems, by the early nineteenth century Worcester still had a highly developed retail environment, partly due to its historic prominence. How this affected the distribution of working-class clothing shops will now be examined.

Geography of the City and Distribution of Shops

The main shopping streets of the city were the High Street, Broad Street and the Cross, which was at the intersection of the two. Foregate Street extended beyond the Cross on the same line as the High Street, with important civic buildings such as the court and museum and later the railway station.[25] By the late eighteenth century, it was seen by some as one of the finest streets in Europe.[26] Towards the cathedral, streets still followed the medieval pattern. However, from the late eighteenth century, improvements began to be made with, for example, the development of College Street in 1794.[27] By the nineteenth century, the area from the High Street down to the river contained poor housing, where the majority of glove workers lived and worked in slum conditions.

From an analysis of the trade directories of the period, it seems clear that the shopping environment had developed some complexity over the course of the eighteenth century.[28] By 1800, respectable shops catering for genteel customers were concentrated on the principal streets, part of the process of geographical specialization and spatial segregation that took place in many towns over the course of the eighteenth century.[29] The main drapers vied to have their shops in Broad Street or the High Street, the most prestigious location seemingly being the Cross, at the intersection of several streets. As the earlier directories do not give street numbers it is not possible to be exact in plotting locations of shops. However, it is significant that salesmen and second-hand clothes dealers catering for the less genteel were to be found concentrated in particular streets, often those which had not been redeveloped during the eighteenth century, such as Lich Street (also variously spelt as Leech and Leach) and Friar Street. Salesmen or saleswomen, terms used from at least the second half of the seventeenth century, were clothes dealers and brokers. Some were also manufacturers and they retailed both old and new ready-made clothing. They often dealt in new and second-hand clothing at the same time, relying partly on the exchange of old clothes for acquiring new stock.[30] Their spatial concentration was affected by economic factors, for example, the cheaper rents in the back streets. Land values affected retail patterns and the visual nature of the shops in different areas, dependent on whether they were housed in a 'modern' or a timber framed 'old-fashioned' building (see Figure 1.1).[31]

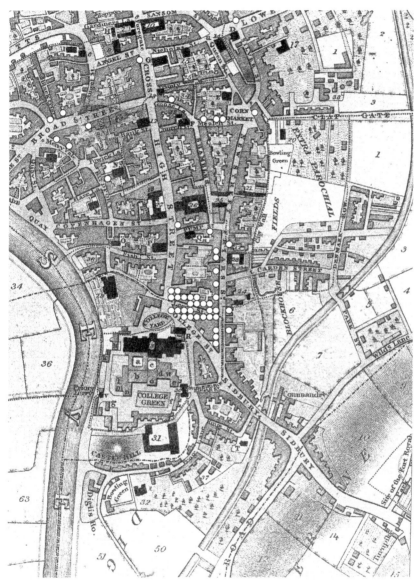

Figure 1.1: Approximate locations for clothing dealers and salesmen in Worcester Trade Directories, 1820–47, map, Samuel Mainley, 1822, image courtesy of Worcestershire Record Office.

Lich Street and Friar Street were at the heart of the medieval part of Worcester on the edge of the Cathedral grounds. They were streets of unfashionable timber black and white houses, unlike the newly built Georgian terraces of the more desirable central streets of the city. By the nineteenth century, these old-fashioned houses had been divided into tenements.[32] Many of the leases were owned by the church, including that of Mrs Whewell in Lich Street, a clothes dealer.[33]

Merryvale was also a common location for clothes dealers. It was the site of the shop of the pawnbroker, James Walter, who in 1820 also described himself as a salesman.[34] This was in the heart of the slum district of Worcester, with pubs and brothels scattered down towards the Severn. Shops listed in this area were likely to cater directly for the needs of the working-class consumer. There were also clothes dealers listed in Broad Street, but by looking at the street numbering where given, it becomes apparent that they were generally at the lower end, towards the river and therefore directly adjacent to Merryvale and the slum areas in the parish of St Andrews (see Figure 1.1).[35] Sprigg's 'Ready-made Clothing Warehouse' advertised a removal in 1831 from number 26 Broad Street to number 30, 'four doors lower down, on the corner of Doldy St', the edge of the slum district, his advertisement stating: 'Particular attention paid to the workmanship of the ready-made article – the lowest price that can be afforded for ready money'.[36] This type of establishment appealed directly to working-class consumers in an area where many resided.

The pattern of low-status clothing retail development as plotted in Figure 1.1 seems logical once the topography of the city becomes apparent. Such shops were generally confined to unfashionable areas and located in streets close to the slums and living areas of their working-class customers. Mrs Henry Wood, a novelist who was brought up in Worcester, certainly regarded Friar Street as a back street when writing about it in the mid-nineteenth century. It was a safe street for her upper-class protagonist to pass along to avoid being seen by people who would know him in the city.[37]

However, both the type of trade practised and the status of the business could be more complicated than this spatial segregation suggests. For example, Richard Sanders ran a shop at number 1 Lich Street. In Lewis's *Directory* of 1820 he is listed as a woollen draper; in Pigot's *Directory* of 1828 he is listed as a woollen draper, salesman, hatter and hosier; in Pigot's *Directory* of 1835 he is listed as a linen draper and tailor; in a guide to Worcester from 1837 he is listed as a linen draper, silk mercer and tailor;[38] his own billhead from 1837 describes him as a 'wholesale and retail Salesman, woollen and linen draper, hatter, hosier, and men's mercer, At the original Warehouse, No. 1, bottom of Leech St, established 1712'.[39] The 'warehouse' was a term for a type of shop and way of selling that had become popular over the course of the eighteenth century. Warehouses offered a large stock of goods, used fixed prices and accepted only cash to enable a high turnover in stock to generate profit. An urban phenomenon and an innovation for fashionable towns of the eighteenth century, for example Bath, this 'modern' way of shopping had declined in status by the first half of the nineteenth century,

Figure 1.2: Richard Sanders shop, Worcester, photographed 1960s, image courtesy of Worcester City Council.

and although still popular, warehouses were increasingly associated with cheap goods, fraudulent selling and pushy advertising.[40]

When Sanders died, aged sixty-seven, in 1837, at his house in Lich Street (presumably above the shop), the announcement of his death appeared in the *Worcester Journal*, stating that he was a man 'whose real worth was appreciated by all who knew him'.[41] At the time of his death, his stock was valued at £1,892 12*s.* 9*d.*, his household furniture and wearing apparel at £210 6*s.* 9*d.*, his clothing later valued separately at £15 14*s.*[42] The value of this stock was just above the median figure for bankrupt drapers' stock in records of this period surveyed by David Alexander. However, only one clothes dealer had stock worth over £1,000. Drapers tended to accumulate stock in order to offer a range of goods in all departments, changes in fashion leaving them with unsaleable goods. Nevertheless, the amount of stock that Sanders held showed he was operating on a par with drapers in other large provincial centres and London, and giving customers a wide range of goods to choose from including clothing.[43]

The relationship between Sanders's status and the focus of his trade was thus uncertain. He clearly had standing in local society both in economic and social terms. A photograph of his shop survives from the 1960s, before it was demolished as part of slum clearances (see Figure 1.2). It occupied a coveted corner position, but on the corner of Lich and Friar Streets, both undeveloped, lower status streets. William Ablett, in his *Reminiscences of an Old Draper*, suggests that all drapers wanted a corner shop as it offered a bold frontage for display to attract customers.[44] Sanders's shop was rebuilt at some point, probably in the early eighteenth century. This may have corresponded to when it was first opened in 1712, the date of which was proudly inscribed on the wall. His family business had been part of the retail boom in eighteenth-century Worcester, and he continued to trade on that fact and heritage, even when his shop was no longer at the vanguard of retail developments and seemingly in the wrong part of the city for quality trade.

Although he presented the shop as an old established clothing warehouse and himself as a salesman and so specifically serving the needs of the working-class consumer, Sanders appears to have been a well respected individual of some wealth and standing. Bills for outstanding debts at the time of his death have survived and show that a shop of this nature had a nationwide supply network. His suppliers included manufacturers in Manchester, Gloucestershire, Shrewsbury and Leicester for various items of drapery.[45] His wealth and status reflect the complexity of investigating shops which appear to be positioned to sell to low-status consumers but with finance and contacts arguably on a par with shops selling to consumers higher up the social scale within the same city. No evidence has been found as yet to verify the establishment of Sanders's clothing warehouse in 1712 aside from his own claims. However, his ancestor John Sanders was selling inexpensive ready-made male clothing to the parish of St Nicholas, Worcester in the 1770s and John Hawkes Sanders was listed as a 'Salesman &c'. in *The Worcester Royal Directory of 1790*.[46] Selling items for low-status consumers seems to have been a profitable business for the Sanders family over several generations.

Worcestershire Towns

There were seventeen towns in Worcestershire defined as such by the directories of the period. These ranged in scale from Chaddesley Corbett, with a population of only 1,404 in 1831, to Dudley in the very north of the county, whose population of 31,232 in the 1841 census had already overtaken Worcester's.[47] They were extremely varied in their social and economic circumstances. The Black Country, with its associated industrial activity, encroached on the north of the county and had a profound effect on towns such as Dudley. The metal trades of nail making and needle manufacture were important for Bromsgrove and Redditch respectively. There were also traditional market towns surrounded by agricultural landscape, for example, Pershore and Evesham, dependent on market and fair days for their business.[48] Upton and Bewdley on the River Severn were reliant on the volume of river trade for their prosperity. Kidderminster was a centre of carpet manufacture, though much like Worcester, it faced a decline in the first half of the nineteenth century due to its failure to quickly take up mechanization of the weaving process.[49] Within a fairly narrow geographical area there were therefore towns expanding and declining at the same time. This would necessarily affect the fortunes of the inhabitants of these towns and the consumer goods that they would be able to purchase. How this manifested itself in the type of clothing shops available will now be examined. The validity of basing findings for working-class clothing provision solely on evidence from trade directories will also be investigated.

It might be expected that the towns of industrial north Worcestershire would cater in a large part for the needs of the working-class consumer, workers coming into the area to take advantage of industrial employment opportunities. Indeed, Dudley had a salesman listed in Holden's directory of 1809–11 and eight clothiers by 1820 centred on Queen Street.[50] There were only thirteen drapers listed in 1820, so in contrast to other towns there were a larger proportion of clothiers or clothes dealers in comparison to drapers.[51] Newly expanding Dudley did not have the historically fashionable areas of Worcester and so the trade of clothes dealers was not confined to particular streets away from the central area.

Also in the north of the county, Kidderminster had the outward trappings of a thriving town. Pigot's *Directory* noted in 1835 in relation to its two main streets, 'both are well paved & clean, & the town altogether has an aspect of respectability & comfort'. Its prosperity was linked to textile manufacturing trades and as might be expected in a manufacturing town, several salesman and clothes dealers were listed in the directories.[52] For example, a clothes warehouse was mentioned in 1820 as run by Isaac Chadwick in Mill Street.[53] As in Dudley, there was no defined street for the trade. Although both towns were medieval in origin, their main growth had been during the second half of the eighteenth century. However, despite the apparent prosperity, the general population of Kidderminster had a poor standard of living exacerbated by industrial unrest, including the weavers' strike in 1828. At the time of the strike, a weaver could expect to earn 16*s*. 8*d*. per week. Out of that he had to pay his business expenses, including the draw boy's wages, coal, candles and rent for where the loom was housed, leaving on average only 5s. 9½d. to live on, 3 to 5 shillings less than an agricultural labourer in the same area.[54] It remains open to question whether the significant presence of salesmen, clothiers and pawnbrokers was a reflection of these towns' industrial prosperity or the poor living standards of their workers.

In contrast, in the agricultural south of Worcestershire, clothes dealers and clothiers were noted less frequently in the trade directories. Pershore had one listed main dealer, Benjamin Farley, who was categorized in different ways across a twenty-year period. In 1820, he was a breeches maker in the High Street. His business was situated in Broad Street in 1828 and 1835, but by 1838 had moved to Bridge Street. By that date he was described as a 'slop seller', having a clothes warehouse and being an agent to the Phoenix Fire Office. In 1841, he was a clothes salesman and distributor of stamps as well as the Phoenix agent. This may not reflect a real change in business, but may merely be an illustration of the looseness of the way terminology was applied to this part of the clothing trade by different directories.

The term 'slop seller' is ambiguous. Historically it referred to ready-made garments made in bulk primarily for the navy, although they could also be sold on to the general public.[55] However, 'slop' could also mean 'smock' as in smock frock, the outer wear of agricultural and other non-industrial labourers.[56] Although the smock frock is associated with hand embroidery and rural crafts, by the early nineteenth century smocks were generally ready-made. There were centres of production in Newark, Nottinghamshire and Haverhill, Suffolk and also on a smaller scale in local areas.[57] For example, in Banbury, Oxfordshire, smock frocks were being sold by a tailor, William Baker, from at least 1813. By 1818, his account book appears to show that he had developed standardized patterns and sizing for them, ready-made examples being listed as N1–N8: N1–3, priced between 8s. 9d. and 7s. for adults; N4–6, priced between 5s. and 4s. 4d. for youths; and N7–8, around 3s. for boys. He also sold 'best work' and 'full work' ready-made smock frocks, presumably with additional embroidery, for 9s. 6d. and above.[58] Pershore was in the centre of an agricultural and market gardening area, and as Farley was also listed in the same directory running a clothing warehouse which would have sold second-hand or ready-made clothing, the 'slop' in this instance was as likely to refer to smocks as to ready-made clothing. Smocks were necessary protective clothing for agricultural labourers and they could be bought ready-made from various shops across the midlands.

Clothing dealers or salesmen who sold ready-made clothing therefore existed in varying numbers in the majority of the towns listed in the directories.[59] Some were associated with pawnbroking, as in Tenbury, where another Richard Sanders, pawnbroker, also ran a 'clothes shop'.[60] Only five towns out of the seventeen had no such trade. Three of these were small settlements that were not particularly well documented by the directories: Blockley, Feckenham and Chaddesley

Corbett. The other two, Malvern and Droitwich, were aspiring spa towns and a very visible trade in second-hand or ready-made clothing might discourage the genteel customers the directories sought to attract. Indeed, the accuracy of the information contained within the directories primarily depended upon the way that they were collated. As Jane Norton says: 'It would be misleading to regard them [directories] as either precise or accurate'.[61] Bentley sums up the frustrations of collating a trade directory in the preface to his Evesham volume in 1841:

> ... that difficulties of great magnitude have required subduing, and labor of no common kind performing, to collect the information it contains; the mere fact of above 5,000 houses, scattered over 78 large parishes, having been visited, (some of them 5 or 6 times before the information could be obtained in a satisfactory manner) is sufficient evidence of itself, to show this.[62]

Not all collators were as thorough as Bentley, either in the information collected or in the area covered.

The directories were compiled only for commercial reasons. Agents would cover main streets, but in the larger towns were unlikely to venture into working-class districts.[63] They were unlikely to garner sales and there was also a difficulty in categorizing working-class areas. Many shops there were not rated as retail establishments as business was informally carried out from the front room. Houses were multi-occupied and addresses such as courtyards of houses were difficult to quantify.[64] The motive of the directory compilers was to enumerate the important people and the businesspeople of the neighbourhood. It was, in effect, an idealized description of a town. Smaller communities also received little attention.[65] As Bentley noted, they were difficult to get to and would not be expected to achieve many sales, so it was not usually economically viable to include them. Directories therefore tend to be biased towards the middle classes and commercially successful occupations and trades, framed in a respectable way, and located in centres of general commerce.

The problem with collating information from the directories becomes apparent when comparing their contents to evidence from the *Worcester Journal*. Businesses from outside the city of Worcester were generally slow to advertise until the second quarter of the nineteenth century. However, other information about businesses in the county can be gained from bankruptcy and auction notices. In Chaddesley Corbett, John Tetstell, tailor, draper and grocer went bankrupt in 1810. His stock in trade at the time of his bankruptcy included utilitarian items such as: 'kerseymeres, velveteens, corduroys, patent cords ... waistcoat pieces ... some ready-made clothes, smock frocks ... cottons ... shawls', along with grocery items.[66] John Tetstell's business failed too early to be listed in the directories; in 1820, only a single mercer was listed in the town; by 1835, six clothing businesses were detailed.[67] However, the advertisement for the auction of Tetstell's stock showed that the people of Chaddesley Corbett were able to buy ready-made clothes and smock frocks prior to 1810, despite the lack of evidence in the trade directories. The absence of a listing in the trade directories for clothing dealers and salesmen should therefore not be read as evidence of absence of their trade within a town.

Similarly in Droitwich ready-made clothing was available from many of the main drapers. This is demonstrated by a series of bills to the overseers of the parish of St Peter's, Droitwich, dating from the first three decades of the nineteenth century.[68] For example, James Horsley, listed as a draper in Queen Street in 1820 and 1828, was selling the overseers shirts and smocks frocks. On the 11 October 1813 he sold them a smock frock for 'Partridge' for 9*s*. 6*d*. In the same year, he also sold the overseers two cloth jackets and continued to sell them comparable items into the 1820s.[69] This suggests that in smaller towns the distinction between a salesman and a draper was often rather artificial.

Likewise, John Pumfrey was listed in the trade directories as a woollen draper from 1828 to 1841 in Droitwich.[70] However, his billhead from 1830 also listed him as having a 'readymade clothes warehouse'.[71] This was evident in his transactions with the overseers, for whom he supplied not only the ready-made staples of shirts and shifts,[72] but also in 1830, a 'fustian jacket & trowsers' at 13*s*. and a 'Mans Kersey Flannel Frock' at 9*s*. 6*d*., and in 1831, a 'jacket & trowsers of moleskin' at 14*s*.[73] Local elites, such as farmers, were also buying ready-made clothing, perhaps more acceptably purchased from a local town draper than from a salesman or clothes dealer. Bills survive from 1805, when John Pumfrey senior sold George Marshall, a local farmer, a 'pair of breeches' for 16 shillings, presumably ready-made.[74] It is, of course, unclear whether such clothing was bought to wear by the purchaser or for another recipient. The price of Marshall's breeches suggests that they were of a certain quality, overseers generally buying breeches from around 5 to 7 shillings.[75] Thus the Pumfrey family business had a long history of selling ready-made items, although this trade was rarely promoted or publicized in their advertisements. The complexity of occupational classifications between directories, newspaper advertisements and surviving documentary evidence obscures the real labour and roles that were actually carried out to make a living.[76] Only if all three sources are comparatively analysed, is it possible to see past the promotion and elaboration, the aspirations of a shopkeeper, and find the routine mundane sales that were made everyday: the 'bread and butter' trade so to speak.

Pumfrey's claims to respectability were emphasized with a move of premises in 1830 from the shop where 'his ancestors carried on the business for more than half a century'.[77] An illustration of his 'newly erected' shop survives from a billhead of W. G. Gabb,[78] who took over Pumfrey's business in 1843.[79] The shop is shown with large display windows, opposite the entrance to the Salt Water Baths and the George Hotel. It was located on the main Worcester road, away from Droitwich's medieval high street. The fashionable exterior of the shop and his advertisements in the *Worcester Journal* for the newest modes did not highlight the fact that he was still selling ready-made garments to the overseers of the poor until at least 1831, and probably to others too. In 1836, he partially acknowledged this with an advertisement announcing that 'his Plain Stock, for which he feels thankful his shop has long been famed' was to be supplemented by a more extensive assortment of goods.[80]

Despite their fashionable exteriors and billheads, inexpensive ready-made clothing could be purchased from the main drapers' shops in Droitwich. Styles offers a note of caution in assuming that the practices of the overseers of the poor mirrored the patterns of acquisition of the independent labouring poor.[81] However, in small towns such as Droitwich (population 2,176 in 1821), traders such as Pumfrey were aiming to sell to the working-class consumer through outlets such as his Clothing Warehouse, in addition to the local overseers. Droitwich had its own traditional industry, the production of salt from brine springs. This involved laborious work for both men and women in poor conditions, particularly during the evaporation process.[82] Such workers would require cheap clothing which the drapers of the town could provide. The opinion of Mr Laird in 1818 was that Droitwich was 'a small straggling dirty looking town on the banks of the Salwarpe'.[83] This may have reflected its industrial core in contrast to the positive comments in the later trade directories. They focused instead on the promotion of Droitwich as a resort from the 1830s onwards, the salt baths established in 1836 as a cure for gout and rheumatism.[84] This wide social focus by retailers was not unusual. In provincial France, Marie Gillet has found that shopkeepers stocked different ranges of goods to attract all social classes. As she points out, diversity of stock was important for a shopkeeper's success in a provincial town, to cater for a socially differentiated customer base whose taste and financial means varied widely, and with perhaps a very small elite market.[85]

Despite the bias of the directories towards high-status shops, they still reveal that working-class clothing provision was widespread across the county. In places where they are not overtly listed, for example Droitwich, other evidence shows how provision was made. This additional provision was likely to be similar in other towns where few retailers' bills survive. Thus, lack of evidence for working-class retailing in the trade directories should not be taken at face value. It appears that a considerable number of drapers and tailors also sold to the working-class consumer. However, few were willing to promote this area of their business through print advertising.

Hereford

The city of Hereford is sometimes seen as distinct from the rest of the Midlands, given its economic focus towards Wales, the border counties and beyond.[86] Indeed, with no Welsh newspapers until the 1820s, the *Hereford Journal* established a monopoly in south Wales and subsequently carried much advertising and news relating to this area of influence.[87] However, there was also a close connection with Worcester, certainly for some shopkeepers.[88] The city's role was as a marketing centre for the produce of the surrounding agricultural countryside, particularly hops and cider, also cattle, sheep, cereal crops and especially wheat. The impression was of a wealthy county, with Hereford at the centre, serving traditional functions as a market and trading centre.[89] It was a focus for county life for the aristocracy and gentry, as well as all the social ranks beneath them. There had been cloth and gloving industries, but by the nineteenth century these had virtually died out. Rural industries such as bark stripping, along with tanning, were still carried out, trade being conducted by barges down the river Wye. The only canal was not completed until 1845, but was soon superseded by the railway in 1852, when the Hereford to Shrewsbury line opened.[90] As with Worcester, in the first half of the nineteenth century, the city lacked the economic advantages a railway might bring.[91]

Hereford was also a medieval cathedral city with crowded courts and poor housing, although it did not have Worcester's population density.[92] In 1831, it had just over 10,000 inhabitants, about half of Worcester's, and the city's population grew slowly but relatively steadily thereafter. Although the retail sector was not as strong as in Worcester, the trade directories highlighted the shops as an attraction of the city, perhaps with an element of self-promotion. In Pigot's *Directory* of 1822, Hereford was described as follows: 'The city contains a great number of very superior shops, supplied with every article desirable for domestic comfort'.[93] In Hunt's *Directory* in 1847, this was expanded to: 'its retail shops are numerous and respectable, being for the most part fitted up in the modern style, and supplied with the necessaries and luxuries of life in great abundance'.[94] However, as with Worcester, those with contacts in London criticized the range of goods available in the city's shops. For example, in the 1820s, William Wordsworth's sister-in-law, Sarah Hutchinson, complained that Hereford was 'the most barrin [*sic*] place in the Island' and it would take twelve months 'to furnish a cottage to ones mind' from the city. She too gave commissions to those she knew in London for her clothing to be made there and sent on to her, perhaps reflecting a more realistic view of what the shops in provincial Hereford had to offer.[95] Although there were large numbers of gentry estates, the retailing environment of the city of Hereford was therefore found somewhat lacking, not able to supply the fashionable and tasteful goods that the gentry expected.[96]

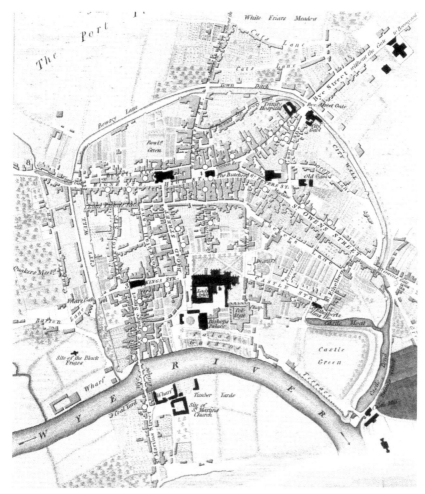

Figure 1.3: Approximate locations for clothing dealers and salesmen in Hereford Trade Directories, 1822–50, map, Cole and Roper, *c.* 1806, image courtesy of Herefordshire Record Office.

Geography of the City and Distribution of Shops

The main shopping areas of Hereford were the High Town (or High Street), which also served as the marketplace, and the streets radiating from it, Widemarsh Street, Eign Street, Broad Street, Bye Street and St Peter's Street. As would be expected, due to lower population numbers, there were fewer traders noted in the directories than for Worcester and a reduced number of specialized traders. In contrast to Worcester there were no defined areas for salesmen or clothes dealers. They were scattered across the city, sometimes combining dealing with other clothing trades such as woollen drapery, their activities more openly advertised than in Worcester (see Figure 1.3). Unlike Worcester, where a pattern of particular shops grouped together to attract the local elite seems to have arisen during its eighteenth-century development, Hereford still displayed the traditional retailing arrangement of a variety of shops clustered around the market place.[97]

The directories do not cover Hereford in detail for the first two decades of the nineteenth century, so court records have also been used to determine the presence of salesmen in the city. For example, Peter Williams was noted as a salesman when he was sued for £29 10s. 4d. by John Garnett, a banker from Hereford in 1812.[98] Williams was also a tailor and had the contract for making prisoners' clothes for Hereford Jail for much of the first decade of the nineteenth century. He did not supply the cloth, only made up the clothes.[99] He was also sued by a clothier, Joseph Wood of York, for £21 for goods sold and delivered, showing that he was part of a national network of supply.[100] Such evidence shows that ready-made clothing was available in Hereford from the start of the nineteenth century, if not earlier.

Pigot's 1822 *Directory* was the first to cover Hereford in detail. Thomas Bishop and William Spriggs were the only salesmen noted. A 'Cheap Clothes Warehouse' at the 'Original Manufactory', previously run by Thomas Bishop, was advertised in 1828 when it was taken over by a new owner, J. E. Turner.[101] This advertisement made much of its 'most astonishing' low prices. It also encouraged other buyers of working clothing such as overseers, to use the shop. The title of the shop as a manufactory suggests that ready-made clothing was fabricated there and had been for some-time, perhaps under Bishop. Their wide range of male clothing held as stock, '1000 Mens' and Boys' Frocks, full and plain worked ... 250 Fustian and other Jackets; 200 Mens' and Boys' Breeches and Trowsers', suggests a sizeable outfit, the emphasis being placed firmly on male garments.[102]

Spriggs's shop was in the High Town and he had directory entries as a clothes dealer until 1844. The first advertisement found for his business in the *Hereford Journal* dates to 1840, again when the shop was taken over by new owners:

> Re-opening of Spriggs Clothing Establishment, the clothing warehouse established by William Sprigg at the corner of Cabbage Lane, opposite the old Town Hall, No. 14. High Town, has been rebuilt and is now opened by H Watson with a new stock of drapery, hosiery, hats, mens and boys frocks, as cheap as any other establishment and readymade clothing of every description, well sewed and of substantial materials.[103]

The shop was run by Martha Watson in 1845 and advertised itself as a 'Ready-made Clothing Warehouse'.[104]

Alongside the salesmen, there were three pawnbrokers listed in Hereford across the period covered by the directories: Soloman Lazarus, Samuel Exon and

Abraham Myer. Myer initially listed himself as a clothes dealer in 1830 before adding pawnbroking in 1838. He advertised in the *Hereford Journal* in 1845:

> Unredeemed pledges, Bye St, 2 doors from the National Provincial Bank, A. Myer, has constantly on sale an immense assortment of wearing apparel of every description for Town and Country all at extremely low prices: Pilot and other coats in great variety ... No business transacted from 6 o'clock Friday evening until 6 o'clock Saturday evening.[105]

The hours of his shop would seem to indicate the observance of the Jewish Sabbath. Jews were noted for pawnbroking and associated with the second-hand market, trades which they could enter without restriction.[106] In 1846, Myer advertised in the local newspaper as having returned from London with an assortment of ready-made clothes. He also stated that he had 'a quantity of second hand clothes, remarkably cheap'.[107] However, in 1847 he placed an advertisement in Hunt's *Directory*, listing himself as a 'Jeweller, Silversmith, Watch Maker and Fashionable Clothing Establishment'. This advertisement failed to mention either his second-hand business or pawnbroking, although he was classified as a pawnbroker in the same directory.[108] The difference between how people ran their businesses and advertised locally, as opposed to how they tried to promote themselves on a national level in a trade directory is clear. They were perhaps trying to appeal to distinct audiences through different media. Using evidence from only one source may not give a representative view of what goods were being sold by a trader.

Lazarus also periodically held sales of unredeemed pledges, the majority of which seem to have been apparel, suggesting that this was possibly what his pawnbroking business mainly dealt in. For example, in 1816 he advertised for sale items including coats, waistcoats, ladies riding habits, pelisses, gowns, corsets and shirts.[109] Certainly, this pattern of dealing extensively in clothing is reflected in studies of pawnbrokers in other areas of the country, most notably, George Fettes in York.[110] Trade could be increased by offering clothing which had not been pawned, as Myer did, and so becoming a general clothes dealer. For the Jewish pawnbrokers of Hereford, clothing seems to have been a significant part of their business.

Thus the working-class consumer was well served by various traders in Hereford. In contrast to Worcester, these shops were dispersed throughout most of the main streets of Hereford. It was a less spatially segregated shopping environment in comparison to Worcester, but still offered various types of outlets to attract consumers seeking everyday clothing.

Herefordshire Towns

Seven towns outside the city of Hereford were covered by the directories of the period. Weobley and Pembridge were the smallest, Leominster, Ross and Ledbury the most substantial. They were traditional market towns, the focus for their rural hinterlands in a county where around 100,000 people lived.[111] The five larger towns of Herefordshire had various clothes dealers. Leominster had several traders over the period including John Jenkins, listed as a tailor, draper and clothes dealer in the contemporary trade directories. He went bankrupt in 1837, although he was subsequently listed in later directories trading again. His ready-made stock in 1837 included smock frocks, moleskin jackets, toilinet and swansdown waistcoats, some garments in different sizes: men's, boys and youths.[112] Ross, Ledbury and Leominster also had pawnbrokers.[113] The pawnbrokers in Ross were related to the Levi family, who were connected with the Jewish community in Gloucester, some eighteen miles away.[114]

Agricultural wages for labourers, although not the worst in the country, did not reflect the wealth of the local gentry. Wages in Herefordshire in the period were between 7 and 9 shillings per week against a national average of between 6 and 15 shillings. Average general wages in 1837 were 10s. 4d., rural workers falling behind manufacturing wages by the mid-nineteenth century. In nearby Birmingham, average wages in 1812 were 30 to 40 shillings per week, and in 1842 24 shillings per week, substantially more than agricultural labourers.[115] Agricultural labourers therefore needed cheap clothing. How far this need was satisfied by urban or rural traders will now be investigated.

In Ross, in the south-east of the county, there were always between two and four clothes dealers during the period covered by the directories. With just over 3,000 inhabitants in 1831 this may seem excessive. However, Ross was the nearest town to the Forest of Dean and the industrial and mining areas within the forest. Aside from serving workers from its rural hinterland, perhaps this was why this sector of the clothing trade was so defined in what was essentially a market town famed for its picturesque aspect and the starting point for tourist trips of the river Wye.[116] However, away from the sightseeing locations necessary as part of the Wye Tour, such as the view from the Prospect in the churchyard, the town itself garnered little positive response. Comments about narrow and dirty streets, with no paving and signs of dilapidation, were common to diarists on the Wye Tour across the period.[117] The industrial aspect of the hinterland was perhaps hidden from 'polite' visitors to the town but its economic importance to local retailers could not be disguised.

Other tailors and drapers in Ross also supplied working-class clothing, competing for a share of what seemed an extensive market. Tailor and draper Thomas Morgan went bankrupt in 1830. Amongst his stock auctioned off was a supply of 'readymade clothes'.[118] However, he recovered from this setback and continued trading in a different street in the 1830s and 40s, presumably in a similar line of business. In 1815, Nathaniel Morgan was calling himself a 'Cheap Linen and Woollen Draper and Hosier', selling for cash utilitarian items such as cords, velveteens, cottage poplins and kerseymeres and also 'a variety of muslin dresses', a rare mention of female ready-made garments.[119] He was listed in Pigot's *Directory* of 1822 and 1830 as a linen and woollen draper and silk mercer. As in Droitwich, it seems that some of the town's drapers were also selling ready-made clothing along with their drapery stock.

Indeed, Sarah Levitt suggests that it was drapers and haberdashers who developed women's ready-made clothing into the mid-nineteenth century, after little expansion in the previous thirty years.[120] References to women's ready-made dresses certainly become more extensive during the 1840s. In 1842, Sarah Marshall stole a dress valued at 10 shillings from Edward Penner of Ross, listed as a woollen draper in the contemporary directories.[121] Also in Ross, in 1845, Elizabeth Clarke was charged with obtaining a dress, a pair of stays and other articles under false pretences with intent to cheat and defraud Jane Gardner and partner Eliza Jones, again listed as drapers.[122] There were references to ready-made dresses throughout the first half of the nineteenth century, for example: in 1827 a draper and silk mercer named Hornby in Hereford was selling cotton dresses for 3s. 6d;[123] and in 1820, at the Manchester and Scotch Warehouse, Broad Street, Worcester, William Powell bought back from Manchester 'coloured and white dresses' as part of his new stock, which as they were highlighted in his advertisement, were presumably distinct from his normal drapery fabrics.[124] As noted by Beverly Lemire, Manchester seems to have been a centre of production for ready-made dresses from the late eighteenth century.[125] By the 1840s, many more drapers, including those in Ross, seem to have been offering ready-made dresses for sale, although it is not often clear whether these were made locally or bought wholesale from Manchester.[126]

Bromyard was situated in the north-east of the county and in contrast to the frequent flattering observations about local towns, several editions of Pigot's directories made unusually derogatory comments, reflecting its inferior status and unfashionable nature. The town was situated in a poor agricultural area on sandy soil. In 1830 the author of Pigot's *Directory* commented that: 'The town does not present either well built houses or regular streets ... [Its] trade confined to the reciprocal requirements of the inhabitants & those of the neighbourhood'. In 1844 the *Directory* stated that it: 'boasts neither well built dwellings nor regular streets, & its appearance altogether is far from pre-possessing'.[127] Its annual mortality rates were comparable to the urban areas of Hull and Rotherhithe due to defective sanitary arrangements.[128] By the first quarter of the nineteenth century, the rents for cottages on the downlands surrounding the town were so low that it was more profitable to send paupers from other parts of the county to live there, rather than keeping them within their home parish.[129] This became illegal after the Poor Law Amendment Act of 1834, leading to a slight population decline. The population of just under 3,000 in 1831 had fallen by fifty-six people by 1841.[130] Bromyard was a deprived area, with limited agricultural employment opportunities for the resident population compared to other areas of Herefordshire. There was little development to advance its status within local society.

This was reflected in its clothing retailers with a cluster of clothes dealers and brokers recorded in the trade directories for Bromyard, many of whom were at some point also classified as tailors and drapers.[131] This represented one dealer for every 245 people in Bromyard in 1822, the population figure in the 1821 census being 1,227.[132] Other suppliers of ready-made clothing are revealed by tenders offered to the Bromyard Union in 1837. The Union required ready-made clothing including smock frocks, trousers, jackets, waistcoats and gowns in two different sizes to bid for the tender, although it was noted that 'all the different sizes will at times be required', suggesting more complex sizing of clothing in day to day administration.[133] In the first year of the Union's existence the contract was held by a Mr Vale, although he was unable to execute it and had to pay the Board of Guardians a £20 penalty.[134] Vale subsequently went bankrupt, his stock advertised in the *Worcester Journal* in June 1837.[135] The tender was subsequently given to Philip Taylor, the Guardians stipulating prices and a penalty of £50 if Taylor failed to deliver.[136] Both Vale and Taylor were local drapers, Taylor listed in directories from 1822 to 1844, Vale in 1842 and 1844. Further evidence needs to be uncovered to ascertain how these tenders were carried out, whether ready-made clothing was bought in from further afield or orders sent to local out-workers to make clothes up. It is a matter of conjecture but it would appear that Vale was unable to supply the capital outlay required to purchase a large quantity of ready-made clothing at the outset or perhaps had overstretched himself to try and do so without being able to finally deliver the order, leaving the rest of his business vulnerable. The trade of speculating in ready-made clothing was still risky, even with a guaranteed purchaser at the end.

This evidence suggests that both ready-made and second-hand clothing were widely available in Bromyard. Certainly a shopkeeper outside the town perceived there to be a gap in the market for more upmarket clothing. In 1834, H. Woakes, a draper and mercer from Pershore who employed a foreman from the 'west end' of London, advertised to the 'nobility, clergy and gentry' that he would be visiting the Bay Horse in Bromyard the first Monday in every month to attend and receive orders.[137] This suggests he supposed that the existing clothing shops were of low-status and not suitable for respectable society.

Worcestershire and Herefordshire Villages

The concentration of historians so far has been focused on urban settlement with, for example, Lemire suggesting that there were 'thousands of clothes dealers scattered through the urban landscape'. Consumers needed to come into large towns and cities in the early nineteenth century to purchase their clothing.[138] However, Frederick Eden claimed in his survey of the state of the poor in 1797:

'In the Midland and Southern counties, the labourer in general purchases a very considerable portion if not the whole, of his clothes from the shopkeeper'. He added that around London the clothes purchased were generally second-hand and little was made up within the home.[139] This section will examine the nature of the retail provision in the countryside of Herefordshire and Worcestershire and will question how accessible clothing was to buy in rural areas or whether consumers had to journey into local towns and cities purchase it.[140]

Two surveys of traders in all parishes across the county were carried out for Worcestershire by Lewis's Directory in 1820 and Bentley's History in 1840–1. A similar survey was carried out for Herefordshire by Lascelles's Directory in 1851. Whilst it is debatable how accurate and how comprehensive the directory sur-

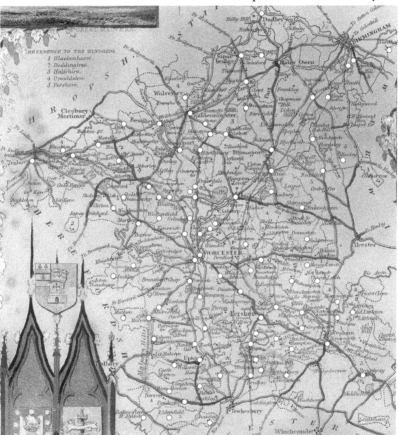

Figure 1.4: Map of Worcestershire showing distribution of tailors, from *Worcestershire General and Commercial Directory for 1820* (Worcester: S. Lewis, 1820) and *Bentley's History and Guide and Alphabetical and Classified Directory of Worcester ... Evesham ... , Dudley ... , Stourbridge ... , and Bentley's History, Gazetteer, Directory and Statistics of Worcestershire*, 3 vols (Birmingham: Bull & Turner, 1840–2), map Thomas Moule, 1836, private collection.

veys actually were, the results do show some general patterns. Any village with a population of over 300 had trades people involved with clothing. The greatest majority of these were tailors, with 124 found in total for the Worcestershire surveys and 117 in Herefordshire.

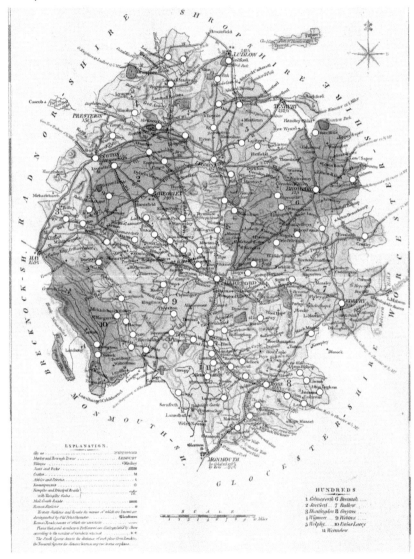

Figure 1.5: Map of Herefordshire showing distribution of tailors from *Directory and Gazetteer of Herefordshire* (Birmingham: Lascelles & Co., 1851), map Cole and Roper, 1805, private collection.

As can be seen from Figure 1.4 and Figure 1.5, where each circle represents the location of a tailor noted in the surveys, they were scattered relatively evenly across the two counties. If a village did not have its own tailor, there was likely to be one in a nearby settlement.[141] It is perhaps questionable how many of these were actually retailers, or whether they were working for part of their time for the larger retailers in the towns, manufacturing the ready-made clothing that most of the latter seemed to be selling. However, some certainly were retailing, if perhaps more informally than their urban counterparts. These included those making up clothing from customers' materials, often with a small stock of drapery on the side, and repairing and altering garments.

The accounts of one such unnamed rural tailor survive from the north Herefordshire/Shropshire/Radnor border, who drew on a clientele from over a ten-mile radius.[142] His customers came from the larger towns of the district as well as small hamlets, most easily accessible along the river valleys to the west of Leintwardine.[143] The anonymous tailor must have built up a good reputation. In the larger settlements of Knighton and Leintwardine there were other tailors operating too. Customers in Knighton in particular, seem to have chosen to patronize him rather than perhaps more conveniently placed tailors in the town. However, the need to traverse more hilly terrain to reach the tailor and the draw of the town of Ludlow, seven miles from Leintwardine, seems to have prevented customers from the east of Leintwardine using his services.

The accounts show the tailor mending, altering and making men's clothes, with the occasional lady's habit, and a stock of ready-made clothing offered for sale too. He catered for a range of customers of all social ranks, from members of the local gentry to tradesmen and labourers on local estates. He was certainly not an out-worker for a business in a large town, but ran a thriving rural tailor's business.[144] This parallels the evidence that Anne Buck found for Bedfordshire in the late eighteenth century, where all social ranks, from the gentry downwards used local village tailors.[145]

His customers were dealt with in different ways in the account books. Some servants were detailed impersonally, as in 'Mr Cookes Groom'. Others were customers in their own right. For example, Mr Davies, a keeper at Clungunford, had an account with him for several years, purchasing items such as in 1845 a jacket and trousers for £1 3s., a waistcoat for 11s. and a coat for £2 10s., all seemingly ready-made.[146] Where items were made by the tailor, the fabric, trimmings and time used to make the garment were detailed. Other items were simply sold with a note of the total price, suggesting that they were ready-made.[147] He was thus selling clothing to both types of consumers of working clothing: the independent working man as well as to the local gentry who bought items on their employees' behalf.

As might be expected, to help generate income all the year round, especially in rural areas, some tailors had a further occupation such as farming.[148] Some of the most common secondary occupations were associated with public houses, victualling or beerselling. The inn or public house was the focus of village life, the place where villagers met – especially men – and where newspapers were read aloud[149] and local meetings held.[150] With a ready-made clientele of male customers, the combination with tailoring would have appeared natural. It seems to have been taken up by several tradesmen both in villages and smaller towns.[151] Barry Reay notes that the trade lent itself to a combination with another craft, as the women of the household could carry out much of the victualling business.[152] In such circumstances, the men could concentrate on tailoring. However, unlike farming, the combination with victualling was unlikely to be due to seasonal employment patterns. The often low volume of trade from whichever was the primary occupation suggests that a secondary occupation needed to be under-taken for economic reasons. Advertisements from the *Hereford Journal* from 1835 detail one tailor, Timothy Hilo Mathews, who was also a shopkeeper and retailer of beer and cider from Fownhope. He was noted as being in the debtors' jail, but a few weeks later was advertising for two journeymen tailors, implying a not insubstantial business.[153] The inn or pub, at the centre of the community, often acted as a forum for informal pawnbroking and a shop as well. In a court case reported from 1830, stolen articles of clothing were sold at a public house between Worcester and Leominster, reflecting the idea of pubs as places where goods could be traded, especially clothing.[154]

Accounts remain from one tailor and victualler, Joseph Blewitt, for the years 1816–29. He was based in Coseley in the Black Country, on the Staf-fordshire border, but sold to customers in Dudley. His business seems to have been a mixture of making and repairing male clothing along with selling some items of ready-made clothing, including waistcoats and baragon jackets.[155] There does not seem to have been a great variation in price between ready-made and made-to-measure items, and this was also found to be the case by Fowler in her study of a similar Hampshire tailor. She suggests that where prices were similar between bespoke and ready-made items, the ready-made items were new, not second-hand, the accepted value for second-hand clothing being a quarter of their original price or less.[156] The accounts of Mr Thomas Wilson of Dudley in 1826 show how the two sides of the business were combined. During the course of the year, Blewitt made a pair of trousers and a top coat for him. He also sold him pints of 'wiskey' and brandy, the total for the year coming to £4 18s. 8d., nearly £4 of which was on alcohol.[157] This suggests that for him, tailoring was the sideline in economic terms.

Another example of such a combination of trades is from Evesham in 1820, although it is perhaps instructive that the business ultimately failed. Thomas

Harris, a bankrupt, was described as an innkeeper, dealer and chapman.[158] When his goods came to be auctioned to pay off his creditors, it emerged that he had a 'valuable' stock described as, 'superfine broad cloths, narrow ditto, kersey-meres, cords, waistcoatings and other valuable property in the wool trade'.[159] He appears to have been both an innkeeper and a woollen draper or tailor. Although these detailed examples were from larger towns, it seems to have been a common combination of trades, particularly in rural areas.

Evidence for a small-scale tailor working in a village setting in 1836 has only survived because he was a witness in a murder case. Francis Fidzer worked in Astley, near Stourport, north Worcestershire, was seemingly just about making ends meet. William Lightburn, a sawyer from nearby Areley Common, ordered a suit six weeks before Christmas. He supplied the cloth and Fidzer the labour and trimmings. The tailor had not allowed Lightburn to take his suit home without payment as he had heard that he would then never be paid. Lightburn called for his clothes after Christmas with the money, but Fidzer had in the meantime pawned them, presumably to raise additional capital. Fidzer gave him the pawn-broker's ticket to go and redeem his clothes himself.[160] Unfortunately, there were no further details about the suit or its cost, but the use of pawnbrokers to cover a possible bad debt shows one strategy used by small-scale traders. The nearest pawnbroker listed in Pigot's *Directory* of 1828 was in Bewdley, three miles away, although there were probably others working on a more informal basis.[161] Pawn-brokers could be vital for keeping under-capitalized small traders afloat and, in effect, acted like a bank for them, their stock used as currency.[162]

In contrast to tailors, although drapers were scattered throughout the villages of the two counties, they did not have the same number of outlets. Sixteen have been found in each county. Twenty-six of these were noted as combining drapery with another trade, usually grocery, sometimes hardware or general shopkeeping. This would suggest that the proliferation of small shopkeepers that Hoh-cheung Mui and Lorna Mui found across the country continued into the nineteenth century, some enterprisingly adding drapery to their general stock.[163] There were some larger village establishments. In Ombersley, north of Worcester, which had a population of around 2,500 by the 1840s, William Corbett was a linen and woollen draper as well as a grocer, tea dealer and tobacconist. His elaborate billhead drew on classical and exotic images designed to appeal to local respectable society. However, he was able to supply ready-made smock frocks for 4 shillings as well as a wide assortment of textiles, as evidenced in surviving bills to the local parish overseers.[164] Such local village shops served all sections of society, including overseers buying for the poor. Overseers were respected upstanding members of the community, so that they chose to buy from a shop that they knew should probably not be surprising. As Buck comments, such shops became general outfitters for the largest family in the parish, those receiving relief.[165]

The advertisements for two drapers' businesses for sale sheds further light on rural clothing provision. Both were sold earlier than their respective county directory surveys, so they would not have been able to advertise in them. Each business was located beside the Hereford to Worcester turnpike. An advertisement from the *Hereford Journal* in 1825 details the stock of a business at Newtown. The owner, Mrs Mary Ross, seemed to carry a large supply of goods for a settlement consisting of a few houses with, for example, 500 shawls and 1,000 yards of cotton print. Along with fustian and duck, she also sold ribbons, gingham, handkerchiefs and muslins. Her choice of stock, with its emphasis on cotton prints and check aproning, essential for protecting female clothing, would have appealed to the working-class consumer, particularly to women. Newtown was on the crossroads of the Hereford to Worcester and Gloucester to Leominster roads, which may account for the volume of business.[166]

The second advertisement appeared in both local newspapers in 1816 for the business of John Saunders of Cradley, a grocer, linen draper and slop seller. Like Mary Ross, his stock seems to have been extensive for a small village shop, with, for example, 105 flannel jackets with sleeves, 152 waistcoats, 55 cotton gowns, 40 smock frocks and 109 pairs of stays.[167] His shop was also located beside the main turnpike and at the crossroads of the Bromyard to Ledbury road. The passing trade may have provided a good source of custom. An auction of drapery and a large stock of ready-made clothes was previously advertised in 1814 in Cradley, when Mr Spooner went out of business.[168] The local population may have been accustomed to buying clothing ready-made. As Cradley was one of the villages where gloving was 'put-out' from Worcester, providing work for local women, perhaps such clothing outlets were more of a necessity. Of course, it is difficult to find the specific details all historians search for in advertisements such as these. The stock is not stated as second-hand so it seems likely that it is new ready-made clothing. The fact that two ready-made clothes sellers also went out of business within the space of three years in one village, may also make the evidence atypical. There was clearly some sort of demand for ready-made clothing in the area for such a stock to have built up in that location. However, ultimately it proved difficult for the two retailers to make enough return on their investment to survive for the long-term.

In the mid-nineteenth century, in the village of Eckington, Worcestershire, a grocer and draper leaving for another part of the country advertised his stock for sale. Alongside his grocery stock was a large quantity of prints and 'muslin de laine, cashmere, Coburg, tweed Orlean and other dresses of the newest design, shawls, stockings, stays ... bonnets, caps, ribbons, handkerchiefs'.[169] A comparative study of Buckinghamshire in the south Midlands, using newspaper advertisements to look for evidence of rural clothes retailing, suggests a similar pattern. Although the newspaper evidence is not so strong as that from Herefordshire and Worcestershire, the Buckinghamshire newspapers being newly established in the second quarter of the nineteenth century, by the 1840s, there is some evidence of rural ready-made clothes retailing as part of grocery shops in Stewkley and Wingrave.[170] Perhaps if rural shops were able to stock necessary groceries and hardware, for example, customers could be drawn in to buy other goods at the shop at the same time, including clothing and particularly smock frocks and items for female dress.[171]

Dressmakers and milliners were also more sparsely spread across the two counties. Like tailoring, it is unclear whether they were retailing to their local communities or were principally out-workers for larger concerns in the towns. They became more common in the second quarter of the nineteenth century, with only one milliner in Worcestershire in 1820 compared to nine in 1841 and likewise no dressmakers in Worcestershire in 1820 and five in 1840.[172] As female rural fieldwork became increasingly less acceptable, dressmaking may have become a more distinct full-time occupation, rather than carried out as a sideline.[173]

However, despite the small numbers listed in the directories, a court case from 1822 shows that dressmakers not listed in trade directories were used by working-class consumers, including those in rural areas.[174] In 1822, Hannah Attwood stole twenty-one yards of cotton print and took it to Hester Done, a 'mantua maker' in Birlingham, a village outside Pershore. The dress had been partly made up when the cloth was recovered.[175] Jane Tozer and Sarah Levitt point out that in the first half of the nineteenth century making female clothing was a complicated matter. Tape measures were a rarity and paper patterns and the sewing machine were developed only from the mid-nineteenth century onwards.[176] Dressmakers were not just used by the middle classes but would make up clothing for anyone, including those on relief. They were sometimes receiving dole among themselves.[177] Nevertheless, it appears that they were unlikely to advertise themselves in directories until the mid-nineteenth century outside the main towns of the area.

Conclusion

By 1800 both Hereford and Worcester were well-established retail centres. Although only twenty-four miles apart, each city developed a different shopping environment. Worcester had been an important city until the beginning of the nineteenth century and the number and quality of its shops reflected this. Over the first half of the nineteenth century, there appears to have been a decline in the status of the type of consumers it attracted, although its population continued to grow. Worcester has arguably never regained its pre-eminence and is still eclipsed by local rivals Birmingham and Cheltenham, the latter developing particularly from the first quarter of the nineteenth century as a fashionable spa and shopping centre.[178] In contrast, Hereford remained more stable both in terms of the number of shops and in population growth. Although the city did receive tourists passing along the Wye valley, this was not a predominant industry. The city principally serviced the needs of its local, largely rural population.

By 1800 ready-made clothes were widely available across the two counties. This might not be evident from the billheads of some drapers but is visible through the stock detailed in the same bills. Selling this type of clothing could be highly profitable, as shown by the businesses of Richard Sanders in Worcester and John Pumfrey in Droitwich. In the majority of towns by this date, the working-class male consumer would have had the opportunity to purchase ready-made or second-hand clothing, either from specialist dealers or tailors and drapers who did not necessarily advertise the fact that they offered this stock. In the north of England, ready-made clothing, certainly in the eighteenth century, was harder to come by in market and country towns than in urban areas.[179] However, by 1849, in Evesham, Worcestershire, for example, a traditional market town, the stock of James Wright, a draper and outfitter was advertised for sale. It included ready-made coats, jackets, trousers, leggings, gaitors, white and brown frocks, shirts, as well as 'a large assortment of slops', which seem to have been of a lower quality than his other ready-made stock. His stock was valued at £875, a sum which might allow a significant quantity of ready-made clothing.[180] Thus backing up the comments of Eden that labourers bought a considerably quantity of their clothes from shops, the retail environment for selling male clothing was well-developed across both counties by the first quarter of the nineteenth century. It was focussed on towns but there were rural outlets too, catering for those who were more isolated and perhaps unable to journey into town frequently.

References to ready-made female clothing were less common than those to male ready-made clothing. However, there are examples of large stocks, for instance, the fifty-five cotton gowns and thirty-seven muslin gowns in the stock of John Saunders in 1816.[181] These date to the period when female dress construction was relatively simple in comparison to after 1820.[182] It seems likely that many women made their own clothes or took material to a local dressmaker, who did not necessarily advertise herself as such in the contemporary trade directories, perhaps using neighbourhood contacts and word of mouth instead. Although little evidence has survived, it seems probable that there were dressmakers in local communities who provided clothing for all social classes, in both urban and rural areas. These community dressmakers have escaped attention, although they are visible in some court cases and in poor law evidence which will be examined in more detail in Chapter 4. They do not appear in the trade directory listings, which as noted in the introduction, are problematic with regard to the roles of milliners and dressmakers.[183] Dressmakers gave working-class women access to new clothes, particularly, as during the 1830s and 40s styles became increasingly structured and more difficult for an amateur to attempt.[184] Although ready-made dresses had been available since the eighteenth-century, a growth in their manufacture seems to have occurred in the mid-nineteenth century, when they were often sold as part of the drapery trade in towns and in more rural areas.

The number and wide distribution of shops selling working-class clothing suggests that working-class customers were accepted as shoppers in their own right and were perhaps sought after. Court records confirm that working-class women in particular, frequently entered drapers' shops and were shown selections of items without raising particular comment.[185] Shoplifters and fraudsters were able to carry out crimes, precisely because their appearance in such shops was acceptable in the first place. Styles has found evidence of such cases occurring in large urban drapers in Newcastle.[186] From court records, this research shows that by the nineteenth century, the practice of working-class consumers entering high street drapers' shops was also well established in smaller market towns. For example, a court case from 1825 described how Sarah Jones, aged thirty-four, was accepted as a potential customer in the main drapers' shops of the market town of Tenbury and given textile samples to examine. She was accused of stealing printed cotton and a piece of muslin from Thomas Benbow's drapers' shop.[187] Jones appears to have been well-known locally, making illicit deals and taking lodgings in the small town (population 1,768 in 1831). Despite what seems to be a precarious way of living, she was still welcomed as a potential customer in the drapers' shop. Tammy Whitlock has argued that working-class shoplifters assumed the identity of middle-class women in order to carry out their crime. Whilst this may have been true for larger anonymous cities, in towns such as Tenbury, populations were still relatively small. People were known to each other through a variety of ties, arguably making such fraud a less viable option.[188] It also seems that the shopkeeper was as dependent on purchases by those of a lower status as those higher up the social scale to keep their business afloat, so many could not afford any snobbery about who they would serve.

Some fraud was carried out in the two counties as in other areas, with people using perceptions about social status as a disguise for illicit gain. However, as a case from Leominster in 1850 shows, fraud was more often tried through borrowing a name and forging an order in a letter rather than entering the actual shop.[189] Shopkeepers received working-class consumers as shoppers seemingly without comment, presumably knew many personally, and expected them to come in and buy. Fowler has also found that this was the case in rural Hampshire, with no obvious segregation of shoppers into differing social bands in her study of a rural tailor's shop in 1811–15.[190] For clothes retailers, especially those who had invested up-front in ready-made clothing, the working-class consumer was the main focus of their business. As Giorgio Riello has suggested in his study of the shoe trade, 'the polarization of shops into different social categories should not be exaggerated'.[191] Many targeted a wide variety of individuals and different types of stock and qualities of that stock were sold by the same shop.[192]

Comparative studies need to be carried out across other areas of the country in order to determine how common the selling of ready-made clothing was across all areas, urban and rural, by the mid-nineteenth century. However, although choice and price competition was perhaps greatest where there were clusters of similar shops, that is in urban areas, entering a shop and being able to choose between buying ready-made clothing or fabric to be made-up appears to have been a normal and routine activity for both male and female working-class consumers across large areas of England. This also confirms Eden's observation of 1797 that many labourers bought their clothes from shops. Provincial clothing shops were thriving across all areas of the Midlands, available both in urban and rural localities, giving working-class people the opportunity to purchase the clothing that they needed and perhaps desired.

2 THE SHOPKEEPER AND THE WORKING-CLASS CONSUMER

Chapter 1 established that there was a wide distribution of clothing shops across all areas of Herefordshire and Worcestershire that could have been used by working-class consumers. This chapter will examine the business of these shops in more detail. By using case studies of businesses in Worcester and Hereford, it will investigate and compare how important the trade of working-class consumers was for these shopkeepers. It will consider whether there were specialist shops purely catering for such consumers or if they were more integrated into the general retail environment. The variety of ready-made clothing on offer to customers will also be examined. A discussion about promotion and advertising directed towards the working-class consumer will follow. It will question if shops made a concerted effort to attract working-class consumers or if they did not want to or need to. Conclusions can then be drawn about the range of shops that sold clothing to working-class consumers.

Worcester

This section will trace how Stephen Burden, a tailor and draper in Worcester, made the transition from salesman to royal warrant holder over the course of the first four decades of the nineteenth century. It will discuss how important the working-class clothing trade was for Burden and how he used it to enhance his own status. It will also seek to ascertain what competition he had from other tailors and drapers in the city. Finally, it will assess how Burden's business was promoted, in contrast to other salesmen in Worcester.[1]

Salesmen had been established in Worcester from at least the late eighteenth century and Burden initially worked for one, Thomas Freame. Freame was also a wholesaler, draper, hatter, hosier and pawnbroker, as well as dealing in furniture, and Burden's signature appeared on one of his bills in 1798.[2] Freame retired from the pawnbroking business in 1805 and appears to have died soon after.[3] Burden first opened his own business on a fair day in 1809, probably to garner maximum custom. His shop, situated in Goose Lane close to his old employer's, sold drapery and ready-made clothes.[4] The Freame family appears to have sold off the remainder of their unredeemed pledges in clothing later that year and from then on concentrated on the furniture side of the business.[5] It is possible that Burden took over the clothing side.

Burden was initially in competition with John Hooper, who had a shop opposite the entrance of the nearby Shambles, which he had opened in 1807.[6] Two weeks after Burden's opening in 1809, Hooper placed an advertisement notifying the public of his 'cheap wearing apparel', for example, coats from 12*s*. 6*d*. upwards and breeches from 8*s*. He claimed that his tailoring 'will do away the prejudice of gentlemen having their Clothes made at a Slop Shop …' and thanked his 'country friends' for their recommendations.[7] In 1810 he changed emphasis, presenting himself as a draper and tailor, his foreman returning from London in the spring, where he had 'selected specimens of the newest fashion and had experience from the first abilities in cutting general wearing apparel'.[8] Hooper then seems to have fallen foul of the Company of Master Tailors, a remnant of the medieval guild system.[9] He was forced to publish a rebuttal to allegations made about the quality of his tailoring and in doing so, called himself a salesman. He stated that he had been told to 'desist' from carrying out the business of a tailor but will 'still honour those who think it proper to honour him with their commands' and he 'employ[s] a number of the best workmen'.[10] A couple of weeks later, the same advertisement was published with the addition 'it has been indiscreetly reported to delude Public Trail [*sic*], that JH manufactures nothing but sops [*sic*] but he feels confident he can produce specimens of work as good as any in the kingdom and cloths, not to be excelled by any'.[11] Hooper was not a member of the Company of Master Tailors and therefore could not claim to be a master tailor in the eyes of the guild. Perhaps he had promoted himself as a tailor in his advertising rather than emphasizing his ready-made clothing business as this might have incurred further censure from the Company of Master Tailors anxious about the increasing size of the men's ready-made clothing business and its threat to their livelihoods. Alternatively, maybe Hooper was trying to enhance the status of his own business with the focus on tailoring, although without sanction from the Company of Master Tailors. This exchange shows the importance of reputation for shopkeepers during this period. As Claire Walsh has noted, in an era before there were many branded products, the shop, and by definition, the shopkeeper, became the brand which needed to be sold to get customers into the shop.[12] Any slur on the 'brand' had to be answered to restore confidence and maintain a commercially successful position.

There was some debate about ready-made clothing in Worcester in 1810, probably emanating from the Company of Master Tailors unsuccessfully trying to control production. Where production was separated from retailing, with outworkers making up ready-made clothing for example, guilds considered this to be an illegal unregulated practice.[13] Penelope Corfield has noted that the authority of guilds was enforced at times of economic difficulty as was probably happening in Worcester.[14] From 1805 to 1810, continual disputes over wages with the journeymen tailors had occurred as reported in the *Worcester Journal*. This attempt at controlling the trade was manifested through comments published in the local newspaper. For example, Alexander Pope was a member of the Company of Master Tailors, and as 'tailor and draper to HRH Prince of Wales', seems to have been at the other end of the social scale to Hooper and Burden. He stated pointedly at the end of his advertisement: 'NB Pope's customers may be assured they shall never receive from him Slops or Yorkshire Broads'.[15] During the eighteenth century, the Yorkshire woollen industry, of which 'broads' or broadcloth was a part, had been based on the production of cheap goods. This was in contrast to the other woollen cloth-producing areas of Norwich and the West Country.[16] Bespoke tailoring as practised by the Company of Master Tailors was perceived to be under threat from those who sought to sell ready-made clothes. It was perhaps the last attempt to protect the traditional way of operating. It does not seem to have had much effect. By the late 1830s, the influence of the Company of Master Tailors had diminished further. From twenty members of the company in 1828, including Burden, it had declined to six members by 1837, the records ending in 1841. The Statute of Artificers had also been repealed in 1814, meaning apprenticeships were no longer necessary for entry into trades such as tailoring, thus loosening guild control still further.[17]

Perhaps due to the adverse publicity that he had attracted and the effect that this had on his reputation as shopkeeper and the stock within that shop, Hooper experienced financial difficulties and was declared bankrupt in 1812. He was able to start trading again a few months later, having engaged staff from London,[18] but by 1815 it seems that he had had enough, as he sold up and left the city. There is an advertisement for a business in *Berrow's Worcester Journal* of 1815 which was probably his:

> To drapers and tailors – to be disposed of for a moderate premium, a respectable drapery and tailoring business, now in good repute and worthy the attention of any person who can command a capital equal to the undertaking, as the tailoring department alone employs 6 to 10 men. The premises are most desirably situated for any trade, particularly that of a Pawnbroker and salesman, the latter business being now carried on. The stock which is not very extensive, to be taken at a fair valuation. [19]

The business was purchased by Stephen Burden. He engaged Hooper's foreman, Mr Craig, who claimed to have worked for Weston's in Bond Street, London.[20] Burden was now advertising himself as a woollen draper with a 'Fashionable Apparel Warehouse'.[21] He appears to have avoided the controversy in 1810, although he too was selling ready-made clothing. It is conceivable that Burden had served an apprenticeship under Freame and so was now a freeman. He was listed as a member of the Company of Master Tailors by the 1820s, which would imply that this was the case.

Indeed, by 1820 Burden's emphasis was firmly on tailoring, engaging another foreman 'who has derived his instruction ... from the most celebrated master in London ... with mathematical precision ... so obviously superior to all others now in practice'. The advertisement did not mention his trade as a salesman or retailing ready-made clothes.[22] By 1830, he had achieved a royal warrant, 'tailor to his Royal Highness, the Prince of Saxe Coburg', claiming to have executed several orders for Prince Leopold while at Malvern.[23] It was the first of many such advertisements that followed during the 1830s. It would appear that he had redefined himself as tailor by royal appointment, dealing with the elite end of the market. In 1832, Burden took over Pope's old shop and business at 2, Foregate Street, opposite the Hop Pole Inn,[24] as he strove to enhance further his status as a premier tailor in Worcester. His son had taken over the day to day running of the tailoring business in 1829, having worked in 'several of the most fashionable houses in the west end of town' for five years.[25] Burden himself died in 1844 and his business was passed onto William Lewis, a tailor and draper who had already been established several years in the city.[26]

Therefore by the 1820s, Burden did not need or want to advertise the ready-made clothing side of his business. In Lewis's *Directory* of 1820, he was listed as a woollen draper and clothier, the only tradesman in Worcester to be classified as such. Historically, a clothier was a cloth merchant and middle man, the go-between for manufacturers and buyers. By the nineteenth century, they were increasingly associated with ready-made clothing, linking textile manufacturers, labour markets and retailers.[27] Others were noted as clothes dealers suggesting perhaps an association with the second-hand trade that Burden did not wish to publicize.[28] In 1825 he had acted as assignee for Thomas Beaman, a salesman from Stourport. It is therefore conceivable that he had become a wholesaler rather than a retailer for this end of the market by that date.[29] A wholesaler was seen as higher in status than a shopkeeper so perhaps this was the way he chose to move out of the ready-made retail market.[30] He could still run a ready-made wholesale business but concentrate on the elite market in his city shop. Bills from him to overseers of parishes in the surrounding hinterland in relation to the supply of ready-made clothing survive from the 1820s, but then disappear. For example, in 1822, Burden supplied the overseers of Hindlip with a flannel jacket, leather breeches, smock frock, shirt and other items for James Merrill.[31] The decline in the purchase of clothing from Burden may however have been an effect of changes in the Old Poor Law provisioning of clothing with the passing of the Sturges Bourne Acts of 1818 and 1819.[32]

Burden was trying to promote himself as a tradesman for 'respectable' society before 1820, even though he was still retailing ready-made clothes. He certainly seems to have been very aware of his image, using relatively elaborate billheads from early on in his career, especially in comparison to his rivals.[33] Burden appears to have seen his long-term business aim as supplying clothing for the elite end of the market. Presumably, he regarded this as more profitable and it would certainly have given him a greater social standing within Worcester society. By the 1830s, he had achieved his aim.[34]

The sale of ready-made clothing was left to his competitors, one of whom was Richard Sanders, briefly discussed in chapter 1. In contrast to Burden, he did not advertise in the press and failed to move his business premises away from unfashionable Lich Street. However, his printed billheads from 1837 emphasized that his was 'The Original Warehouse' established in 1712,[35] also highlighted by his successor, John H. Sanders.[36] In a way, the trajectory of his business was the antithesis to Burden's. Sanders's shop had already been in existence for nearly 100 years by the time Burden went into business. The only bills that have been found from Sanders's shop prior to 1837 are all handwritten, suggesting a less sophisticated operation than Burden's.[37] While Burden strove to become part of the elite network of Worcester tailors over a twenty year period, Sanders continued to concentrate on his core customers, working-class consumers.

On his death in 1837, Sanders had several outstanding bills from suppliers, which reveal how his business was part of a national network of supply. These included 'Armstrong & Phillips, Manufacturers of Woollen Cords, Fustians &c., 12 George Street, Manchester', from whom in 1836 he had two orders amounting to nearly £30 of various cords and moleskins. The note on the bill from August 1836 stated: '... hope pleased with the colors [*sic*] of the cords sent'.[38] A similar manufacturer, 'William Anthony, 16 Bread Street, Manchester', a fustian manufacturer and merchant, sent a bill in November 1836 for the purchase of thicksetts and moleskins, for £16 3*s*. 2*d*., transported to Worcester by Pickfords. Sanders was less satisfied with this supplier. Writing on the back in a different hand noted: 'Moleskin very close measure in 2 pieces and a rent [tear], 3 yds short'. Likewise, from 'Charles Cross, Fustian, Calico &c., Manufacturer and Printer, 24 High Street, Manchester', a bill exists, dated 1 January 1837, just three weeks before Sanders's death. He had purchased twelve items, including drab twilled nankeen, drab drabbett and ducks, again transported by Pickfords, for a total of £29 12s 2d. The note on the back of the bill, written by Sanders or one of his employees, stated: 'The annexed order is far from the prices ask'd. The nankeen was made at 8½, charged 9 ¼ brown twill made at 7, charged 7¾, which must be a mistake (Examine it) only 28 inches'.[39] Another of Sanders's suppliers was 'Charles Stephens & Co., Stanley Mills, Gloucestershire', with warehouses in London and Manchester and with whom he had an account.[40] In 1836 he bought black, blue and dahlia-coloured woollen fabrics and black 'mill'd' cas-simere, with deductions for holes found in the fabric.[41] As would be expected, manufacturers and shopkeepers bargained to get the best prices, their notes to each other on the bills also displaying developing relationships.

The fabrics Sanders purchased from his suppliers across the country included many used for everyday clothing, such as cords and moleskins. What is not clear from the surviving evidence is whether these fabrics were sold as part of his drapery business or if they were subsequently made up into ready-made cloth-ing for his clothing warehouse. The surviving bills do not note any ready-made clothing being bought wholesale, although he was known as a salesman.[42] It is probable that clothing was made up locally to sell ready-made in the clothing warehouse.[43] The 1841 census reveals that Sanders's successor, his nephew John Hawkes Sanders, lived in a small household with just one female servant. There were no workers within his household who could have made up the clothing. However, in Lich Street and Friar Street there was a concentration of tailors, dressmakers and seamstresses, the last occupation in particular associated with making up ready-made clothing. In 1841, twenty-one tailors, five dressmakers and eight seamstresses were listed.[44] As they did not appear in the directories, they were almost certainly employed as out-workers for all or part of the time and probably linked to local retailers selling ready-made and second-hand cloth-ing, for example, Sanders's clothing warehouse.

Burden and Sanders, along with Sprigg's Warehouse and James Walter, who also ran a pawnbroking business emerge from the surviving evidence as the larg-est traders selling ready-made and probably second-hand clothing in Worcester before 1850.[45] Like Burden, Spriggs Clothing Warehouse used newspaper adver-tisements, promoting the sale of ready-made clothes, cash sales and fixed prices.[46] Spriggs used tickets fixed to individual garments, presumably to display fixed prices.[47] James Walter did not advertise his clothing business in the local newspa-per, evidence for this business only emerging from Poor Law bills and reported court cases. He appeared to be a well-known figure in the local community and his personal reputation may have been more important for him than newspaper advertising.[48]

The shops of Burden and Sanders were promoted in very different ways. Sanders did not use press advertising while Burden frequently promoted his business in the *Worcester Journal*. Sanders remained in a street which was not part of the city redevelopment in the late eighteenth and early nineteenth centu-ries, whilst Burden ultimately ended up with one of the most sought-after retail addresses in Worcester, reflecting his diversification into the male elite clothing market. However, for at least the first quarter of the nineteenth century, these shops provided the working-class consumer, particularly the male one, with choice. This choice included deciding which shop to enter in the first instance, and presumably, once inside, selecting garments from a wide variety of stock. The influences of the shop's history and its location, its reputation and the personality of the retailer, the breadth of stock carried with the price of clothing, would also undoubtedly have had a bearing on the decision of an individual consumer, influences always difficult to quantify.

Hereford

Ready-made clothes were not advertised in the Hereford press until the 1830s. Salesmen in Hereford existed earlier in the century, as noted in Chapter 1, although evidence is less readily available than it is for Worcester. Prior to the 1830s, some tailors in Hereford also sold ready-made clothing, for example, John Gardiner.

Noting that he had had experience with the first houses in London, Gardiner took a room at the premises of Mr Williams, a plumber, of Eign Street, Hereford, to start his tailoring business in 1820.[49] At the end of that year, he was doing well enough to move into an old printer's house in Broad Street, and also to add the woollen drapery trade to his business.[50] In 1823 he moved to Bye Street next to the Judge's Lodgings.[51] Later he opened a branch in Bristol and finally a branch in Piccadilly, London, in 1848, displaying royal arms.[52]

Much like Stephen Burden in Worcester, Gardiner had moved to the elite end of the tailoring trade by providing a cross-section of society with clothing, including ready-made items. Both appear to have concentrated exclusively on the elite market in the latter part of their careers. However, the household bills of Captain Patershall show how Gardiner also sold ready-made clothes when he started out in Hereford. Patershall had a house in London and a listing in the directories under 'gentry'.[53] He patronized several tailors and most of his bills were for altering or repairing his clothes or making up garments to measure. However, in 1825, he purchased from Gardiner in Bye Street, 'two fashionable waistcoats complete, £1 16s, blue gros de Naples slop, 7s 6d, plaid balencia slop, 7s 6d', the latter presumably waistcoats too.[54] Other items, such as coats and trousers, were also purchased 'complete' the same year, suggesting that they were ready-made. In addition, Patershall bought 'complete' items such as trousers, shooting jackets, coats and waistcoats from other tailors such as Richard Pritchard and Samuel Bullen.[55]

Another tailor and woollen draper, Robert Mallit of St John's Street, in 1826 deducted £1 10s. from Patershall's total bill of the year of £3 11s. for 'old cloth', and likewise £2 in 1829 for 'old clothes',[56] suggesting that the tailor perhaps dealt in old clothes as a sideline to his main business. Beverly Lemire has detailed this practice in reference to London tailors.[57] She also suggests that such an exchange in second-hand clothes helped to contribute to the demand for new clothes and increase the distribution network of second-hand clothes.[58] These are hints that such dealings in 'slops' and second-hand clothes were more widespread across the city's clothing trades than the directories and newspaper advertisements at first portray them to be. There is further evidence for this with an advertisement placed in 1830 by Joseph Mallit, senior, also of St John's Street, a tailor for twenty-seven years, who advertised that he had bought the house and stock of the late John Cooke, a tailor and salesman for the last twenty years.[59] Likewise, Luke Edwards of Broad Street was a man's mercer and hosier, who retired in 1831 advertising his stock for sale. Alongside the stockings and drapery, there was also a large quantity of boys and men's' ready-made clothing including coats, jackets, trousers and smock frocks, which he noted were 'warranted home manufacture', that is, said to have been made up locally.[60] Ready-made and/or second hand clothes may have been a common sideline for many tailors in Hereford.

Of course it cannot be ascertained who these clothes were bought for and worn by. Patershall may have bought clothing for his servants. However, the ready-made fashionable waistcoats were not cheap, at over twice the price of the 'slop' waistcoats. There may have been differences in quality and finishing for which no evidence now survives. It may also have been acceptable for the elite to buy local ready-made garments to wear whilst resident in Hereford, a practice, for example, also found in Bedfordshire.[61] Certainly in the case of shoes, Giorgio Riello has found that ready-made ones were not always the lowest quality and possessed other advantages, such as being able to try on a variety before immediate purchase.[62] The same would be true of garments, available in a wide range of styles, prices and ready to take away once paid for, with no need to wait for an order to be made up. The prevalence of the ready-made clothing trade would suggest that its use was widespread and popular with the city's male population.

Nevertheless, the ready-made clothing market in Hereford was not deemed significant for national advertisers in the provincial press. After the end of the war with France in 1815, auctions of surplus ready-made army clothing were advertised for sale in huge quantities. 20,000 jackets, 17,000 waistcoats with sleeves and 10,000 pairs of trousers were sold on just one occasion, with at least five auctions held in London. These advertisements were placed in the *Worcester Journal* but not the *Hereford Journal,* perhaps suggesting that Hereford was not regarded as a good market for this business.[63] To give an idea of the quantity of clothing released into the market, approximately 240,000 items of various clothing were auctioned over two years. Whilst such auctions may not have been regarded as important to the local Hereford trade, as part of a national network, such a dumping of clothing onto the market would affect supply and demand ratios, and ultimately reduce the price of clothing in the city. This does seem to have occurred over the second quarter of the nineteenth century, stemming from continuing over-production in the textile and clothing industries once the

French wars had ended. The effect was felt in Hereford, as will be detailed, with the incoming of cheap clothing warehouses from outside the area.

Although ready-made clothing was not publicized in the press, the advertisements of the large drapery warehouses in Hereford highlighted that there was already competition in the selling of cheap textiles within the city. The genesis of this competition can be traced though the history of two businesses. The first of these was the Manchester Warehouse run at first by Elizabeth and Mary Anthony, their earliest advertisement placed in the *Hereford Journal* in 1818.[64] Situated in Widemarsh Street, they advertised in 1820:

> The following is stated as a specimen of the low price. Two thousand shawls of different descriptions from 10d. upwards, White Calicoes 3d., 4d. and 5d. per yard; Fine ditto 6d. and 8d.; Four-fourths, very stout 9½d. and 10d.; Prints 8d. and 9d.; ditto on Cambric Cloth 11d. and 1s. 2d.; White Jeans 11d. 1s. to 2s.; Four-fourths and Six-fourths Cambric and Jacconnet Muslins 10d. to 2s. 8d.; Six- fourths Satin checked ditto 1s. 2d. and 1s. 4d.; Tamboured and Satin spriged [*sic*]; Muslins of all descriptions, equally cheap ... Kerseymeres 7s.; Ditto very superior 9s. 6d.; Bennet's best Patent Woollen Cords from 4s. 6d. to 7s.; Corduroys and Velveteens from 1s. 2d. to 2s. 6d.; three-fourths Broad Velveteens and Broad Moleskins from 1s. 10d. to 2s. 10d.[65]

By 1823 they had two shops, one in Widemarsh Street and one in High Town, which may have been connected as they were round the corner from each other.[66] The cheapness of their goods was continually emphasized although Charles Anthony was to state in 1830 that: 'CA carefully exclude from his stock, that miserable description of goods which to entrap the unwary, are sold at low prices but which invariably prove to be "rubbish".[67] In 1828, Charles Anthony advertised the fact that he had a brother who was a manufacturer in Manchester so he was able to get quality stock at cheaper prices.[68] This appears to be William Anthony, whom Richard Sanders in Worcester also dealt with, as he is the only textile manufacturer of that name in the contemporary trade directories.[69] Anthony was also the first draper in Hereford to use an illustration for its advertising. A representation of their shop was placed in the *Hereford Journal* in 1828.[70] It shows a double-fronted building with large display windows, the open doorway revealing a man examining fabric. Anthony sold the business to Edward Morgan in 1832, who then sold it on to Frederick Newman in 1837.[71]

The second business to focus on the sale of cheap clothes was opened by Daniel Evans in Bye Street in 1839, where he sold a wide selection of general drapery goods as well as dresses and smock frocks. He called his shop a 'Cheap Mart', the name of his shop emphasizing his main selling point, low prices.[72] Newman, then running the Manchester Warehouse responded later that year with a somewhat incongruous advertisement depicting a train with the title 'Just arrived by railway' and then the usual list of his current stock.[73] Where his stock had arrived by railway is not clear as the railway was over ten years away from reaching Hereford. However, his advertisement played with ideas of modernity and quick turnover with up-to-the-minute new stock.

Evans also regularly used newspaper advertisements. He advertised fifteen times in the *Hereford Journal* in 1840, with different offers and highlighting various aspects of his stock. For example:

> Extraordinary Attractions!!! Surpassing everything yet offered in cheapness, novelty and design, Daniel Evans ... has purchased his Spring stock ... a splendid choice of dresses, shawls ... stays ... men and boys hats and frocks at half the usual price, small profits for ready money only.[74]

Tammy Whitlock has noted the growth of cheap shops targeted at the non-genteel shopper in London from the 1830s. Hallmarks included aggressive advertising, plate glass windows, garish displays and low priced lead items to entice shoppers. They were criticized for crossing the line between good business and fraud, promoting dishonest retailing.[75] It seems probable that Evans, who had recently moved to Hereford, was attempting something similar in a provincial context. He certainly seems to have upset the long resident tailors and drapers with the way that he went about his business.

By December 1840, the Manchester Warehouse was bankrupt and the stock sold off,[76] Newman moving first to Kington and then to a shop in Westgate Street, Gloucester, where he became a linen draper's assistant.[77] It appears that Evans had seen off his main competitor. The same edition of the newspaper that detailed Newman's fall from grace carried the first mention of Evans's ready-made clothes business. He had obviously been selling items such as smock frocks prior to this and now claimed: 'Also the largest stock of Readymade Clothes and Frocks in the County'.[78]

Evans continued with the aggressive promotion of his cheap prices and this appears to have drawn others in the ready-made clothing sector into advertising for the first time. For example, James Bosworth was described in his newspaper advertisement as a 'hair dresser, broker, appraiser and general salesman' as well as running a 'museum of curiosities' and 'clothes warehouse'. He had regularly supplied overseers of the poor with ready-made clothing since the 1820s,[79] but his first newspaper advertisement was not placed until 1841, when he used a particularly large, two-column-wide, nearly full page one consisting of sixty rhyming verses detailing his stock. Written in a humorous vein, it was certainly eye catching and would take quite a long time to read out loud, as seems to have been the intention in the tradition of broadsheets and popular ballads.[80] Read to an audience in a pub, it appealed to his target customer, the working-class consumer in search of second-hand and ready-made clothing, Bosworth also advertising the fact that he would take 'goods in exchange' and would give the best prices 'in money or goods'.[81]

In 1842, Daniel Evans diversified further by entering the bespoke tailoring business but again emphasized his low prices: cassimere trousers from 10 shillings; dress and frock coats from superfine cloth from 21 shillings.[82] The newspaper advertisements placed in the spring of 1843 show the increased competitiveness of local clothing shops. For instance, a 'Clothing Establishment' was opened by Edward Jones in Wye Bridge Street, 'two doors from the Black Lion', a visual prompt for his customers. He stated that he was the son of John Jones, a tailor and draper of Broad Street, and appeared to position himself in direct competition to Evans. He, probably indirectly, reveals what Evans stocked:

> He will not offer to their notice Goods bought of Myers of London or Hyam & Co. of Bristol, but assures them that the Goods shall be of his own materials & made up under his own superintendence & will be in the end cheaper than any cheap mart in England.[83]

The use of the term 'cheap mart', and the fact that Evans was the only trader who seemingly used this term in Hereford, suggests that he was selling the cheap ready-made clothing of large London manufacturers.[84] Based in London, firms such as Hyam and Moses were descendents of Jewish salesmen. They branched out into the large-scale manufacture of clothing with the growth in the market for ready-made clothing for those who were emigrating. These clothes were then also purchased by the working population for general wear.[85] Such businesses had been growing in size during the 1830s and 40s, their urban 'show' shops helping with promotion. The distribution of their stock in the provinces before they set up their own shops in larger towns and cities later in the 1840s has been little detailed. If not Evans, in 1843 some retailer in Hereford was already selling their clothing.

Evans responded to Jones's advertisement by again highlighting his major selling factor: his cheapness, '50% below any other house in the trade'. He detailed the prices of certain items, for example, waistcoats from 9*d*. and coats from 2*s*. 6*d*. Smock frocks varied depending on the fabric and embellishments, 'extra prime worked' being the most expensive from 5*s*. 6*d*.[86] These compared favourably to the prices that Moses charged with ready-made suits for 8*s*. 6*d*. in 1846.[87] In Aylesbury, Buckinghamshire, F. Elmes advertised his cheap ready-made clothing in 1840, with prices within a similar range to Daniel Evans. For example, he offered white and coloured smock frocks in two sizes from 2*s*., waistcoats from 12*d*. and a whole variety of jackets, in 'worsted and silk shag', fustian, cord and velveteen, prices unlisted. With a large red signboard over his door for easy identification, Elmes too, perceived there to be a growing market for male ready-made clothing and felt it worth advertising in the local newspaper to highlight the fact.[88] Although Evans claimed to have the cheapest prices in Hereford, other retailers in different areas were selling similar clothing at comparable pricing levels.

In the next edition of the newspaper, Watson, who was now running Spriggs Clothing and Drapery Warehouse entered the fray, claiming: 'no mart or other Establishment can sell well-sewed and home made garments ... at lower prices'. Having emphasized the quality and so durability of his stock, he continued:

> ... nor will he insult the understanding of his customers as the proprietors of such cheap marts do, by affecting to sell Goods at from 40 to 70 % below the cost prices, whilst they are enabled by such pretended sacrifices, to enlarge their premises and pursue a flourishing trade.[89]

It was the start of what appeared to have been a besmirching both of Evans's stock and the way he sold it, carried out through press advertisements by competitors. The reputation both of his shop and his sales techniques were under attack, certainly in print and presumably through word of mouth too. Watson continued to emphasize the fact that his clothing was 'well sewed and got up under H. Watson's inspection',[90] in the same vein as Jones, suggesting that they had workshops on their retail premises or in the immediate environment of the city.[91] The new London manufacturers of ready-made clothing were presumably felt to be of inferior quality and under less control than ready-made clothing manufactured within the city, as well as threatening local livelihoods. Pamela Sharpe has noted that ready-made clothing was often marketed in the provinces as 'London fashion' and 'London made', even if the reality was that it had been manufactured locally.[92] However, the shopkeepers of Hereford appear to have ignored the London connection as a selling aid.

Watson continued the campaign against very cheap prices, appealing to the common sense of his customers: 'the public must clearly perceive that if Prints be advertised at a farthing or 1d per yard, hose and gloves at 1d per pair or waistcoats at 9d each and Frocks 1s, they can be of no possible use to the purchaser'.[93] These prices were a direct reference to Evans's advertisement the previous April. Watson attempted to use the quality and so the durability of his stock as the main selling point rather than the price. This chimed with contemporary alarm, as noted by Whitlock, about large cheap drapery establishments underselling goods and threatening the business of an entire neighbourhood, from the late 1830s to the 1850s.[94] To some extent, the press campaign must have worked, as Evans announced in July, 'A Genuine Selling Off' as he was 'removing to London',[95] presumably where he expected to find a more receptive market for his style of retailing and he would be able to restore his reputation.

In the tradition of this type of selling, dependent on price and special offers, it took Evans almost another year to complete the sale of his stock and business. This led to queries about when this would actually happen, which he responded to in his advertisements. The underlying suspicion was that it might be just another selling ruse. In the *Hereford Journal* of 14 August 1844, it was announced that Samuel Sillifant had taken over the 'Cheap Mart'. He continued to deal in ready-made items but renamed the shop 'Albion House' and, perhaps consciously heading off criticism, detailed the prices of his menswear. Prices were higher than Evans's, with satin waistcoats from 15*s.* and tweed trousers from 10*s.*, the starting price for Sillifant's trousers being higher than the top price charged for trousers under Evans.[96] The emphasis of the business had changed to higher quality items and tailoring, and away from selling purely by price.

The reluctance of Hereford shopkeepers to promote their ready-made clothing as having an origin outside of the city continued into the late 1840s. In 1848, John Jones of Broad Street was advertising his return from London with new stock.[97] However, he still advertised his ready-made clothing as '(home-made)'. The type of consumers he intended to appeal to is revealed in his advertisement from 1845 when he advertised a quantity of hay for sale, further evidence of mixed trades, but noted that for twenty-five years he had been tailoring for the 'Hay trades and will still endeavour to continue'.[98] As a clothes dealer and tailor, his appeal to hay-trade agricultural workers would seem to indicate that he too was primarily concerned with supplying rural workers with essential items such as smock frocks.

The sale of 'London-made clothing' was announced with the arrival of Richard Davis, 'late of London', in 1848 who set up the 'London Clothing Establishment'.[99] His selling point was firmly fixed on both his personal London connections and the metropolitan manufacture of his stock. By March the following year, this had proved unsuccessful and he dropped his London associations, perhaps to try and follow local custom.[100] He began to use his original name, 'London Clothing Establishment' once more, later in 1849, perhaps having had time to reassure his customers about both his own merits and those of his clothes.[101]

Local ready-made clothing was thus promoted by the shopkeepers who controlled its production, seemingly to the detriment of London-made clothing. Whether this was successful is open to speculation as the evidence for the volume of clothing actually sold in various Hereford shops does not survive. For those who did not work in the industry, it was presumably difficult to know the origin of a garment by looking at it. This controversy does demonstrate how prevalent ready-made articles were in Hereford, both for men and, to a lesser extent, women, most clothing retailers seemingly having some dealing in such clothing. The items Evans advertised illustrate how cheap some new clothing was, with waistcoats from 9*d.* for example. The working-class consumer would be welcomed into such shops and was probably thought of as the shopkeepers' main customer.

Promotion to the Working-Class Consumer

The press advertisements of shopkeepers in Hereford in the early 1840s show how the lure of cheap prices and the durability of clothing were used to entice consumers. However, it is impossible to know how much effect these notions actually had on consumers. Advertisements show the preoccupations of the shopkeepers involved and how they wished to be perceived by consumers. The following section will investigate further the advertising methods clothing retailers used to appeal to the working-class consumer. [102]

The primary concern of newspaper advertising was to influence the middle classes.[103] The lists of the newest fashionable goods were detailed at length in advertisements, not only promoting novelties, but also giving the consumer an idea about the status and layout of the shop, often located in the main streets of a town.[104] Revenue from advertisements was the mainstay of the newspapers' profit, circulation sales covering costs.[105] It was expensive to advertise, being subject to government duty, at a reduced rate from 1833 of 1*s.* 6*d.* until duty was abolished in 1853.[106] Only shopkeepers who could afford the expenditure were therefore likely to place newspaper advertisements which would appeal to their core customers, the respectable middle classes.[107] Such promotion was therefore not representative of the whole trade, excluding those whose business was focused lower down the social scale on customers unlikely to read the newspaper and those who could not afford to, or did not want to, advertise. During the late eighteenth century, well-established retailers who used conventional methods of selling did not generally advertise unless announcing alterations in circumstance, such as a change in ownership or premises. Instead, new types of business, such as the drapery warehouses, which asked for 'ready money' and had fixed prices, used frequent newspaper advertising.[108] Advertising the method of sale could save a customer being embarrassed by asking for unavailable credit.[109] Such promotion could therefore be a sensitive issue, associated in the minds of high-class customers with the pushy sales techniques of the new drapery warehouses and patent medicines.

Newspaper advertisements were, however, also readily accessible to the working-classes. Ivon Asquith has estimated that every newspaper in the first half of the nineteenth century would have been read by around ten to thirty people, as it was passed down through society.[110] Public houses at the centre of the community also took newspapers, which could then be read out to anybody interested.[111] For example, in advertisement for a take-over of the New Duke's Head Inn, Leominster, noted: 'NB Two London Newspapers every Evening except Monday, and on that day, the Glocester [*sic*] Herald, which are publicly read at Eight o'Clock.'[112] There were also items that appeared in newspapers which showed they may have been aimed at a wider audience. In the reporting of court sessions, warnings to others not to fall into the same traps were an example of this. For instance, in 1847 the *Hereford Journal* published a caution for licensed hawkers as one had been prosecuted in Hereford for selling shawls at the City Arms Hotel without a licence once his master, licensed hawker 11a, had left town.[113] Also, there were direct appeals to specific sections of the lower orders, for example gin drinkers in 1835, which noted the money that they were wasting on alcohol, suggesting that it could have been better spent on clothing.[114] Practical information with details about applications for hawker and ale licences suggested a broader audience, along with news items such as a weaver's wife giving birth to five babies.[115] The geographical prompts for addresses of shops appealing to the less literate were used, although they decreased across the period.[116] As Hannah Barker has stated: 'Neither the inability to read nor the high cost of newspapers necessarily prevented the bulk of the population from discovering their contents. Reading aloud ... was a common activity and the shared purchase and hire of newspapers, coupled with their presence in coffee houses, pubs and shops ... made them accessible to many'.[117]

Nevertheless, out of the sixty-eight individuals listed in the directories across the period 1800–50 in Hereford and Worcester as either ready-made or second-hand clothes dealers, only ten placed any advertisements in the local newspapers, two of which were notices of business take-overs. The implication is therefore either that they could not afford to advertise in the local papers or that they did not need to. Perhaps they had enough potential customers without the expense of such promotion, for example, through word of mouth and an established reputation. The question of whether such businesses did not need to advertise because they were not dealing in fashionable or novelty goods then arises. However, the stock of such shopkeepers did not remain static, new items being ordered every few months, as shown by the accounts of Richard Sanders, whose shop did not use newspaper advertising.[118]

Despite the evidence that the working-class consumer could access newspapers, very few advertisements directly appealed to them. Burden, for example, chose to emphasize the higher-status tailoring side of his business after 1810.[119] In 1849, Henry Meredith, a draper in Kington, advertised that he had a stock of 'cheap goods for the supply of the Labouring Classes and for Clothing Clubs'. This was presumably items such as the 1,000 'de laine' dresses advertised the previous month at 3s. each.[120] However, this unusual promotion appears to have been more of an appeal to those who ran organizations such as clothing societies, rather than to the 'labouring' classes themselves. Likewise, ready-made clothing could be purchased by local elites, as demonstrated by the bills of Captain Patershall.[121] The mention of ready-made clothing in advertisements should therefore not necessarily be read as directed exclusively at working-class consumers.

The Bosworth advertisement, discussed above,[122] was one of the rare examples of advertising targeting the working-class consumer, along with one placed by James Tranter of New London House in 1832. Tranter ran a drapers shop, although he was not listed in the contemporary directories, as he only remained in Hereford a couple of years. He stated:

> To servants – this being the period at which most of your purchases for the year are made, much depends on the well-laying out of your hard earned gains ... fully impressed with the necessity of this, JT in the selection of his Goods has not forgotten to consult your interests.[123]

This suggests that some servants did not rely solely on perquisite clothing or cast-offs, and as mainly young unmarried adults, were perhaps likely to have the most cash left over to spend. They were seen as potential consumers in their own right, at least by one shopkeeper.[124] This advertisement was also placed in April, maybe to cash in on servants who might buy new clothing to create a good impression at the hiring fairs held in early May. This could include both domestic and farm servants.

As there were few direct appeals through newspaper advertising to the working-class consumer, perhaps other methods were used to promote individual shops to this sector of the market, for example, word of mouth, handbills, criers and through window displays. In *The Natural History of the Gent*, cheap metropolitan tailors were noted as advertising through ephemeral flyers, 'thrown with such unsparing liberality through the windows of railway omnibuses'.[125] Presumably, something similar might have happened in provincial towns and cities, although the evidence does not survive. Clothes were certainly hung on rails outside salesmen's shops, advertising their stock to passersby. In 1850, for example, Michael Osborne, aged seventeen, was convicted of stealing two pairs of trousers from Edward Wood, Dudley. They were hanging on a rail outside Wood's shop when he was caught in the act of theft.[126] Likewise, in 1844, James Harper stole a pair of breeches from the clothes dealer and tailor Thomas King in Friar Street, Worcester, 'exposed for sale' at the shop door.[127] In Hereford, James Bosworth, a general dealer as well as a salesman, was fined in 1846 after frequent cautioning for having chairs and other goods 'exposed before his door'.[128] This type of haphazard display was associated with downmarket shops, the plethora of goods suggesting cheapness. In an age of civic improvement, shops which spilt out onto newly paved walkways or which had cluttered façades were not seen as respectable. Inside the shop, the profusion of stock often continued. Goods were not enclosed in cases, also meaning that less interaction with shop workers was needed, speeding up the sales process.[129] Unfortunately, few street scenes that record Hereford and Worcester's clothing shops from this period survive.

In contrast to the chaotic displays of salesmen was Richard Lillington's shop, in the fashionable part of Worcester, near the Cross. His trade card was published in Lewis's *Directory* of 1820, showing the elaborate window display of his shop.[130] The main items of his trade, hats, gloves and hose were artfully placed, the door of his shop invitingly open to show fashionable customers examining goods across a counter (see Figure 2.1). Such trade cards set out to entice customers in, combining fantasy and reality: the genteel customer you might hope to meet there but a true depiction of the shop exterior to aid identification from the street. The trade card also reflected the cosmopolitan nature of trade, placing their customers in an international consumer network, with Welsh, London, Brussels and Turkey goods on offer, playing on the seductive image of an attainable world of material goods a consumer could purchase if they visited Lillington's shop.[131] It was also an alternative way to window-shop, with the pleasures that this entailed, for anyone who saw the trade card.[132]

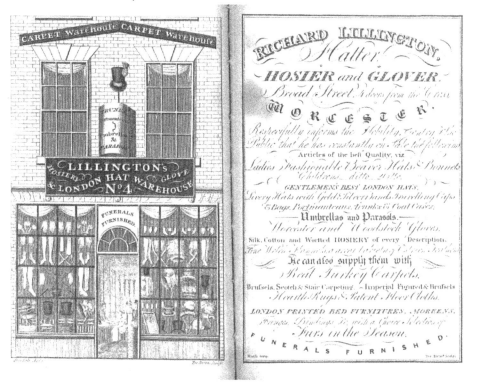

Figure 2.1: Richard Lillington's Trade Card, published in *Worcestershire General and Commercial Directory for 1820* (Worcester: S. Lewis, 1820), image courtesy of Worcestershire Record Office.

Shops such as Lillington's held goods that were less expensive than traditional drapers' shops, but also included fashionable items such as silk ribbons, lace and gloves, which had general appeal.[133] Whitlock notes that in cheap shops targeted at the non-genteel female shopper, show and display were more important than quality, inexpensive items being sold with the pomp usually reserved for expensive goods.[134] Although he rarely advertised the price of his goods, Lillington seems to have been attempting something similar, both with his trade card and presumably his window display.[135]

Thus the way Lillington advertised and the goods that he stocked represented an example of how to sell and promote to the working-class consumer while maintaining a fashionable business for 'polite' society. He advertised constantly from 1816 onwards in *Berrow's Worcester Journal* and took up new lines of goods with a willingness that perhaps went with this way of selling novelties.[136] He highlighted innovative products, becoming an agent for Mackintosh within five years of the patent being granted[137] and promoting new 'zephyr' coats in 1840.[138] He was first defined as a glove manufacturer in *Robson's Directory* of 1838, eventually becoming a royal warrant holder, a fact thenceforth emphasized to give his business added kudos.[139] The royal association gave his stock certain elite connotations, adding to its status and respectability. However, in the same advertisement, he noted that he had just returned from 'town' with 'gentlemen's tweed upper coats and jackets', which were presumably ready-made.

In 1846, in an advertisement which emphasized his royal connections, Lillington noted he was now selling Nicoll's registered paletôts, as well as 'Tasty' single and double breasted waistcoats.[140] Nicoll's were one of the large London manufacturers of ready-made male clothing that had been criticized in the *Hereford Journal* by Edward Jones.[141] Stanley Chapman has noted the manufacturing details of H. J. & D. Nicolls, who produced some 500 paletôts per week. He states that they retailed for a modest 12s., but this was still considerably more than the 2s. 6d. charged by Evans as a starting price for coats in Hereford.[142] The names attributed to these paletôts, for example, Oxanian, functioned as a generic system of branding, referring principally to their cost.[143] In a market where ready-made clothing was increasingly common, the naming of a product or noting its derivation from a particular shop or manufacturer, gave a certain differentiation from other similar products, meaning it could be marketed as superior and perhaps merit a higher price tag.[144] Such products were advertised by manufacturers in the press for direct sales or could be purchased from outlets such as Lillington's.[145] This ambiguity about which end of the market Lillington was appealing to is shown further by an entry in Hunt's *Directory* of 1847, where he was described as a clothes dealer and hosier still operating out of his fashionable address on the Cross.[146]

Lillington's business seems to have been founded on the principle of selling goods cheaply, quickly and for cash wherever possible. The goods he chose to sell were often novelties in the true sense of the word, with new textile innovations such as the Mackintosh. Their varied cost, and perhaps quality, suggests that they appealed across the spectrum of society, with small items such as hose and gloves affordable for less wealthy consumers. His shop reflects the diversity of stock needed, and the variety of approaches towards selling it, necessary for success in a provincial city. He had to cater to a socially differentiated customer base whose taste and financial means varied widely and his aim seemed to be to please everyone, from royalty through to those buying ready-made clothing. Thus his glove manufactory, which held royal warrants, appears to have been a distinct business from the shop, although he linked the two in his advertisements to gain general prestige. Despite his royal patronage claim, he still defined himself as a hosier and clothes dealer, perhaps because of his longstanding association with ready-made outer-garments. When he retired in 1848, after thirty-two years in business, I. and J. Moses took over his shop. They stated that they had branches in Cheltenham, Gloucester and Ross.[147] This suggests the existence of links with the Jewish ready-made trade in London, although no other evidence through newspaper advertising has been found prior to 1850.

Lillington was obviously an innovative businessman, not averse to taking risks on novel products and seeking new ways to advertise them, as his decorative trade card shows. Enticing window displays were increasingly being used by retailers of lower status goods such as Moses in London, at least from the 1840s. Written *circa* 1848, 'Cheap Clothes and Nasty' by Charles Kingsley criticizes such show shops as run by Moses, with their 'absurd plate-glass fronts'.[148] These new methods of drawing in customers from across the social scale were also used by Lillington in Worcester to help expand his business over a thirty-year period. He made no direct appeal to the working-class consumer in terms of cheapness in the manner of Daniel Evans, but Lillington's window display and trade card advertised small value goods and practical outerwear available from a respectable retail address in Worcester. These commodities were popular across society. Thus, while there were few specific advertisements to attract the working-class consumer, Lillington could appeal to them in a more oblique manner. Whether such obliqueness was a conscious strategy is a matter of speculation.

Conclusion

Some historians have suggested that specialist shopkeepers in the first half of the nineteenth century relied heavily on affluent society for their business. Due to the limited number of people that could be classed as affluent, this trade would only support a few shops. These shops might collude in pricing stock to ensure survival, differentiation between competitors established instead through the diversity of the products available and variety of service.[149] The evidence from the retailers of Hereford and Worcester shows that many shops sold to a wider spectrum of society than just the affluent, and appealed to the working-class consumer in various ways in order to enhance business. Competition ensuring cheap prices and a wide variety of stock, including everyday items, were part of many shopkeepers' dealings. The appeals of 'cheapness' and 'bargains' in advertising was a common ploy to induce customers from all social classes to come and buy from a shop. However, the prices advertised by some of the shopkeepers discussed show how low some were by the 1840s so that the clothing offered was affordable for all levels of society.

Tradesmen such as Burden may have gradually scaled down their transactions with the working-class consumer to concentrate on bespoke tailoring. Nevertheless, as a wholesaler of ready-made clothing, selling garments to and for the working-class consumer may have still been an important, if less evident, part of business. In general, between a third and a quarter of tailors and drapers listed in the trade directories for the period 1820–50, were openly selling stock for working-class consumers, for example, also being listed in trade directories as salesmen or owning clothing warehouses. However, the number of other clothing retailers who also dealt in similar stock would appear more significant than this, making it difficult to quantify the numbers of shopkeepers who were involved in the trade.

The importance of the ready-made clothing trade in 1840s Hereford is shown by the advertisements of competing retailers. These suggest that there was reluctance from well-established clothing retailers, who also oversaw the manufacture of local ready-made garments, to use a London manufacturing origin as a selling aid. They questioned why London-made clothing was so cheap, and thus questioned its durability and long-term value in contrast to local ready-made garments. The apparent importance of the origin of ready-made garments, at least for the manufacturers and retailers trying to sell them, highlights the economic importance of this market within a local context.

Provincial clothing warehouses had been in existence at least since the eighteenth century, as demonstrated by Richard Sanders's business. However, the progressive specialization of some shopkeepers in the second quarter of the nineteenth century, who renamed their shops from general drapery to businesses with names such as 'Clothing Establishment' and 'Ready-Made Clothes and Smock-Frock Warehouse', suggests that lower status clothing was increasingly recognized as a viable commercial opportunity in provincial towns and cities.[150] They appealed directly to working-class consumers and promised them affordable new clothing with a wide choice of stock. This included customers in the rural hinterland, who needed garments such as ready-made smocks, in order to work.[151]

Stanley Chapman has noted that opportunist London drapers, led by James Morrison in the 1820s, set up a new style of high turn-over warehouse on the back of falling textile prices.[152] Although it is extremely difficult to quantify precisely and analyse the true cost of clothing in terms of real wages over a period of time, the general price of clothing had fallen substantially, particularly after the end of the Napoleonic Wars, with the over-production of the northern textile manufacturers.[153] Sir Frederick Eden's survey at the end of the eighteenth century, for instance, listed the prices paid in a London slop shop for a 'common' waistcoat as 6s. 6d. and a good foul weather coats as 13 shillings. Evans was charging 9d. for waistcoats and selling coats from 2s. 6d, around six times less than Eden's prices.[154] Whether Evans's very low advertised prices were 'puffery', to entice customers in, is a matter of speculation. However, with the general fall in the price of new clothing, such garments were affordable to many more people, which presumably helped fuel the growth of this market.[155]

Working-class consumers were sought after and desired as customers in this expanding commercial network and shopping for new clothing was an essential part of working-class clothing acquisition networks. Such consumers had a choice in the type of garments they could purchase, in quality, price and style. Consumers certainly had options about what shop to visit and from which to obtain new clothing, particularly male ready-made garments. The next chapter will investigate further the retailing of clothing for the working-class consumer, but trade carried out beyond the shop by itinerant clothing sellers.

3 SELLING BY NON-FIXED TRADERS

Selling clothing beyond the boundary of the shop remained an important part of clothes retailing in the nineteenth century. The early consumer market in clothing accessories, as traced by Margaret Spufford, had been principally developed through the efforts of pedlars and hawkers and they continued to play an important role in the dispersal of clothing across the countryside.[1] Indeed, at various points, they came into direct competition and conflict with retailers, resulting in legislation designed to curb both their activities and reach.[2] There is a growing recognition by historians of the complexity of the retail trade and the coexistence and close interaction between different retail circuits, which require both integrated and comparative analysis, a concept which this book seeks to address.[3] This chapter will thus focus on the itinerant trade and its links to existing retail provision.

There are problems in examining the itinerant or ambulant trade, both in terms of sources and in definition. For example, it could be an informal trade, taken up when times were hard with little capital investment, as part of the economy of makeshifts, which left little trace behind. The evidence for hawkers and pedlars, however, is often focused on those who were licensed and therefore have left a paper trail behind.[4] Numbers of licensed itinerants have been extrapolated to give an idea of how prevalent the trade was and how it changed over the centuries. This chapter will argue that the licensing system is at best a weak pointer to the state of the itinerant trade and at worst not indicative at all. There is evidence from contemporary government records about how the licensing system was perceived, both by itinerants and government agents, and how this affected the way it was used in practice. Both contemporaries and subsequent commentators and historians have also noted problems with defining those who participated in itinerant selling. This chapter will examine in turn three broad subsections: pedlars and hawkers, credit drapers and market traders. After examining the definition of hawkers and pedlars, the licensing system will be investigated. Two types of pedlar will be considered: individuals who were officially licensed and those without licences. A discussion about the types of goods sold and their relationship to shop retailing will then follow. Were travelling sellers in competition with shops or did they focus on gaps in the retail market? The trade of travelling or credit drapers will then be explored. Their origin will be analysed along with the way that they operated. The chapter will finish with a study of the importance of markets as a way of providing clothing, considering how traders selling from market stalls were linked to shops. The scale of itinerant sellers' operations in Herefordshire and Worcestershire will be investigated and linked to the shopping environment in both rural and urban areas. The crossover in definitions can be considered along with how working-class consumers used non-fixed traders for the acquisition of clothing.

Defining Hawkers and Pedlars

In contemporary sources, the terms 'hawker' and 'pedlar' covered a wide range of itinerant salespeople. They were not a homogenous group but sold different products to different types of people using various communication techniques.[5] David Brown has tried to define people covered by the terms hawker and pedlar.[6] As he notes, a 'precise definition tends to obscure their [pedlars'] adaptability and the multiplicity of their interests'.[7] For example, Robert Menzies was a licensed hawker from Dumfries who stayed at the White Hart Inn, Sidbury, Worcester, to sell items for a short period of time. These included ladies' pelisses and habit clothes along with tartan.[8] Likewise, 'R. Pledge, cheap linen draper, Licensed Hawker No. 440, Cheapside', had a sale for ten days at the Coach and Horses, the Tything, Worcester. He advertised that he had attended sales in London and claimed to have a £1,000 of goods, advertising gown and waistcoat pieces, although 'no patterns cut'.[9] Both appear to have carried with them a fashionable and fairly valuable stock. At the other end of the scale, some itinerant sellers were described as barely better than vagrants, especially when convicted of a crime. Itinerant selling could be part of the casual labour market with its seasonal fluctuations. It was a way of making ends meet or, after a difficult period, a means to get back in business. This has been especially noted with regard to urban street sellers, but seems equally applicable to rural areas.[10] The fact that many itinerants were of Scotch or Irish origin helped foster hostility, particularly as the authorities were struggling to cope with an influx of poor immigrants from Ireland during the 1830s.[11]

Selling items at an inn or pub was not unusual, especially if on a long tour away from home as Menzies and Pledge appeared to have been. As in the case of Pledge, sales could often last for several days and were often in the form of auctions, drawing in crowds to the itinerant's sale as well as increasing custom for the innkeeper.[12] Holding the sale in such a location could sometimes backfire. In 1843, William Pitman was trying to sell stockings at the Talbot Inn, Upton-upon-Severn. Three pairs were stolen leading to a court case in which a description of the scene was recorded: '[the] whole company [was] in a state of intoxication and were hiding the stockings about the kitchen ... [Pitman] missed many other pairs which have not been found'.[13] A similar case occurred in Dudley at the Crown Inn, where Matthew Mallin was selling his wares and a struggle ensued over a piece of cloth with Francis Rogers, a miner.[14] The necessity of finding a ready-made market for stock, in this case the customers of the inn, was balanced against the state of mind, and intoxication, that those consumers might be in. However, inns did provide a venue in which male consumers in particular could easily purchase clothing. They were also centres for carrying services, both for transporting goods and the itinerant traders themselves out into the countryside.[15] George Elson, whose parents were hawkers of haberdashery and drapery in the 1830s, notes that they lodged at the principal inn of a market town for a week, before setting off into the surrounding countryside each day.[16]

The minute books of the Stamp Office offer some insight into why people turned to hawking. Acts passed in the 1780s had allowed hawkers to settle in any town and open a shop without the guild requirement of apprenticeship, as long as they displayed their name and licence number correctly.[17] Francis McGedy was convicted at Worcester for not displaying the sign 'Licenced [*sic*] Hawker' in his shop in the correct manner.[18] He had previously been a resident of 18 Park Street, Bristol, but 'bought out of his house during the fires at Bristol'. This may relate to the Bristol Riots that began on 29 October 1831, a popular uprising in favour of the Reform Act in which part of the city was burnt down and many people were killed.[19] He had been hawking his remaining stock as a licensed hawker from that time. His address was given as 62 Broad Street, Worcester.[20] On appeal, he was refunded half of his fine.[21] Hawkers and pedlars could therefore encompass a broad swathe of society, from vagrants selling a few cheap items to make ends meet, traders who moved systematically from inn to inn, through to shopkeepers on the main streets of a town, settled in a place for an extended period of time.

Circumventing the Licence

Hawking and peddling was felt by some shopkeepers to be an 'unfair' trade, both because shopkeepers had to pay rates and taxes on their fixed abode, and also the ease with which pedlars could undermine established business. Aside from commercial competition, one reason why some shopkeepers were so hostile towards hawkers and pedlars was the various methods that could be employed by itinerants to legally circumvent the need for a licence, thus avoiding any tax.

A court case from Dudley in 1830 involving a tea dealer shows one such method. Ivie Macknight, described as a 'servant' to Mr Grey, a tea dealer, was accused of being a hawker of tea without a licence. On appeal against his conviction with a £10 penalty fine, he was able to prove that he took orders and then delivered the goods a fortnight later, when he then took further orders. In the court's eyes, a hawker or pedlar was someone who sold goods immediately, not someone who carried goods to fulfil an order. It was noted that otherwise it would be necessary to 'legalize the transactions of travellers for London houses'.[22] This was an important distinction especially for the growing sector of commercial salesmen who worked exclusively for one firm. 'Manchester Men' and later Scotch and tally men and other travelling drapers took advantage of this loophole in the law, as did shopkeepers who hawked their own goods as a method of boosting sales.[23] As long as the ordering and delivering of goods was not done concurrently, registration as a hawker and pedlar could be avoided regardless of whether the individual was working for him/herself, a small local company, a large Manchester cotton factory, or a London wholesaler.

Alternatively, if pedlars were able to prove that they had manufactured the goods that they were selling or were wholesalers, they were not liable for a licence.[24] This loophole seems to have often been invoked as a defence against being fined for not having a licence, but unless proof was produced, the penalty still seems to have been levied. In 1821, John Broadbent of Kidderminster was caught travelling with a horse, selling a parcel of cloths and shawls without a licence. In his defence, he said that he was the manufacturer of these but could produce no further evidence and was fined the statutory £10.[25]

Enterprising shopkeepers seem to have realized that by taking their wares directly to consumers in the surrounding countryside they could increase their sales. In Ross, when Thomas Morgan, tailor and draper, was declared bankrupt, his goods included, 'household furniture, useful horse, Light Covered Cart, stock of Drapery and Hosiery, Ready Made Clothes &c', suggesting that he went out into the countryside with his horse and cart to sell stock from his shop.[26] Samuel Sillifant, who sold ready-made clothing in Hereford,[27] advertised in 1845 for a draper's assistant, a young man, 'well acquainted with the Welsh trade, & who can speak the language'.[28] Either there were a considerable number of Welsh-speaking customers in Hereford, or Sillifant was selling directly to Welsh customers just over the border by travelling to their homes with his order book or stock. This practice has been documented in other trades, such as jewellery and maps.[29] The central Welsh market was ripe for exploitation by traders from Hereford. Its geographical isolation meant that Hereford was one of the nearest and most accessible towns. Several drovers' routes crossed Herefordshire, used for bringing sheep down from the uplands to the borders and points further east.[30] Chester, a town in a similar situation to northern Wales, had certainly exploited its geographical position during the eighteenth century.[31]

A court case from Pershore, a market town in rural Worcestershire, also demonstrates how narrow the boundary could be between hawkers and shopkeepers. In 1827 William Whitehouse, a linen draper, was prosecuted for owing tax amounting to £20 and fined £10. He was also accused of being 'a hawker and trading person', hawking 'a parcel of silk handkerchiefs' without a licence. He appealed against the conviction unsuccessfully, his defence being that he had a right to hawk, having taken over 'the house in which he exposed to sale, goods wares and merchandise', in other words a shop. He was then fined another £10, and it was reported in the local newspaper that he had taken the shop with the fraudulent design of evading the licence.[32] Whitehouse was not mentioned in the contemporary trade directories for Pershore, suggesting that either his business was relatively short-lived or that he operated on a small scale.

Some shopkeepers may have found themselves in the position of being a hawker and pedlar in order to make enough sales to keep their businesses afloat and pay the taxes that running a shop involved. They were essentially becoming the very people that shopkeepers in general so vociferously complained about.[33] The dividing line between the trade of hawkers and shopkeepers was thus very fine.

That said, hostility to hawkers and pedlars should not be underestimated. There was a perception that the majority avoided purchasing a licence. In 1840, for example, the *Worcester Journal* quoted a letter from the *Salopian Journal*, which had a very similar tone to the late-eighteenth century diatribes against hawkers detailed by Hoh-cheung Mui and Lorna Mui.[34] This suggests that, contrary to David Alexander's opinion, peddling in rural areas may not have declined by the 1840s.[35]

> ... while the hawker, the man who is undermining and ruining the fair dealer, has only a nominal tax of 4l [£] put on him, in the shape of a licence, and which includes all the burdens he has to bear. How is it possible the tradesman, paying 50l [£] to 100l [£] per annum in rent and taxes, besides the keeping up an extensive establishment can compete with such opponents? ... [hawkers] ought to be taxed treble the amount. But the most unfair part of the business is that scarcely one in ten pay the licence: they are not looked up. In the manufacturing districts, where I reside, there are nearly forty pass my door on a Monday morning, and scour the country, while I am warranted in saying that not above two, before the present year, have taken out a licence ... [the] new police would be [wise] to look up these abuses.[36]

The correspondent implied that these hawkers lived in urban areas and then went off into the countryside to ply their wares rather than selling in their immediate urban industrial locality. Thus hawking may have been an urban occupation, but not always carried out in an urban location. James Jones was one such pedlar, travelling out from Birmingham to Bewdley. He was asleep by the side of the road in the evening, when his parcel containing neck handkerchiefs and other items was stolen.[37]

In old-established medieval towns and cities, restrictions on trading could be prohibitive for hawkers. In Worcester, only freemen could trade except on market days under an act dating from 1785, with a £20 penalty liable for those who ignored this.[38] Tolls for coming into the city to trade could also be expensive. The 'Ancient Duties and Customs' paid by all 'foreigners' were noted in a history of Worcester, published in 1816. They included 1*d*. for 'a person hawking the streets with goods', 1*s*. for 'a hawker or pedlar selling by hand or auction' and 1*d*. for 'every roll of cloth brought into the City upon a fair day, or eve'.[39] It therefore made financial sense to buy stock in the city and sell it outside, where there were no urban tolls. According to the letter printed in the *Worcester Journal* in 1840, such hawkers were also not bothering to purchase licences. The following section will investigate why this was so.

The Licensing of Hawkers and Pedlars

This section will investigate how the licensing system operated within each county. The routine functioning of the system will be analysed as well as the role of the licensing office.

Brown contends that the licensing office was inefficient and badly managed, concerned with bringing in sufficient revenue to pay for the increasing remuneration of its staff, rather than enforcing the licensing law. In addition, he estimates that only a quarter of pedlars and hawkers were officially licensed.[40] It has also been noted that it tended to be country pedlars who took out licences, urban street sellers not bothering to do so.[41] The minutes of the Commissioners of Hawkers and Pedlars Licences, the Commissioners for Hackney Coaches and the Stamp Office, who at various points over the course of the first half of the nineteenth century ran the pedlars' licensing system,[42] all show that the supposed regulators did not know the numbers of hawkers and pedlars operating within England and Wales, and that this was not their primary concern. As a government department under the authority of the Treasury, their main aim was to raise revenue while avoiding unnecessary costs. The circumvention of the licensing system might have worried shopkeepers and other traders, including licensed hawkers themselves, but it was not practical, either in physical or economic terms, for the government to try to license all hawkers and pedlars.

Until 1832, the main agents both for selling licences and catching evaders were the riding surveyors. In 1800, there were only thirteen for the whole country. By the 1820s, this number had doubled, each taking a different region. They were paid an annual salary of £100 and an allowance of 2*d*. in the pound for every licence they sold. They were also entitled to part of the fine if an unlicensed hawker was prosecuted successfully. Generally recorded with the status of 'gentleman', they often had another occupation, commonly that of solicitor. Usually they were the more mature members of the community: in a list of 1822, only four were under the age of fifty.[43] They were assisted by licence inspectors, who were unpaid, but took a percentage of the licences they sold and of the fines from prosecutions they helped to bring about.

When the department was taken over by the Stamp Office in 1832, the riding surveyors lost their position. From then on only the licence inspectors actively sought out unlicensed hawkers and pedlars and no annual salaries were paid.[44] This might have resulted in inspectors being vigilant and selling and inspecting as many licences as possible. However, it is very clear that it was only worth targeting those hawkers who could actually pay the fine. If hawkers ended up in jail because they could not afford the fine and the selling of their stock could not raise it either, then nobody got any money and it was a waste of time prosecuting them.[45] The whole point of the licensing system thus seems to have been to raise revenue, not to regulate the trade of hawkers and pedlars. As early as 1810, it was suggested that riding surveyors in London should be abolished and licences be ignored, presumably because of the impracticalities of checking them all in the metropolis. However, the Lords of the Treasury refused to sanction the idea.[46] Those who turned to hawking in times of need and desperation were unlikely to be prosecuted.

Another change took place when the Stamp Office took over the licensing system in 1832. From then on, any person wishing to become a licensed hawker and pedlar had to supply a certificate of good character with references from a clergyman and two householders. Those who already had licences could simply renew them.[47] To become a licensed hawker, it was therefore necessary to have local connections and to be of some social standing.

Herefordshire and Worcestershire seem to have been typical of what was going on across the whole country in relation to the licensing system. Until 1819, there was one riding surveyor for the whole of Wales, and the nearest to Worcestershire was based in Staffordshire.[48] By 1820, John McCallum had been a licence inspector for seven years. He was then based in Birmingham and petitioned the Commissioners, backed by 'the mayor, magistrates and many inhabitants and traders of Worcester' to become a riding surveyor for Worcestershire and Gloucestershire. In the government records, Worcestershire and Gloucestershire were described as previously having the greatest number of unlicensed hawkers, but since McCallum's efforts, 'it is rare to meet with one at this time in this [part of the] country!' Thomas Shepherd, 'gentleman', was instead appointed riding surveyor for Worcester, aged about sixty-seven, having secured important local backing.[49] The creation of this new post of riding surveyor suggests that unlicensed hawking was perceived as a problem in the Worcester area. By 1821, Shepherd recorded seventeen successful prosecutions, raising £197 6s., of which he kept half, the highest figure in the country for that year, nearly 15 per cent of all prosecutions.[50] At least four of those prosecuted were selling clothing-related goods.[51]

A group of records in the Worcestershire Quarter Session papers, from 1801 to 1848, provide details of hawkers and pedlars selling clothing and textiles, caught without licences and prosecuted successfully, with the £10 statutory penalty being imposed. The majority of the surviving prosecutions were from the north of the county (see Figure 3.1). In general, the hawkers were relatively local to the area where they were caught. They were usually travelling out from the larger towns into the surrounding area, rather than travelling long routes away from home at a particular time of year. McCallum had detailed his journey out from his base in Birmingham to survey county towns after Christmas in 1820.[52] Most of those who were caught without licences were likely to have been caught on inspections such as this one.

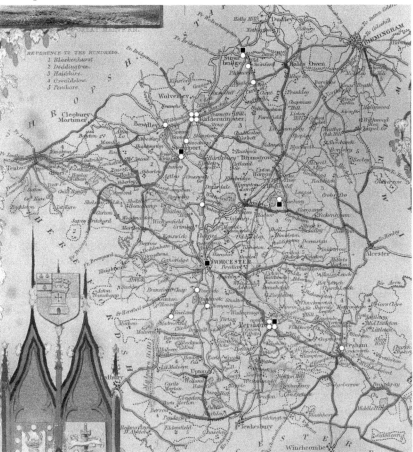

Figure 3.1: Map illustrating the locations in which hawkers and pedlars were caught selling clothing and textiles without a licence [circles], and the location of surveyors of hawker's licences [squares], Worcestershire Quarter Session Papers, 1801–48, Worcestershire Record Office, map Thomas Moule, 1836, private collection.

As can be seen in Figure 3.1, surveyors of licences were based in Worcester, Stourport, Stourbridge, Hanbury Hall and Pershore,[53] very close to where the majority of the hawkers were caught without licences. The south-west and north-west areas of Worcestershire did not have a regular inspector and, perhaps unsurprisingly, no pedlars have come to light in the court records from these parts of the county. From the evidence of prosecutions, Kidderminster seems to have been a popular place in which to be based: Edward Swindley hawked flannels,[54] John Broadbent cloths and shawls,[55] Joseph Rogers printed cottons, bombazins, worsted stockings and other articles,[56] and Thomas Downey, described as a labourer, hawked worsted and cotton stockings, combs, watch seals and other articles.[57] As previously noted, hawking could also be a part-time activity, taken up when trade in other areas was slack. In Kidderminster as in other towns, when there was distress in the predominant industry, in this case carpet weaving, hawking small amounts of wares might be a way to make ends meet either seasonally or over a longer period of time. However, there might be a further explanation for the number of hawkers prosecuted around Kidderminster. This was the presence of licence inspectors living nearby. In reality, the numbers of hawkers and pedlars may have not varied much from elsewhere in the county.

Upton was the only town in the south-west of the county, and had no prosecutions for unlicensed pedlars. There was, however, no surveyor of licences in or near the town. A case dealing with hawking goods in Upton was actually noted in the Minutes of the Stamp Office in 1836, where Mr. J. B. Beck appealed to the Board against his 40 shilling fine for hawking. However, the Board stated that he had breached a local Act of Parliament, not the jurisdiction of the Hawkers and Pedlars Act and so could do nothing.[58] Thus peddling and hawking did take place in Upton, for example William Pitman selling stockings at the local inn as noted above, but it is not recorded in the government licensing records.

From the 1830s, the Stamp Office also turned to the Stamp Distributors and Sub-Distributors for help. A circular letter to them from the Stamp Office noted:

> As without the co-operation of local officers it is impossible, effectually, to collect the Duty on this Branch of the Public Revenue, the Commissioners rely on yourself and Sub-Distributors ... to detect Persons trading in your District without the proper Licence.[59]

Two stamp sub-distributors in Worcestershire, Daniel Edge of Evesham and Benjamin Farley of Pershore, were linked to the clothing trades. Edge was a draper and Farley variously a slop seller, breeches-maker and clothing warehouse owner.[60] For those who probably already sold stock to itinerant traders, selling licences would perhaps have been a profitable sideline.

Unlike Worcestershire, there is very little evidence for hawking and peddling in Herefordshire. Before 1832, the area lay between licence inspectors in Brecon and Worcester, both having large industrialized areas to deal with. The Worcester inspector dealt with a substantial part of the densely populated Black Country and the Welsh inspector covered South Wales, implying there was little time left to check more sparsely inhabited rural areas. The lack of prosecutions from Herefordshire suggests that pedlars in this area were probably left alone to ply their trade. Only in 1832, when the Stamp Office took over licensing, was an official network introduced to Herefordshire. Distributors and Sub-Distributors of stamps could now sell licences and help detect offenders.[61] To some extent, the county was ignored by the various offices for licences, being a relatively sparsely populated area that would not garner much easy revenue for them, even after the more systematic regulation of the trade in the 1830s.

In contrast to Worcester, there was no suggestion noted in any official minutes that a Riding Surveyor was necessary for Herefordshire. This perhaps indicates that pedlars and hawkers were not in such direct competition with shops. Although Herefordshire had an early turnpike system from the first half of the eighteenth century, local roads were in poor condition.[62] Correspondence published in the local newspaper noted in 1825 that the state of the roads had recently improved. It had previously taken six hours to get between Leominster and Kington with a hack chaise and four horses, a distance of only fifteen miles.[63] In terrain such as this, the hawker and pedlar working on foot probably had an advantage. As demonstrated by the pattern of prosecutions in Worcestershire, the lack of evidence for peddling in Herefordshire should not be taken for absence of the trade in general. The county simply did not have the mechanisms of official regulation. Historically, itinerant sellers had been active in the county. For example, Spufford details the activity of one, Oliver Jones, travelling out from Monkland, near Leominster, in the seventeenth century.[64] Itinerant quacks were also prevalent in the county, their advertisements littering the pages of the local newspapers. As noted earlier, other hawkers, of jewellery for instance, also plied the county for trade. It would seem an ideal landscape to practise an itinerant trade but due to the lack of enforcement of the licensing system in the early nineteenth century, there is little tangible evidence, certainly with regard to the clothing trade.

Perhaps because of this lack of official sanction, letters from 'tradesmen' intermittently appeared in the local newspaper warning of the pitfalls of using itinerant sellers. In 1831, a female itinerant vendor of women's attire was described as 'very successful', selling shawls and lace for £4 and £5 when they could be bought in the shops for seven and ten shillings. She spoke French and pretended not to understand English. The newspaper stated that the cheapest and safest practice, so as not to be duped, was to buy from a respectable shop.[65]

Likewise in 1833, a shawl merchant described as a Turkish Jew, who bought his stock from drapers in the city and then sold the shawls in the surrounding countryside for double the price in the shops, disappeared to Oxford without paying for his stock in full.[66] The use of words such as 'dupe' and 'cheat' in the newspaper reporting, suggests an outrage against honest respectable shopkeepers who had to pay rent and taxes, vying both with this unfair competition and the gullibility of the public in allowing such charlatans to ply their trade. The fact that there appears to have been so little official regulation of itinerant sellers in Herefordshire may have meant that the shopkeepers felt that they needed to publicize this perceived problem, leading to these distinctly biased accounts. This point of view was not common to all shopkeepers however. Charles Anthony's 'Manchester Warehouse' in Hereford appealed directly to hawkers and pedlars for their business. He advertised in 1826 that allowances would be given to country shopkeepers and hawkers, suggesting that he would offer them good wholesale prices.[67] For this shop, hawkers and pedlars appear to have complemented their trade, taking their goods out into the hinterland to customers that the retailer themselves could not usually reach.

No doubt the main reason for not getting a licence when it could be avoided was the expense. The settlement examination of William Shorey of Broadway in 1810 details how he trained as a journeyman breeches-maker in Evesham. He then took a shop by himself in All Saints, Evesham, at a rent of a shilling per week.[68] His total rent for the year was therefore just over half the amount required to obtain a pedlar's and hawker's licence. It can be assumed therefore that there were many small-scale hawkers and pedlars who could not afford the expense of a licence. As such, they were unlikely to be able to pay any penalty imposed, and so were not usually targeted by the inspectors. These hawkers and pedlars have left very little sign of their existence. However, where evidence has come to light, it shows that they were probably commonplace across the two counties.

Goods Sold

The majority of hawkers and pedlars probably bought their stock from their local towns or cities, in shops such as the Manchester Warehouse in Hereford. There was therefore not always competition between pedlars and shopkeepers but often commercial integration.[69] It is difficult to discern a clear pattern of what stock pedlars and hawkers carried. However, when the Worcestershire prosecutions are taken in conjunction with the countywide surveys of tradespeople in the Worcestershire directories of 1820 and 1841,[70] the surviving evidence suggests that outside the larger towns, pedlars were selling items not commonly stocked by shops in the immediate locality. Whereas tailors were fairly evenly distributed across the county, drapers were under-represented. It could be argued that, to a certain extent, pedlars and hawkers fulfilled the role of drapers, particularly in selling female clothing, fabric and trimmings. For example, the stock of Kidderminster hawkers seems to have been mainly textiles, including flannel, linen, woollen drapery and cottons, along with various yarns. As noted, accessories sold by drapers such as stockings, handkerchiefs and shawls were also sold by several itinerant traders from the town. The gender bias in stock towards feminine articles was also the case in other areas of Worcestershire: Joseph Williams, caught in Hagley and Pedmore, was selling lace, cotton handkerchiefs and stays,[71] Cornelius Mills of Worcester, caught in Pershore with a licence but not displaying it properly, was hawking handkerchiefs, shawls and dresses,[72] John Burns of Stourbridge was hawking cotton gown pieces,[73] and Robert Brown of Worcester, caught at Kempsey, was hawking shawls, dresses and tea.[74] In March 1847, a Castlemorton farmer noted in his diary, 'A flash woman called and obtained a quantity of bed feathers off Mrs L. [his wife] in exchange for new dresses ...'[75] Respectable customers such as Lane, a local overseer, could accept such unlicensed itinerant selling, as the method was enforced by legitimate licensed hawkers with little to differentiate them.[76] Similarly, unlicensed hawkers were caught at Eaton Bishop, Herefordshire, selling shawls and dresses in return, or part exchange, for bed feathers.[77] So it appears that some dresses were being sold ready-made by itinerant sellers. There is little evidence of masculine clothing such as waistcoats or breeches being sold.[78]

Pedlars and hawkers appear to have identified gaps in the market, particularly in female clothing, which was not so readily provisioned by rural retailers. It would have made commercial sense for itinerant sellers to pursue sales and develop this market rather than competing directly with the existing trade of local shopkeepers. For example, in 1848 Robert Brown of Worcester, whose items included dresses and shawls, was caught at Kempsey. There had only been tailors noted in the village in the directory survey of 1820, and one combined tailor and draper by 1847.[79] Henry Bradford of Birmingham was caught hawking linen cloths at Hanbury in 1824, where there was only one tailor recorded in 1820.[80] Of course, directory entries were probably not comprehensive, especially with respect to those traders serving the lower end of the social scale, but they do give a general indication of how retailers may have interacted.

Mui and Mui have noted that hawkers and pedlars in the north of England provided a complementary rather competitive service to shops. In southern England, pedlars were perceived to be in competition with shops.[81] From the surviving evidence, Worcestershire and Herefordshire would appear to fit with the northern pattern, certainly in their rural areas. Male working-class consumers were probably already well catered for both in towns and rural areas, and were often able to buy ready-made, workaday clothing from tailors and woollen drapers across the two counties. The implication is that the retailing of lower status men's clothing through shops was more established outside town centres than that of women. Pedlars may have enabled women to access consumer markets from their homes. This idea was to be exploited further by travelling drapers, a new form of itinerant seller, in the second quarter of the nineteenth century.

Travelling Drapers

By the mid-nineteenth century, a new form of itinerant seller had emerged, travelling drapers, also called tallymen, after the stick carried to tally up accounts, or scotchmen.[82] The derivation of the term 'scotchman' is unclear and may have been connected to the 'Scotch' cloth that was sold during the eighteenth century. However, by the nineteenth century, there was a firm association between scotch drapers or 'scotchmen' and Scottish nationality.[83] Such traders worked strictly on credit, customers paying by prearranged installments across a period of time. They circumvented the licensing laws by travelling out from a shop to target a specific area, or by taking orders to deliver at a later date.

How much difference there actually was between a travelling draper and a pedlar is a matter of debate. The main disparity was that pedlars traditionally carried their stock with them. However, the case of Robert Brown shows that there was an overlap between the two occupations. He was prosecuted as an unlicensed hawker and pedlar selling shawls, dresses and tea on foot at Kempsey in 1848.[84] Presumably he was carrying some of his stock with him, as he was not able to successfully defend himself with the plea that he was only delivering goods previously ordered. Nonetheless, he was listed in Hunt's *Directory* of 1847 in the section for 'tea dealers and travelling drapers', the first time such a category appeared in listings for a Worcester trade directory.[85] Ten were listed thus, in contrast to fourteen drapers selling from shops. Conceivably, pedlars and hawkers who had previously traded without a licence began to call themselves travelling drapers.

The occupation of travelling draper first appeared in the Worcestershire trade directories in Dudley, in the industrial Black Country. Thirty-two travelling drapers were listed in the directories of 1835 and 1840, fifteen combining the trade with tea selling.[86] William Harrison, for example, was listed as a wholesale travelling draper and tea dealer in 1840. He had been listed in the Dudley directories since 1820 as a draper, so perhaps he used stock from his shop to expand into the itinerant wholesaling business in the second quarter of the century.[87] Ivie Mcnaught [Macknight] was listed in 1840. He had probably set up in business in the intervening ten years, after being involved in the court case in 1830 detailed above.[88] The connection between selling tea and drapery was close. Both were easily portable and durable consumables desired by the lower orders, who could only afford to buy small quantities at any one time.[89] Margot Finn also notes that there was a general expansion in numbers of travelling drapers during the 1830s, when a reduction in excise duty made the sale of domestic cotton more lucrative than that of tea.[90]

Dudley had a sizeable community of drapers of Scottish origin, evidenced from the 1841 census. Most were twenty-five to forty years old. Half of the thirty-two drapers listed in the directories that were traced in the 1841 census were of Scottish origin. However, of the ten names listed in the directory from 1835, only three had Scottish origins, John Campbell, James Harrison and James Murdoch, suggesting that there may have been a larger influx of Scotchmen into the area in the late 1830s, perhaps reflected in William Harrison's expanding wholesale business.[91] Many of the drapers had small children under the age of ten, generally born in Dudley. In the 1841 census, for example, Robert Blair, living in Newhall Street, was of Scottish origin, although his son, aged six, was born in the county. Likewise, in the household of James Harrison from Queen's Cross, his wife and young children were born in the county, integration into the local community perhaps helped by marrying local women and starting a family. Scottish apprentices were also brought to live in Dudley along with other members of the family. William McMillan of Stafford Street was listed in *Bentley's Directory*. He was also listed a year later in the census, aged twenty-five, with James McMillan, aged thirty, a draper, John McMillan, aged twenty, tea dealer, Gordon Barbere, aged twenty, and William McMellan, aged fifteen, both drapers' apprentices, and all Scottish.[92]

Likewise in Hereford, in Hunt's 1847 *Directory*, all those listed as travelling drapers who have been traced six years earlier in the census, were either of Scottish or Irish origin.[93] One of these was William Harris Maclean who traded out of St Peter's Street in the centre of Hereford, and who was also listed in the same directory as a hosier, glover and clothes dealer. Presumably his trade in the surrounding countryside was in all these items. Maclean was listed in the 1841 census as a draper of Scottish origin. Then aged thirty-five, he lived with his wife from Herefordshire, two children not born locally and two that were. He also had a Scottish apprentice, Hugh Murray, and two locally born female servants.[94] In an embezzlement case in 1846, Peter M'George was accused of stealing tea from his employer, Maclean, whom he worked for as a hawker in an allotted district. He was originally from Kirkcudbrightshire. A witness, Quintin Mitchell, was also in Maclean's employ, working the 'drapery round'.[95] It appears that men were sent out from Hereford into the surrounding countryside on specific routes, selling particular items. By 1848, Maclean was running the 'London Hat and Ready-Made Clothing Warehouse' in St Peter's Street, selling items such as overcoats and mackintoshes.[96] Mrs Maclean ran a 'French and English Stay and Bonnet Warehouse' from the same street, catering for female consumers.[97] The

Macleans could fully supply the men doing 'rounds' in the countryside for them. By the late 1840s, apart from his Scottish ancestry and his listing in the new category of travelling draper in the trade directories, there was little to distinguish Maclean from other shopkeepers in Hereford selling a similar range of goods. He was fully integrated in the commercial environment of Hereford, using all retail methods to further his business.[98]

A large proportion of travelling drapers that came to settle in Dudley were therefore not natives from Worcestershire, but were Scottish. Likewise in Hereford, being a travelling draper would seem to indicate a Scottish or Irish ancestry. Presumably, like any good businessman, they would have drawn on contacts in Scotland and in this way, perhaps promoted the Scottish textile industries.[99] These included linen and shawls, which, by the mid-nineteenth century, were increasingly popular. As skirts became more voluminous during the 1830s and 1840s, coats became increasingly difficult to fit. Shawls became normal outerwear for women of all social status. The Scottish shawl industry had been strong since the late eighteenth century, particularly developing in Paisley where it was famous for imitating Indian patterns. Scotland also produced 'Scotch plaids', checked shawls which were used for more everyday wear.[100]

The scotch drapers seem to have integrated quite quickly into communities, some taking up market stalls and eventually high street shops. The growth of Dudley made an attractive economic proposition for setting up a business. Its population had grown from around 10,000 in 1801 to over 30,000 by the 1830s. Even by the 1840s, it still had one of the highest ratios of population per shop in Worcestershire, revealing a relative lack of retail provision.[101] The scotch drapers seem to have partially filled this gap, catering for the growing population of industrial workers at a time when emigration from Scotland was commonplace.[102] In a move away from the geographically remote areas they were traditionally associated with, itinerant sellers had become more interested in areas where population density had rapidly increased and there was a dormant market for cheap goods ready for exploitation.[103] In other areas of the country too, for example Stockport, like Dudley, a newly expanded urban area, travelling drapers were increasingly common, selling on credit but said to charge 50–100 per cent more than shops.[104]

Over the course of the nineteenth century, the terms 'credit draper' or 'tallyman' became more common than 'travelling draper'. Increasingly, they attracted criticism for the way that they operated. Hawkers and pedlars were seemingly acceptable for contact with consumers across society. For instance, Parson Woodforde often bought haberdashery and textiles from hawkers and pedlars; on 17 September 1802, he bought thread from Mrs Falling.[105] The wide range of both people involved in itinerant selling and goods that they sold was reflected in diffuse attitudes towards them.[106] However, the persistent criticism that many hawkers and pedlars were little more than rogues and vagabonds continued, particularly as evidence shows that, for a variety of reasons, they were often caught up in court cases. By the second quarter of the nineteenth century, this moral sanction was turned towards credit drapers, partly as they were seen to be targeting labouring women, persuading them to buy fashionable rather than practical clothing. In their defence, credit drapers argued that they sold masculine clothing too.[107] For contemporary commentators such as the novelist Mrs Henry Wood, travelling drapers tricked women into buying fashionable finery that they could not afford and which was perceived to be unsuitable for the wives of labourers. Her 1862 novel, *Mrs Halliburton's Troubles,* was set in the fictional town of Helstonleigh, her alias for Worcester, and focused on a group of gloveworkers, or 'gloveresses', in the mid-nineteenth century. She described the operation of a credit draper:

> A twelve month previously, some strangers had opened a linen-draper's shop in a back street of Helstonleigh: brothers, of the name of Bankes. They professed to do business upon credit, and to wait upon people at their own homes, after the fashion of hawkers. Every Monday would one of them appear in Honey Fair, a great pack of goods on his back, which would be opened for inspection at each house. Caps, shawls, gown pieces, calico, flannel, and finery would be displayed in all their fascinations. Now ladies, you who are reading this, only reflect in the temptation! Suppose Halling, Pierce & Stone (or any other house you may think of) brought their wares to your residence every week, and laid them out on your dining room table, right before your longing eyes, and said 'Choose what you please, madam, and pay us at your own convenience'. I am not given to insinuation but I do not think it impossible that even you might run up a score. The women of Honey Fair did; and it was three parts the work of their lives to keep the finery, and the system, from the knowledge of their husbands. 'Pay us so much weekly' Bankes's would say. And the women did so: it was like getting a gown for nothing. But Bankes's were found to be strict in collecting the instalments; and how these weekly payments told upon the wages, I leave you to judge. Some would have many shillings to pay weekly.[108]

Although a fictional account, this reflects middle-class concerns about travelling or 'credit' drapers, in this case shown operating in the immediate locality of their shop and targeting female working-class consumers with fashionable clothing.[109] Credit drapers were noted for enforcing debts, taking a husband to court for his wife's illicit spending.[110] Mrs Henry Wood's short story, 'Jellico's Pack', reflects this in its description of village women near Evesham trying to hide their mounting debts to a credit draper from their husbands.[111]

In the same way that some tailors and drapers saw increasing commercial opportunities in the sale of ready-made clothing specifically targeted at working-class consumers through specialized retail concerns,[112] a similar process appears to have taken place with itinerant clothing sellers. The growing demand for ready-made clothing, particularly in the second quarter of the nineteenth century, seems to have led to its further distribution, in both rural and newly urbanized areas. Many traders were already within the clothing trade before turning to the new category of travelling draper.[113] By the late 1840s, the number of drapers or hawkers who recognized the itinerant clothing market as a viable commercial opportunity had substantially increased. This new economic dynamic afforded them a new category in the trade directories. There is little evidence about the actual social status of their customers. The stock which is detailed in surviving evidence, for example ready-made dresses, and the number of travelling drapers who were also clothing dealers or market stall holders, would suggest a bias towards lower status clothing. Both their importance in distributing such stock and the strength of this clothing market is thus highlighted. However, they left themselves open to censure from middle-class critics, uneasy about the supply of such working-class clothing on credit.[114]

Markets

Previous research into clothes retailing in the first half of the nineteenth century has revealed little evidence of clothing sold through markets, suggesting that they were no longer important for the sale of clothing by this date.[115] This section will investigate whether this was the case in Herefordshire and Worcestershire during this period. While the trade directory descriptions and surveys of towns detail different types of food for sale at various weekly markets in Herefordshire and Worcestershire, contemporary authors often used generalizations such as 'most other articles' which might include clothing.[116] Evidence from surviving market accounts in Hereford suggests that this market was indeed used for the sale of clothing during the first half of the nineteenth century.[117]

Although scattered about the streets of the city, Hereford market was concentrated in the main square, the High Town, where the ground floor of the sixteenth-century market house provided the only covered space.[118] Market accounts survive for the period between 1810 and 1835, but although they list the surnames of those who paid rent for stalls, they do not list their occupation or what they were selling. However, it is apparent that non-perishable goods were sold. For example, a note in the 1821–2 accounts shows a stall was let weekly to an unnamed shoemaker.[119] Most surnames are too common, without a Christian name, to effect a reasonable identification to cross reference with other sources, but there are a few which can be linked to specific people. MacMullen was one such name that was listed and there were no other MacMullens in the 1841 census. He was first noted as taking a stall in 1829 with a Mr Bennett.[120] The following year he took two stalls by himself, at a rent of £4 each per year and similarly in 1835,[121] the first year the name John 'M'Mullen' appeared listed in Pigot's *Directory* as a travelling tea dealer and draper. This was almost certainly the same person building up a business via the market, perhaps having arrived in Hereford during the 1820s. Similarly, Burns was also listed as renting a stall, first with Lloyde in 1821–2, then by himself by 1830 and as T[?]erry Burns in 1835.[122] His entry in the census as a 'cloth dealer' would suggest that perhaps he was selling second-hand clothes or drapery in the market, before becoming a travelling draper by 1847.[123]

Thus, a few traders probably sold at markets with a view to acquiring fixed shop premises or focusing on itinerant selling. Combinations of various selling techniques were used by others. Hereford's twice-weekly market, every Wednesday and Saturday, was a good opportunity for the working-class consumer to purchase clothing, especially for those coming in to trade other goods in the market from the surrounding hinterland. A mixture of selling methods was noted in a court case from 1848. John Preece was a dealer in shoes and clothes with a business in Bye Street. He also took stalls in the 'New Markets' on Wednesdays, Saturdays and Fair Days. Preece was not noted in the trade directories, so presumably his business was relatively small-scale. Perhaps he did not even have a proper retailing space, hence the need to take market stalls. Although described as a clothes dealer, Preece was not just selling second-hand items. Some of his new waistcoats were noted as being from Samuel Sillifant's old stock, sold off when Sillifant went bankrupt.[124]

Pedlars and hawkers, working within the boundaries of a borough, were probably increasingly pushed into selling their wares in official marketplaces. By late 1843, the Hereford authorities judged that hawkers did less harm to the trade of the city in the open market than if they were allowed to sell door to door.[125] A case in 1846 details a hawker of brushes being fined when he did not use the market. The hawker argued that as he had bought a licence he could hawk anywhere. The authorities disagreed and, not wanting to set a precedent, imposed a 7s. 6d. fine.[126] By acting in this way, the authorities were reducing further the advantages of obtaining a licence, hawkers essentially having to be market traders. This was not welcomed by all shopkeepers. In 1844, there was a debate about the subject through letters to the *Hereford Journal*. A shopkeeper, for example, argued that hawkers selling cloth a few yards from his door by taking a standing in the marketplace were directly undermining his own business in that trade:

> It was only last Saturday that an itinerant cloth merchant, in a large gig, took his place
> in the open market, not many yards from my shop door ... where he continued during
> great part of the day in an auctioneering style vending his broad cloth at a consider-
> ably lower rate than I can procure it from the manufacturers ...[127]

The perennial complaint, that it was unfair for shopkeepers to be subject to rates and then be undersold by itinerant traders who paid nothing, was once again aired.[128] The editorial notes, however, that they would recommend the modification of hawker's licences to prevent this happening, although how effective this would have been in reality is another question.[129] The following week, in defence of the authorities' decision, it was stated that hawkers often bought goods from the same town in which they sold them; the goods were often damaged or remnants and so not suitable for sale in a respectable shop; hawkers often spent their receipts within the town; they usually had a house somewhere on which they would pay rates and in objecting to competition from the market, the shopkeeper was in effect objecting to free trade.[130] Indeed, Harold Deceulaer has noted a very similar example from 1762 in Belgium when drapers petitioned to stop the selling of textiles during fairs as it was harming the local shop trade. The itinerants sold at lower prices and used wagons to sell from, along with printed publicity advertising their pitches, much like the Hereford example.[131] For the city authorities, the regulations may have been a way of imposing control and order within the city centre, but both hawkers and shopkeepers clearly had reservations about them. The spatial proximity between these two retail networks – shops and market stalls – indicates their interrelatedness, and indeed, their complimentary nature, in terms of drawing customers in.[132] Despite the very black and white arguments presented by those involved on both sides, both networks were intermingled with each other in terms of attracting custom and, to some extent, their stock.

Evidence about markets from the remainder of the two counties is very patchy and often imprecise. It is clear that apart from foodstuffs and livestock, markets were still important as venues for the sale of 'sundries', which could include clothing. Dudley market was described in *Pigot's Directory* of 1828 as 'excellently supplied with all the necessities of life'.[133] William Raynes and John Harris both had stalls there, selling stockings that they had manufactured.[134] By 1838, Harris had moved into a shop, noted as a hosier and haberdasher in Wolverhampton Street.[135] In 1817, Patrick McNaley, a hawker from Manchester, was told by Phebe [*sic*] Moore that Elizabeth Trowman had stolen shawls from his 'standing' in Kidderminster market, including one of spotted muslin.[136] There was only a crockery market recorded at Kidderminster in the surviving market accounts, although clearly the market sold a much broader range of goods and was a base for those bringing textiles direct from Manchester.[137]

Where evidence of clothing stalls does exist for markets in Herefordshire and Worcestershire, there were commonly links to the second-hand clothes trade and to itinerant sellers, who both found them useful and convenient. This was also the case for fairs, where evidence is even sparser. The few examples that have been found suggest market-stallholders might take a stand on fair days too, for example, John Preece noted above; or sellers could use them as a way to get rid of unwanted stock quickly with exposure to a large number of people at one time.[138]

In Hereford, the market may have to some extent compensated for the lack of second-hand clothes dealers. Its importance was perhaps reflected in the higher rents charged for stalls than in Worcester.[139] The opening of the Butter Market building in 1860, a market still in use today, also reflects the civic importance placed on markets as a way of retailing in Hereford.[140] However, the success of individual market stalls appears to have been linked to the existing trade already within a town, with interaction between various retail networks, both in the type of stock sold and the traders, retailers and customers involved. There appears to be a problem with a lack of surviving evidence demonstrating such market trading rather than any absence of the trade itself.

Conclusion

As the nineteenth century progressed, the role of the hawker and pedlar seems to have splintered into different categories, such as commercial travellers or credit drapers, now noted in the local trade directories. These occupations became associated with specific types of goods, different ways of selling and distinctive types of consumer.[141] Their often informal nature, with the circumvention of the licensing system, makes it impossible to know if these associations were correct and how socially diverse their customer base was. This redefinition and targeting of particular markets may not have meant any loss in numbers of traders making a living from itinerant selling. Itinerant sellers remained a highly adaptable group, fulfilling new functions and selling new products, indeed creating new trades.[142] However, for those on the margins of poverty, small scale unlicensed hawking continued as it always had, as part of the makeshift economy. For example, 'travelling with a basket' was still used by agricultural labourers to generate income when out of work.[143] Such temporary traders were unlikely to be prosecuted for being unlicensed.

The proximity of Herefordshire to mid-Wales also represented a large market with little other retail competition.[144] Trade from Herefordshire might solve the conundrum of upland Wales having few pedlars despite being an isolated area, as shown by Mui and Mui in the late eighteenth century.[145] The pedlars that serviced this area may have come from further afield along the Welsh Marches. The *Hereford Journal* had a circulation across mid-Wales with an office in Brecon and included, for example, advertisements for the benefits of sea air at Aberystwyth.[146] With no Welsh newspapers until the 1820s, the *Hereford Journal* established a monopoly in south Wales and focused on its Welsh sales.[147] Itinerant traders could bring the goods advertised in pages of the newspaper directly to the consumers who had read or heard about them in the 'urban desert of Wales'.[148]

Despite problems with sources, this chapter has shown that itinerant selling continued throughout the period in both urban and rural areas. Indeed, it was almost too commonplace to be mentioned. Pedlars were creative in the ways that they operated and sought to get around restrictions, for example, renting rooms or pretending that they had a shop.[149] The very development of the travelling draper shows these metamorphosizing tendencies in action. However, official documentation shows that it was not the aim of the government to tax all itinerant sellers. The illusive hunt for the licensed pedlar and hawker to demonstrate the state of the itinerant trade is shown to be a chimera and leaves it impossible to quantify the number of hawkers and pedlars operating. This obviously makes it difficult to tell if there was a decline in hawkers and pedlars in rural areas during the first half of the nineteenth century. New categories such as travelling drapers and expanding networks of commercial salesmen probably changed the nature of itinerant selling and its definition, rather than there being any substantial alteration in the amount of people who earned their living in this way.[150] The surrounding countryside was still serviced by itinerant sellers, as demonstrated by the example of travelling drapers going out from Hereford.

For the working-class female consumer in particular, not so well served by shops outside towns, pedlars and later travelling drapers may have been useful in bringing clothing and textiles directly to the home. Thus itinerant sellers in the two counties seemed to have filled in retail gaps, rather than have been in direct competition with shops.[151] Combined with some selling at weekly markets and the shops previously discussed in Chapters 1 and 2, itinerant sellers ensured that all working-class consumers across Herefordshire and Worcestershire had access to a range of clothing that could be purchased either by cash or credit.

4 CLOTHING THE POOR: PARISH RELIEF

The following two chapters will examine the informal trade in clothing, where clothing changed hands without the need for cash, usually outside the boundaries of shops and typically carried out by people not professionally connected to the clothing trade. This chapter will first examine how informal exchange of clothing could be part of the economy of makeshifts, before turning to look briefly at the illicit trade in clothing. The main section will investigate Poor Law provision in various urban and rural localities, concluding with a discussion on workhouse clothing. Clothing charities will be considered in Chapter 5.

Informal Exchange and the 'Economy of Makeshifts'

While they acknowledge that informal exchange of non-perishable goods was probably an important part of consumer life, historians have found little surviving evidence of such transactions. For example, gifting has left little evidence, particularly in Herefordshire and Worcestershire.[1] Set within the economic climate of the early nineteenth century, where the limited supply of coin did not accommodate the expanding numbers of people dependent on wages, other methods of commodity exchange were perhaps necessarily sought.[2]

The acquisition of clothing by the poor has been analysed as part of the 'makeshift' economy. For Steven King and Alannah Tomkins, the 'makeshift' economy encompasses self-provisioning to help make ends meet, for example, using income in cash or kind from the parish, local charities, friendly societies, kinship and neighbourly support, along with pawning.[3] As will become apparent over the next two chapters, it was usually a household strategy rather than an individual one, with all family members contributing from various acquisition strands.[4] Clothing was an important part of the makeshift economy, allowing appearance to be maintained. Employment could thus be sought in order to ensure survival and a sense of self-esteem within the community. The value of clothing as a necessity to enable this to happen should not be under-estimated.[5] The next two chapters will take as their basis the idea of the 'makeshift' economy. Thus they will examine clothing acquisition by the working-class consumer in its broadest sense. This included both legal and illicit networks as well as local resources, for instance, charitable bequests. How accessible Poor Law provision, charity and informal trading were, and how frequently they were used by working-class consumers to obtain clothing, will be discussed.

Illicit Second-Hand Exchange

The informal and unregulated market, often including stolen clothing, was most probably a significant part of everyday life for working people. Coming outside official control, participants were usually otherwise not professionally engaged in clothing retail, it was, and remains, an important provisioning channel. As Beverly Lemire has stated, this system of commodity exchange was so pervasive, extensive and necessary, that working people depended on the manipulations of the material goods that they traded as a means to square their domestic finances.[6] Building on the research of Lemire, the second-hand and illicit markets have recently garnered academic attention and will therefore not be considered in detail in this study, which instead focuses on new clothing retailed through shops or given out as part of the economy of makeshifts.[7]

The illicit second-hand market in Herefordshire and Worcestershire occurred in both rural and urban areas, with both men and women trading and participating. Indeed, male clothing was an important part of the network, perhaps reflecting men's already routine consumption patterns of buying clothing ready-made. Of course, evidence from these networks is elusive and patchy, and relies almost exclusively on court records when thieves were caught, along with newspaper reporting of the court case, which often provides detail about the defendant's life. There was probably also an equally important licit informal market involving the exchange of clothes for money or other items or services, around kin and friendship groups, as well as the wider community.[8] This has left even less evidence. It is thus difficult to quantify precisely the extent and reach of the market, but it still seems to have been an important parallel market for clothing acquisition into the mid-nineteenth century and beyond.

The main difference between informal clothing exchange and the retailing of clothing, whether new or second-hand, was the site of the exchange. Informal clothing exchanges occurred in mundane, everyday situations, where people would otherwise ordinarily meet without clothing exchange: in the street or at a place of work.[9] In Herefordshire, for instance, in a survey of Herefordshire Quarter Session Records, 1820–50, approximately two thirds of all clothing theft cases were working men stealing workaday clothes such as smock frocks, shirts and corduroy breeches from men of a similar status.[10] Garments were stolen from fields and barns where their owners were working. For example, in 1820, a linen smock frock, valued at 2 shillings, was left in a barn by Joseph Bowcot while he was hop picking, in Whitbourne, Herefordshire. It was stolen and found in William Jones's box, who fled and was later found a few miles away by the Suckley constable whom he tried to bribe.[11] To realize its potential, stolen clothing had to be sold on, quickly if possible, to help avoid detection. In 1822, two linen smock frocks were stolen from Joseph and Charles Taylor, of North-field, valued by the court at 5 shillings. William Clarke subsequently offered them for 10 and then 6 shillings and a quart of ale by to John Pinfield, a cooper, presumably at a pub, who suspected they were stolen and sent for the constable.[12] This attempted clothing sale was sought out by the seller in a location, the pub, where the potential buyer had gone, presumably for a very different reason, although pubs were also well-known as places for trade.[13]

Stolen clothing was likely to be sold on to make a profit, or licit clothing surplus to requirements was exchanged or sold for cash. A case from 1844 illustrates the opportunist nature of such crimes and perhaps the dire financial situation that might have led to some of this criminal activity. James Newton, aged twenty and described as a labourer, was accused of breaking into various houses in and around Longton, in south-west Herefordshire, with two other men. Their haul for a night's work included shirts, stockings, a smock frock, eighteen yards of cotton print, twenty pounds each of bacon and cheese and a pair of trousers belonging to a servant, left drying by a fire. Most of this property was disposed of to Patrick Gawler, an old clothes dealer in Abergavenny, where the men had been living. In court, Gawler confirmed that he had bought some items from the men, but became suspicious and gave information to the constable. He denied the claim put to him by one of the prisoners in their defence: that he had told them that if they stole items Gawler would dispose of them. James Newton was caught wearing some of the missing clothing and with a book in his pocket called *The Modern Farmer*, which had also been stolen. The defendants were found guilty and were transported for fifteen years to Australia. The crime had taken place in October 1843 and it may be that the motive was the desire for enough money to survive following the seasonal downturn in the casual labour market. The men had been seen begging in the area prior to the break-in.[14] Newton's naivety in actually wearing the clothes that he had stolen probably helped with his capture and prosecution, and may have reflected his destitution. The role of clothing as a basic necessity is emphasized in this case.

When acquired, surplus clothing could be used as an alternative currency or a kind of savings account held in lieu until needed, when it could be sold for cash. This role of clothing has been highlighted and discussed in detail by Lemire and others.[15] A similar role was fulfilled on a more formal level by pawn-brokers, petty bankers for the urban population as Tomkins has termed them, with clothing acting as security.[16] The value of second-hand goods away from the retail market may also have varied. Commonly, the value of second-hand goods was about a quarter of their new cost.[17] However, sellers of the goods were able to create value by selling specific clothes to a person who they knew would require that garment, or who would be able to purchase it for resale at a future point in time. The large market in agricultural labourers selling useful garments such as smock frocks to each other is one instance of this. The context of the sale in an everyday situation, perhaps in the middle of a field or on a roadside, might create value in a garment, presenting it as a bargain or something that may be of use in the future. Such a purchase was possibly something that would not have been considered if it necessitated journeying to and entering a shop to buy similar garments. For example, in 1818, the clothing of Thomas Bubb, South Littleton, Worcestershire, was stolen from a stable when he was out ploughing. William Baylis, the suspect, was sleeping there. John Falkner, who lived nearby, had been offered the clothes by Baylis, comprising two pairs of shoes, a Russia duck smock frock, two pairs of gloves and some shaving items, all items that he may have found some future use for and were presumably offered to him at a good price.[18]

The skill of the seller was to present garments to the potential consumer as something of value for them at that specific point in time.[19] Although new clothing might be as cheap in some cases, a good price for second-hand clothing could still be achieved by offering it for sale in the right, convenient location.[20] Nicky Gregson and Louise Crewe, with their pioneering work on modern second-hand markets, contrast the different spaces of the modern charity shop or second-hand shop, which operates along similar lines to a first-hand sale shop, with displays, fixed prices and the need for monetary exchange, with that of the car-boot sale, an informal, unregulated situation, where a transaction has to be generated between the seller and the buyer, value reached by consent and through accumulated practical knowledge of similar transactions. They found that often the most important characteristic of buying at a car boot sale was to 'capture value', or in other words, to get a bargain, the price often being more important than what the actual goods were which were being purchased.[21] This is similar to the actions of some buyers in the informal trade in clothing during the first half of the nineteenth century. Clothing was often bought apparently on a whim, with seemingly no intention of using it, but in the knowledge that its value could be realized at a later date. In the informal economy, the exchange was not always for cash. Payments in kind or for community kudos and general well-being might also be considered. For example, clothing might be purchased from a neighbour who was struggling, the sale facilitated using notions of charity, whether real or imagined.[22] Profit was not always the motive and there may have been a variety of types of 'value' as well as the economic one. Therefore, it would appear that there was probably also a social and cultural nature to some exchanges, which are extremely hard to quantify or trace in the evidence.[23]

Participants in such networks were operating in an unregulated world. However, there were still obligations upon them, which seem to have been inferred, understood and accepted. These ranged from the necessity of being careful about illicit transactions, particularly in an era when successive convictions for theft, a felony, could result in the death penalty, to understanding neighbourhood obligations and ensuring the well-being of the community as a whole by exchanging commodities when necessary.[24] It is difficult to know whether a consumer set out with the intention of buying second-hand clothes from the informal market or more likely, whether it was a pragmatic decision taken when the opportunity presented itself, along with any community or social obligations felt.[25] Or in the case of stolen clothing, as the case of Charles and Joseph Taylor above showed, loyalty to the victims or to upholding the law may have been just as important in small communities as taking a commercial opportunity, the potential purchaser here sending for the constable.

The presence of this parallel informal market to the more formal retail systems illustrates the complexity of the material goods available to the working-class consumer and the various negotiations they had to undertake to acquire their routine clothing.[26] This could involve payment in kind, a credit in community goodwill or, as will be discussed, an undertaking given to parish or charity officials to behave in a certain way. A careful evaluation of what was required, what the value was, both economically in terms of the new cost of the garment and socially, for example, passing on something at a good price to a neighbour, or perhaps negatively, wearing clothing provided by the parish, was needed for every transaction. This assessment was necessary to negotiate exchanges effectively, both as individuals and as a member of a family group, enabling the continuing use of several provisioning channels at the same time to achieve clothing needs.[27] Without clothing it was impossible to work, or even seek work; it would not be possible to raise extra money when needed, for example, at a pawnbroker; and respectability and dignity would be lost. Nakedness and with that the implied loss of all material possessions, led to absolute poverty and destitution, with little chance of self-help to change the situation. How the authorities approached the clothing of people who were heading towards this situation will be examined in the remainder of this chapter and the following one, along with the way in which working people used such provision for acquiring their clothing.

The Dress of Paupers

The first half of the nineteenth century marked a period of enormous change in the welfare of the very poorest members of the community, those who generally relied on relief.[28] In 1834, the New Poor Law was introduced. Thereafter, there was an increasing reliance on workhouses to look after the needs of the poorest, removing them from their immediate communities. Historians have debated the extent of differences between the two systems, and the question of under which system the poor were better off. Along with food, fuel and shoes, clothing was of primary importance as a form of relief both under the Old and New Poor Laws, although until relatively recently, its importance has been overlooked.[29] King has contended that by the early nineteenth century, the Old Poor Law enabled those on parish relief to obtain a standard of clothing that was to some extent fashionable and better than that achieved by others who did not rely on relief. He has suggested that people who wore ragged clothing were those who struggled to avoid dependence on parish relief.[30] This idea will be examined within the context of Herefordshire and Worcestershire. Lemire has also noted that by studying what clothing was given to the poorest members of society, it is possible to gain a benchmark as to what was acceptable as a minimum standard of dress.[31]

This section will begin with a discussion about why clothing was given in relief and how claimants might apply for it successfully. There will then be an examination of how Old Poor Law clothing provision was used in several localities. Overseers' accounts and records from five parishes in varied geographical locations across the two counties have been sampled, consisting of a market town, two rural villages and two industrial areas. Parishes have been chosen on the basis of the survival of relevant parish records, supplemented where necessary with material from other similar parishes. The chapter will assess how useful parish clothing was to the working-class population. The relationship between parish clothing provision and other clothing suppliers in the area will also be considered. It might be expected that there would be variations in the type of provision between urban areas, where clothing was more readily available, and remote rural areas where there were few salesmen or other clothing dealers. This concept will be tested within the diverse retail environments of Herefordshire and Worcestershire. A brief examination of changes introduced with the New Poor Law and the subsequent workhouse provision of clothing will follow, investigating the type of clothing given out in workhouses and if it differed to clothing obtained via parish relief.

Claiming Clothing under the Old Poor Law

One of the problems with the Old Poor Law, and one reason why it was reformed, was that there was no statutory requirement or standard of relief. Instead, there was a network of customs and local practices over which there was no central control.[32] This meant that rates of relief, particularly in terms of clothing, could vary considerably between parishes. There was therefore no single strategy for using parish relief to obtain clothing, as provision depended on the judgement of the local overseers. This judgement might be influenced by perceptions about an applicant and also how overseers thought their organization of parish provision might be seen by observers from outside the parish. For example, on 3 August 1832, relief was refused to two women in Castlemorton, Worcestershire, as their husbands had been seen drinking all day in the Feathers pub.[33] In contrast, in Bromyard on 31 July 1818, £1 was paid to Mrs Page for clothing Maria Fudger, 'she being almost naked'.[34] It was enough to refer rhetorically to the state of Fudger's clothing to evoke sympathy, rather than be specific about the clothing that was lacking. An absolute lack of clothing, nakedness, emphasized that a pauper needed relief as soon as possible.[35] Aside from genuine concern about Fudger's welfare, if not addressed, this state of clothing would reveal poor parish welfare provision to outside observers. Likewise, in Hope under Dinmore, Ann Jones asked for clothing, including two shifts, a pair of shoes, a petticoat and gown. The comment in the complaints book is: '[ordered] what is thought propper by the overseer'.[36] Clothing was handed out in line with an unwritten standard of what was perceived decent in that particular parish and against the normal clothing worn by people of a similar status in the locality.[37] The overseers might also make a judgement on an applicant's standing from the clothing worn when asking for relief. However, this notion could potentially also be used by claimants to help gain relief by wearing what the overseers expected paupers seeking clothing to wear. Indeed Pamela Sharpe has suggested that some Poor Law officials were more concerned with external appearance, and by implication the respectability of the parish, than with assuring that there was enough food to eat.[38]

Those in need seem to have had an ambivalent attitude to the act of seeking relief. In some cases, to seek parish relief was the last strategy available to make ends meet. Certainly it could mean a loss of respectability in the eyes of peers, with the possessions of a pauper who sought regular relief becoming parish property on their death.[39] However, those who were disadvantaged, such as widows or the disabled, and who relied on relief for long periods of time, often saw it as a right. This is also evident in pauper letters from those living outside the parish. Mary Burns in Worcester wrote to the overseers of her home parish in Droitwich: 'you will oblige ... everything very dear and we are getting [on] in years ...'[40] In this context, the poor were not submissive or downtrodden, but had a concept of rights and self-worth, in which clothing played a major part.[41] The lack of enough clothing to maintain at least a reasonable appearance could be used as a bargaining tool with the parish. Without suitable clothing, claimants stressed that they would be unable to function fully within the community or seek work and may have to return home, where they would cost the parish more.[42]

Thus clothing may have been not just a symbol of social status but also an indicator of behaviour and social value in a community. It could demonstrate that a person was a productive member of that society, working or searching for work. Alternatively, it could show that somebody was at an unproductive stage and could potentially become a disruptive member of that community. The overseers regarded nakedness, signifying destitution, as a threat to the neighbourhood. Ragged dress had long been seen as a symbol of man's sinfulness and tainted soul.[43] Within local society, those clothed in ragged dress needed to be controlled by being given clothing before they could become disruptive 'bodies'. The overseers could also display their compassion to the poorest members of society by helping them to acquire new social value.[44]

This idea of lack of social worth and unproductivity was used to good effect by out-parishioner George Bourn, in his letters to his home parish. For instance, he stated his desperate need for clothes in a letter to the overseers of Droitwich in January 1833. Bourn, who lived in Birmingham and had corresponded irregularly with overseers since his release from prison in 1806, wrote that he was ill and able to 'do but little work'. He continued: 'I am in great distress, for the want of Clothes, particularly so for a pair of Trowsers, a Shirt Stockings and Shoes. Indeed I am so distress'd for the want of those necessaries, that I feel asham'd to be in the House'.[45] A month later he wrote again, threatening to come back to Droitwich in his present state of health, as, although the overseers in Birmingham had received a letter from Droitwich, it had not been clear if the relief was for him or his son.[46] For George Bourn, it appears that it was vital to maintain a decent appearance, even during a period of ill-health and when apparently residing in the workhouse. Unable to work, he was 'asham'd' about his appearance and implied that the condition of his clothing would make it difficult for him to get a job. If successful in his claim, Bourn would have been able to continue his life in Birmingham and use the clothes, either by wearing or selling them as he desired, away from the control of the overseers. A pair of fustian trousers was purchased for 'George Bourne' for 5 shillings from Pumfrey in May 1833: his appeal to the overseers had worked to some extent.[47]

For the people who ran the parish, and later the boards of guardians, the relief system was about spending money effectively and saving it where possible. Clothing was used by the overseers as part of this strategy. Children were given clothes to enable them to become apprentices or work in service, in the hope that they would then no longer be a burden on the parish. Out-parishioners who wrote letters for relief were often sent it in the hope that they would remain where they were and continue to eke out an existence, rather than return to their home parish and become a bigger burden. For example, Mary Bodel wrote from Deptford to her home parish of St John in Bedwardine, Worcester, asking why her pay had been stopped: 'For the times have bin [sic] so bad all this winter that I have not bin [sic] Able to Cloth my children ...' She ended with the threat that if the overseers stopped her pay, she and her four children would have to return home immediately.[48] As will be shown, in some cases men were given working clothing such as jackets and smock frocks. Presumably this was so they could function in work, rather than rely on further parish relief. The following sections will ascertain how much of an impact this strategy of giving out clothing in the hope of future savings for the parish had on the clothing provision for working-class individuals and families, and therefore how useful the Old Poor Law could be for obtaining clothing. It will question if there were certain stipulations that had to be met to obtain relief which precluded the majority, or if it was of benefit to the whole family. The relationship between parish clothing and its suppliers and general working-class clothing will be examined. It will explore whether suppliers were the same, and also the type of clothing that was given out. To what extent these ideas were determined by geographic location will also be considered by investigating provision in five different areas.

The Market Town: Bromyard

As previously noted, the town of Bromyard in Herefordshire attracted derogatory comments from the authors of contemporary trade directories.[49] Paupers from outside the parish were also sent to live in the parish, their home parishes attracted by the very low rents charged on cottages on the downland surrounding the town.[50] The needs of the working-class consumer were already well catered for in the town, with a cluster of clothes dealers, tailors and drapers who dealt in clothing for the lower end of the market.[51] Records of poor relief survive for three parishes which came under the township of Bromyard: Linton, Norton and Winslow. Bromyard therefore provides an opportunity to explore the crossover between parish and independently purchased low-status clothing. This section will examine whether parish clothing was similar to other working clothing, and if it was purchased from the same shops.

Many of the town's tradespeople probably made a large part of their living from providing clothing for those on parish relief. For example, in May and July 1816, James Amiss provided the overseer Mr Page, with two smock frocks, two pairs of breeches, six shirts, three pairs of hose, a hat, five yards of brown cotton and three yards of calico, the bill totalling £3 7s. 6d.[52] William Willcox, who does not appear in the later trade directories, sold frocks, shifts and breeches to the overseers in 1812. In 1843, Thomas Robinson and John Green, labourers of Bromyard, were accused of stealing sixteen waistcoats, value £4, and two pairs of trousers, value 14 shillings, from Samuel Wilcox, listed as a tailor, clothes dealer and draper in the contemporary trade directories. Seven shillings for breeches and five shillings for waistcoats were around the prices commonly charged to overseers, suggesting that shopkeepers such as Wilcox sold similar stock both to the parish and the wider population. Overseers generally bought such ready-made male clothing for paupers locally, from the shops in the town.[53]

Female ready-made clothing, including petticoats, shifts and dresses, was similarly purchased by overseers from local shops. For example, Martha Lane, noted as a clothes dealer in *Robson's Directory* of 1838,[54] presented a bill to the overseers of Winslow on 17 August 1833 for what appears to have been the basic wardrobe of Elizabeth Franks: flannel, stays, gound [*sic*], stockings, cap, chimize [*sic*], shall [*sic*] plus clothing for the child, totalling 16*s*. 7*d*.[55] Lane is likely to have sold similar items to the general working-class population. However, not all dresses were bought made-up. In 1817 and 1818, payments of 1 shilling were made to an unnamed person, probably a local woman, for 'making a gownd' [*sic*].[56] On 7 December 1833, a bill from P. Taylor, a draper, was presented to the overseers. Philip Taylor listed goods for John Taylor's daughter, including calico, print, flannel, hose, tape and cotton, totalling 7*s*. 11½*d*.[57] Dresses could have been made up from the five yards each of cheap calico and print bought from Taylor, costing only 3½*d*. and 6*d*. a yard respectively. Buying the material for the recipient to make up would allow the parish a saving of a shilling, the parish providing two dresses as well as hose for less than 8 shillings for Taylor's daughter.

There were two methods by which paupers could obtain clothing from the overseers. Most of the accounts state 'Paid' to an individual. For example, 'Paid for a pair of breeches for Richard Turner, 8*s*' or 'Paid Wolton's wife towards clothing her daughter, 2*s*'.[58] This seems to imply a certain amount of freedom for the recipient in choosing the clothing, presumably from a shopkeeper who dealt with the overseers, such as James Amiss. However, some entries indicate that the overseer himself bought clothing: for example, on 18 August 1820, 'Bought at Bromyard for Ann Moor one pair of stockings and shift, 2*s* 8*d*'.[59] It is impossible to be certain, but perhaps this difference was due to the perceived status of the pauper. Those that were incapacitated would need somebody to purchase items for them. If they were deemed deserving, such as Elizabeth Franks, perhaps they may have been given more freedom to purchase clothing themselves, the overseers ultimately vetting the payment of the bill. This practice was also noted by King, who speculates that some paupers were deemed to be trustworthy and so could buy their own clothing and be 'proper'.[60]

Franks wrote a letter to the overseers dated 21 July 1833,[61] probably from Birmingham where she had been receiving weekly payments of 4 shillings from the overseers via the Birmingham Tea Company.[62] In it, she voiced her opinion of her son and daughter-in-law who had returned to Bromyard for relief. She saw them as 'undeserving', as they preferred not to work and had pawned their clothing for money to drink. She seemed to see herself as a worthwhile recipient, both of ongoing payments, and of clothing. However, her letter may have been more of an act than a genuine reflection of her feelings for her son. Thus

Franks ensured that those who were paying for her maintenance, the overseers, understood that she was respectable, above blame and able to recognize those that were not, even if they were members of her own family. It seems to have worked, for she received clothing from the parish as well as ongoing payments. Elizabeth Franks demonstrates how issues of respectability and morality underpinned applicants' judgements, both about themselves and about their peers.

As Chapter 1 has shown,[63] Bromyard appears to have had a wide choice of retailers of low-status clothing, including those selling male and female ready-made garments. Perhaps the increase in the population due to the out-parish paupers was seen as a commercial opportunity by retailers of such clothing. It seems likely that clothes dealers were supplying both the overseers and the general working-class population with similar clothing. Of course, without further evidence, it is impossible to tell whether there were differences in quality and finish, but the clothes seem to have come from the same retailers and to have been similarly priced. Unfortunately, the complete overseers' accounts no longer exist, so it is not possible to ascertain what percentage of the population relied on such relief. The poverty of the area, reflected in its retail environment, would suggest there might have been a large number of applicants.

Rural Villages: Castlemorton and Abbey Dore

The parishes of Castlemorton and Abbey Dore will be examined in turn and show differences in clothing provision within rural areas. Castlemorton in southwest Worcestershire, at the foothills of the Malvern Hills, was a small parish of 879 people in 1831, with forty-five paupers receiving parish relief. It still had common land, which may have influenced relief figures, making it atypical in contrast to other locally enclosed areas. The ability to keep livestock on common land was, for example, estimated to be worth 5–6 shillings a week, potentially enough to keep families off poor relief.[64] In 1835, the parish had become part of the Upton Union under the New Poor Law. Thereafter records of outdoor relief gradually cease as paupers were sent to the workhouse erected during 1836, instead of receiving relief within their parish.

Quarterly lists of recipients have survived from 1836, which detail names, ages and status of those who received both weekly dole and payments in kind.[65] The paupers that were listed in the overseers' accounts of 1836 were either 'past work', disabled, injured in some way, illegitimate children or widowed.[66] They had received clothing from the parish over several years and most also received a weekly dole, with clothing a supplement to this payment. These claimants accounted for the bulk of the parish's clothing purchases, which varied between a quarter and third of the total budget. For example, in 1825 sixteen applications for clothing were made to the vestry. Eleven were requests for children, either as part of a family or children being looked after by another party, two of which were refused. Two other entries related to Richard Symonds, described as of 'weak intellect' in 1836 and seemingly needing much care, including lodging, washing and mending. The other three entries could conceivably be injured or elderly people who had died prior to 1836. The accounts show a similar pattern of clothing distribution in other years.[67]

In Castlemorton it seems that relief in the form of clothing was only granted to those who could not otherwise earn money, either through disability or old age, or children, who often seem to have pushed family budgets to breaking point. Historians who have studied economic life cycles note that hardship was worst for individual adults when their dependent children were young, and when they reached old age.[68] The usage of parish clothing provision in Castlemorton reflected this pattern. It may have been local practice simply to grant clothing to those who were unable to work. This system might have influenced the way in which claims were then put to the overseers. For example, applications may only have been made for particular family members. King has shown how women used the Poor Law as only one strand of a make-shift economy, alongside waged work. If women were able to find work, they were more likely to be deemed 'respectable' by the overseers. Thus they could obtain casual relief for their children, the attempt at self sufficiency making them 'morally deserving'.[69]

Overseers purchased most of the clothing and fabric from shops in Upton-upon-Severn, the nearest market town, four or five miles away. The drapers' shops used included Charles and Henry Nash, Henry Cowley and William Barnard. Local women, who perhaps would otherwise have had to rely on relief, were paid to make up shirts, shifts and smocks. The Old Poor Law often created female labour where there had previously been none. The employment of women in this way also became more important with the decline of women in the agricultural labour force.[70] Elizabeth Beale, for example, was paid 5*s.* 9½*d.* for 'making and mending' clothes in February 1825. Later in October the same year, she applied to the overseers for clothing for 'Nuttings child', who was seemingly in her care.[71] Beale continued to receive irregular payments for making up smocks and shirts. This cheap, out-work, organized and subsidized by poor law officials, was found in many other parishes across England, creating employment whilst providing a cheap service for the parish.[72] Other men's clothes which were more complicated to make, such as breeches or jackets, were supplied by local tailors, although presumably not made to measure.

The second rural village is Abbey Dore in south-west Herefordshire, located in a pastoral hilly landscape close to the border with Wales, the population totalling 533 in 1831. The status of those seeking clothing through relief in Abbey Dore is difficult to ascertain, although some were described as 'old' or 'blind'.[73] Claims for clothing were more frequent than in any other parish so far examined. The majority of successful claims were for children, but male clothing in particular, was granted more often than in Castlemorton. In the first decade of the nineteenth century there were around thirty-five payments for clothing per year. In 1808 there were eight for shirts, four for clothing for known elderly people, four for other men's clothes and the same for women, seven for children, five for apprenticeship or service clothes, and two for shifts.[74] On average, about 8 per cent of the population received clothing from the parish. If recipients were part of a larger household, this clothing would have also helped family budgets. Including the clothing for service or apprenticeship, about a third of the clothing was for children. The adult men and women who received clothing may also have had a disability or illness, which is not readily apparent through existing records.

Abbey Dore appears to have been a more benevolent parish than Castlemorton in terms of the number of claims it allowed, the type of clothing purchased and particularly the amount it was willing to spend on clothing children leaving the parish for service. This generous allowance could set them up for life, as well as creating a good impression of parish welfare to outsiders. In times of need, clothes could be sold into the second-hand market. Servants commonly did this, perhaps preventing the necessity of claiming relief as out-parishioners.[75] April was a common time to clothe parish apprentices. This may have been given additional resonance with the tradition of everyone having new clothing to wear on Easter Sunday.[76] For example, in April 1804, five employers of parish apprentices were granted £1 5s. for their clothing, which appears to have been a standard sum.[77] Clothing for apprentices was an important part of the indenture agreement. From the overseers' view, if a suitable position could be found away from their pauper origins, the potential apprentice would have a better chance in life and would be less likely to need relief in later years.[78]

There were other cases of parents applying for their children. Sarah Preece was allowed £2 2s. for her daughter to go to Bristol, John Loyd was allowed £1 11s. 6d. for his daughter to go to London, whereas James Pritchard was only allowed 7 shillings to buy a shirt and smock frock for his son to go into service, presumably as a local farm servant.[79] William Jones gave up his weekly pay of a shilling for a period to obtain 12 shillings for his daughter to go into service.[80] If families were able to place a child in service, even if they needed the help of parish provision to do this, they might enjoy sartorial benefits in the future, such as cast-off clothing. However, servant apprentices or 'parish girls' as they became after the apprenticeship system was abolished in 1814, were some of the most exploited employees in service.[81]

As in Castlemorton, women were employed locally as seamstresses to make up clothing for females in their parish or their own children's clothes. For example, in 1807, 3s. 6d. was paid for linsey for Mary George's petticoat, with Sarah Watkins paid 8d. for making it up.[82] Female clothing was not necessarily made of the cheapest material available. Stuff, that is woollen cloth, was bought to make a gown for 'Mary Woodings child' also in 1807, plus linsey for a petticoat and check linsey for an apron. Lining was also bought for the gown, perhaps seen as necessary with the woollen fabric, costing a total of 8 shillings.[83] Women rarely seem to have made men's clothes apart from loose fitting shirts and smocks. Other male clothing such as breeches, waistcoats and jackets appears to have been purchased from tailors, principally Abraham Jones and 'Mr Dean'. Mr Dean may be James Dean of Hereford, who was also a salesman.[84] There were no tailors noted in the village in the 1841 census, suggesting that male clothing was bought outside the parish.[85]

The frequency of applications to the parish for clothing suggests that this was an important strategy for those in a more isolated area than Castlemorton, particularly with regard to clothing children and setting them up in work. Women often applied for clothing, but usually on behalf of their children, not for themselves. The impression is that women who applied individually tended to be old or infirm, while men applying individually needed clothing to be able to continue working. In the 1841 census, for example, John Brace was described as an agricultural labourer, then aged sixty-eight, with two small children under the age of ten. He claimed successively from the parish for clothing, apparently to allow him to work. In 1816, 1822, 1824, 1826 and 1831 he obtained smock frocks, while in 1813 he was given material, a jacket and leather breeches. He also claimed clothing for his children at least twelve times over the same period. The clothing the family received equates to an item annually, almost every year between 1813 and 1831.[86]

The villages of Castlemorton and Abbey Dore show the varying approaches that could be taken by a rural parish in distributing clothing. Abbey Dore, in a mainly pastoral hilly landscape, was the more geographically isolated and therefore perhaps a more close-knit community. This is reflected in the local knowledge apparent in the parish accounts, where nicknames were used to refer to parishioners. The overseers of Abbey Dore dispensed more clothing than Castlemorton and the parish was a significant source of clothing for its inhabitants. In both parishes, clothing was given to people with social problems, such as widows, those with poor health or the elderly. Parishioners who applied for clothing, either for themselves or on behalf of someone else, probably knew what was most likely to be granted. This need was stressed in the hope that if successful, the clothing provided would help the family budget. By clothing the children of working families, the relief system contributed to the welfare of the community generally. There was not a continuous strategy of providing clothing for working adults via poor relief.

However, in Abbey Dore there appears to have been more emphasis on keeping the whole population working. Women claimants were also often employed by the parish, for example, in making up clothes, spinning hurden and acting as carers, but not receiving direct parish relief.[87] Men were given clothes to enable them to work. The desire to be independent and to work was thus linked to the entitlement to receive some relief, particularly clothing, which was necessary to undertake this work. The ability to remain working and as independent as possible would hopefully allay the threat of higher relief costs in the future for these claimants.[88] This emphasis on clothing for work was more limited in Castlemorton, particularly with regard to male employment. Possibly, the availability of common land around Castlemorton and the extra income this could bring in meant that adults were seen by the overseers as needing less help to generate a living. In contrast to Abbey Dore, Castlemorton was also not geographically remote, perhaps meaning that opportunities to work elsewhere were more widespread. In Castlemorton, those who were able to work, particularly men, were expected to be self-sufficient and not depend on the parish to help them. Specific local employment patterns and how these were seen to affect communities, to some extent, determined how universally clothing relief was distributed across all age groups and to both genders.

Industrial Towns: Droitwich and Kidderminster

The town of Droitwich to the north of Worcester offers a useful comparison to smaller rural communities. The town was around four times the size of Abbey Dore,[89] and although divided into three parishes, the overseers would have to deal with more claimants. Although promoted as a spa town in the trade directories, the salt works were a major industry and offered a harsh life for workers.[90] The parish of St Peter's in Droitwich has surviving overseers' accounts, as well as a series of bills from tradesmen presented to the overseers, which list garments in more detail. The overseers do not seem to have been overly generous. For example, there were more references to mending items of clothing than in the rural parishes previously discussed, although of course this may have been carried out there on an informal basis. For instance, on 16 December 1800, 'Paid for footing Mary Gay's stockings & yarne &c., 1s 7d',[91] or on 24 February 1808, for John Partridge's son, 'pair of leather breeches seated and mended, 1s 6d'.[92] Secondhand clothing was also noted once in 1800 for Thomas Smith, who was given 3s. for an 'old coate'.[93] The condition that some claimants lived in was hinted at, with mentions of clothes being cleaned of lice.[94]

In common with the rural villages, the names of the same applicants and recipients of relief come up frequently, some noted as old or widows. Likewise, some women who also received relief from the parish were paid to make up items of female clothing or shirts and smocks. In comparison to Abbey Dore, taking into account that it was a smaller community, there do not seem to have been many claims for clothing in Droitwich. Apart from 1800 to 1801, when there were significantly more claims, as there were in Abbey Dore, possibly reflecting the general economic climate with the very poor harvests of 1799 and 1800, there were fewer than ten claims a year for the remainder of the decade.[95] However, the surviving bills from local tradesmen, which were presented to the overseers with totals noted in the accounts, show that clothing or material was provided which would not otherwise be visible in the non-itemized overseers' accounts. Thus, the amount of clothing given out by St Peter's, Droitwich, was greater than first assumed.

In Abbey Dore, it was not usual to present tradesmen's accounts to the overseers whereas in Droitwich it seems to have been much more common for the parish authorities to procure clothing via local tradesmen. This is demonstrated by examining St Peter's overseers' accounts for 1816 and 1817, and the clothing references extracted from these two years. These two years were chosen for analysis as three of the bills noted in the accounts have been found. In 1816, there are seven clothing references in the accounts, including the purchase of two pairs of breeches and a smock frock, along with two tradesmen's bills. In 1817, there were six references, including the purchase of stockings, payment to retrieve clothes in pawn and three tradesmen's bills.[96] However, the surviving bill from the draper Horsley from June 1816, details the sale of a frock, jacket, waistcoat, hat, shirts, shifts, yards of linsey, flannel and blue print plus tape and binding to make them up, for a further nine named recipients. His bill from January 1817 has entries for another four recipients and includes a flannel jacket and blue grogram, a textile often used for Poor Law gowns.[97]

The clothing that was distributed directly to the recipient from a parish stock of clothing, the clothing the overseers bought, or when recipients were directed to go and purchase a garment themselves, was shown in the overseers' accounts. However, tradesmen's bills show that sometimes the parish used drapers or tailors to independently distribute clothing to recipients. Between 1816 and 1817, in Abbey Dore, no tradesmen's bills for clothing were presented. Instead there were thirty-three individual claims for clothing in 1816 and fifty-seven in 1817,[98] which were seemingly bought by the claimant as directed by overseers, or perhaps given from a parish stock of clothing. Therefore, where few original bills from tradesmen survive, but they were noted as having been received, clothing distribution through the Poor Law may, in fact, have been more extensive. How these garments were then actually given out is not clear. Perhaps it was up to the recipient to go into the shop to collect them, or maybe they were given out centrally, for example at a vestry meeting, after the initial application had been made.

The Droitwich bills demonstrate that men's clothes were likely to be ready-made and women's were often made up from fabric purchased. Evidence from the accounts also suggests that fabric could be acquired by paupers through other methods, for example from a cheap drapers shop or through charity, and be made up at parish expense. This would account for the extra making up expenses in the overseers' records, which do not link to parish-purchased fabric.

The quantity of bills surviving for this parish allows the frequent successful clothing claims of three individuals to be reconstructed between 1800 and the 1830s.[99] The contrast in the type of clothing claimed by Thomas Poney (between 1816–23) and John Partridge (between 1810–19) highlights the different provisioning methods used by individuals. Thomas Poney appears to have been a young man, possibly illegitimate or orphaned, whose care was provided by the parish. By 1823, Poney's basic working wardrobe of smock frock, breeches and shirt was being renewed at least every other year, with two jackets provided within the period too. This clothing provision does not contain references to the repair of clothing, which may also have been paid for by the parish.

John Partridge had a family, a wife, a father and children including at least one son, who all claimed clothing from the parish. John Partridge had less clothing bought ready-made, although he still had five shirts four smocks, two pairs of breeches, a jacket and waistcoat, but more material bought for unspecified purposes. This was enough to make up the difference in quantity and presumably could be made up independently of the parish, perhaps by his wife. This would alleviate some expense for the parish which was not feasible with Poney. By 1841, there were nine families with the surname Partridge, most of whom were engaged in making baskets to collect salt extracted in Droitwich.[100] Unfortunately it is not possible to establish a definite correlation between these families and those with the Partridge surname who claimed clothing from the parish from 1800 to 1823. However, it seems likely that they were engaged in a similar employment, although clearly this did not provide for all their needs.

Mary Gay also seems to have relied heavily on the parish (between 1800–35) for most of her life.[101] At the beginning of the period, clothing was made up for her but this gradually stopped. Presumably as she became older, she could make up some garments herself, saving the parish money. Although this evidence cannot be conclusive, as there may be bills and detailed entries in the records missing, Poney obtained an average of around four items of clothing via parish relief every year for the period where records survive and Partridge obtained three. Mary Gay had around two and a half items per year. Perhaps women were seen as better at repairing and maintaining clothing, so there was an assumption that they needed less. Gay had substantially more material given fifty-eight entries – in comparison to five for Poney and eleven for Partridge, which she could put to a variety of uses. Possibly Gay was just not as effective as Poney and Partridge at appealing to the parish for relief. However, she still managed to obtain around ninety items of new clothing or cloth from the parish across thirty-five years.

The volume of clothes given, especially in some years, demonstrates that those relying on relief could have a substantial wardrobe. The quality of clothing is difficult to gauge, although obviously not particularly expensive when related to the total sums of parish relief expenditure.[102] However, particularly in Droitwich, the overseers gave out new clothing of a certain standard, as some was durable enough to be deemed worthy of the expense of repair. The items that Mary Gay obtained also suggest that different types of fabric and patterns were ordered, including stripes, prints and two different types of 'cloth' specified on one bill in 1819 but not detailed.[103] A bill from 1807, from drapers Heming and Taylor, is one of the few to provide some detail. It included items such as white calico, grey calico, brown linsey, claret linsey and striped linsey.[104]

A small series of churchwardens' accounts also survive from St Mary's parish, Kidderminster, from 1833 to 1836. These highlight the more pronounced poverty of some industrial areas. The carpet weavers' strike of 1828 had a profound effect on the Kidderminster economy for the next decade. In contrast to other industrial districts the population actually declined by 4 per cent during the 1830s. Living conditions were harsh and commentators noted the decline in the 'moral' state of the weavers as they struggled to survive and thus presumably maintain a decent appearance.[105] These economic conditions are reflected in the parish accounts from this period.

As with other areas, bills were presented by local tradesmen and noted in the overseers' accounts. The bills themselves have not survived, and so there are no details about the garments that were bought. However, some of those tradesmen who presented bills were noted in the accounts as providing second-hand clothes. For example, clothes dealer David Jones provided second-hand garments to the value of £1 19s. on 27 September 1834 and likewise Isaac Chadwick, second-hand clothes and trousers to the value of £2 10s. on 7 November the same year.[106] Other clothing brokers and salesmen were similarly parish suppliers of clothing. Presumably, the state of the Kidderminster economy was such that it was acceptable for officials to clothe parish paupers in second-hand clothing. The emphasis on second-hand items has not been found in other areas of the two counties although records for most industrial areas do not survive. Some new cloth and items such as stockings were given out in Kidderminster, but civic pride in pauper clothing seemed to have been set at a lower standard than in other locations. This appears to have been in direct opposition to the respectable impression the town gave to visitors during the 1830s.[107]

The very differing approaches of parishes in Droitwich and Kidderminster show that clothing paupers in industrial areas had no overall pattern. Solutions to the want of clothing seem to have been dictated, at least in part, by local economic circumstances. Overseers were also dependent on what resources were available in the vicinity and what was most cost-effective and acceptable. The general standard of clothing given out by the parish appeared lower in industrial areas than in rural villages, with second-hand clothing and regular repairs part of the provision. However, smaller rural community networks may have provided such services more informally, not recording them in official account books. Across all areas, there needed to be a good reason for a pauper to be able to obtain clothing from parish under the Old Poor Law. Nevertheless, once a pauper was accepted as deserving, as with the case of Mary Gay, it was possible to expect clothing to be renewed regularly and perhaps to build up a wardrobe of garments.

Clothing Provision in Workhouses

By the mid-1830s, the overseers' accounts ceased as the union workhouse system came into force under the New Poor Law, and clothing was increasingly only provided through the workhouse. Workhouse clothing has been described as a uniform, 'a distinctive dress' of 'printed dresses' and 'corduroy suits'.[108] However, this description could also apply to working-class clothing in general. The following section will investigate how much difference there was between workhouse clothing and independently purchased clothing, as well as the clothing previously given out under the Old Poor Law. Was there a distinction between clothing worn inside and outside the workhouse?

Tenders for workhouse clothing were advertised in the Worcester and Hereford newspapers. In the first few years of the New Poor Law, such advertisements show that there were variations between what different workhouses asked for. This suggests not a 'uniform' but usage of low-status clothing sourced from drapers who were also selling to the general public.[109] The advertisements for workhouse tenders show that the way clothing was provisioned under the Old Poor Law continued. Men's clothing was expected to be ready-made and therefore in different sizes, probably 'adult', 'youth' and 'boy', whilst fabric was supplied for women, presumably to be made up within the workhouse. Droitwich Union's advertisement, asking for applicants to tender for a quarter of a year in 1837, was typical:

> men's strong dark blue coloured cloth coats, waistcoats, and corduroy breeches, men's strong fustian jackets, waistcoats and trowsers, boys and youths ditto, Boys fustian skeleton dresses, worsted hose for men, women and children, bonnets for women and girls, blue chambray per yard, strong linen ditto, hurden ditto, woollen linsey ditto, women and girls stays per pair, strong Welsh flannel per yard, [as also for] check muslin, linen check and strong brown calico, neckerchiefs, strong shoes for men, women and children, per pair.[110]

In 1840, the Droitwich Union also required 'Men's and Boy's stout drabbed frocks' as well as plaid gingham and blue mixed chambray per yard.[111] Smock frocks (frocks), were required in several, but not all workhouses. Bromsgrove Union specified 'strong hurden short slop frocks',[112] whilst Bromyard wanted smock frocks and flannel waistcoats, with and without sleeves.[113] There was also variation in the colour of men's coats, either blue as in Droitwich or grey in the Martley Union.[114] 'Strong red and white striped linsey' was specified in Worcester, maybe similar to the striped linsey detailed in the Old Poor Law bills in Droitwich, along with 'strong brown and white calico'.[115] Variations depended on local guardians' preferences, encompassing both what they thought paupers should be wearing, and what could be supplied easily and at a good price. The items bought by various workhouses may have differed but presumably as the guardians of each were ordering a quantity of the same garments, this clothing would become recognized locally as workhouse clothing and thus a workhouse uniform.

The main difference between clothing obtained at the workhouse and clothing obtained from outdoor relief was that it was up to the discretion of the guardians to decide if clothing could be taken when leaving the workhouse. Clothing was workhouse property and there was a constant worry that people were entering workhouses just to get new clothing. This situation had previously occurred in the Houses of Industry under the Old Poor Law. For example, by the early nineteenth century in Ombersley, clothing was not allowed out of the House of Industry unless the person was going to the Infirmary. This was because any clothing which had previously been allowed out of the House of Industry was usually immediately pawned for money.[116] A case in Ledbury in 1845, which made the national press, highlighted the conflict in the ownership of workhouse property. The Ledbury Guardians gave the master and matron discretionary powers to clothe a baby following its birth at the workhouse. This policy was questioned by the Poor Law Commissioners, who commented that some women were going into workhouses just to get a supply of clothing for their babies.[117] Thus, workhouse clothing did not automatically become clothing that could be used when leaving the workhouse. It might have to be left behind and as such would only be of short-term use. This was in contrast to garments given out under the Old Poor Law. The need for rulings about the ownership of clothing in the controlled environment of the workhouse would suggest that clothing given out as part of parish relief had in the past been sold or pawned rather than worn by the intended recipient. The actual garments given out in workhouses were not a uniform standard. However, the way that they were used and depersonalized, not becoming part of a person's permanent possessions, suggests that they were used as a uniform might be.

Conclusion

The reasons for seeking relief were complex. These varied from the sheer desperation of extreme poverty through to an expectation about the type of claim that was likely to have been accepted by the overseers within a parish. Clothing distributed to paupers may have been basic, but seems to have been similar to other independently provisioned clothing, using the same materials such as printed cottons, corduroy and fustian. King's contention, that there was little to distinguish parish clothing from that of the wider population, seems broadly correct for Herefordshire and Worcestershire.[118] Those on relief and ordinary working-class consumers were often obtaining clothing from the same shops, although using different acquisition methods. However, some evidence survives that suggests that overseers had a clear idea of what was suitable for parish clothing. In a note on the back of a Hereford draper's bill of 1825, the overseer of the village of Stoke Edith states:

> ... the hurden is to [*sic*] much that half the Quantity will do and the Gingham is sufficient to make one for herself, if you can put the right Quantity without it being ill convenient to your self shall be obliged as the parish will think it extravagant.[119]

It was not the quality, but the quantity of the fabric that was being queried here, with the recognition that it was important to spend prudently when purchasing pauper clothing. Indeed, as King speculates, after 1815, as clothing became cheaper, it perhaps became less acceptable for officials to scrimp on clothing and the benchmark of what was expected from pauper clothing may have risen.[120]

Clothing relief within the two counties was not the means by which the majority of the working-class population acquired their clothing. It was generally granted only to specific types of already disadvantaged people. Those who applied usually had particular reasons that would appeal to the compassion of the overseers. However, the Droitwich evidence of successive clothing claims for individuals like Thomas Poney and Mary Gay does show that some paupers, having been accepted as 'deserving', could acquire a reasonable amount of clothing from the parish. The way that clothing was acquired, whether bought by an overseer, ordered from a shop or bought by a pauper with money as directed, would also influence to a certain degree the type of clothing received. This was especially the case with women's clothing, where the second part of the process would often involve independent making up, whether within the family or by a local seamstress.

For those who were perceived as genuinely deserving, the elderly, disabled or sick, obtaining parish clothing was regarded almost as a right, especially in isolated rural parishes where there were few other outlets for obtaining clothing. Clothing relief was also deemed necessary for some small children who were too young to work, their day-to-day maintenance stretching family budgets to the limit. Healthy men and women of working age did not generally apply for parish clothing, unless in extreme circumstances of destitution. Without clothing, paupers were cut off from the world of work and unable to be independent in any way, so clothing relief in these circumstances was seen as a necessary expediency.[121] The Old Poor Law was more generally used in other ways by working adults, for example, by giving women work in making up pauper clothing. This parish employment gradually diminished, as under the New Poor Law paupers were moved away from their home parishes. Mainly due to the tendering and acquisition process with numbers of the same garments bought from the same retailer for each workhouse, a local uniform of dress for the poor then developed in Herefordshire and Worcestershire. However, the garments purchased would have little to distinguish them from those acquired by the general working-class population from the same shops.

5 CLOTHING THE POOR: CHARITY

The 1830s saw a profound change in welfare structures, with the introduction of the New Poor Law and the assessment of existing charity provision by the Charity Commissioners. A new network of charitable elites emerged, who in effect took over from the Poor Law administrators as arbiters of respectability of the poor and of their need within a local community.[1] Regulated charity was an important part of the Victorian welfare system, with the middle and upper classes benevolently helping those not so fortunate, but only those who were perceived to be deserving. The idea of self-help was also increasingly fundamental to charitable provision, whether in monetary contributions to a club or by receiving instruction in sewing, for future self-reliance. Such self-help initiatives sought to discourage dependence on welfare provision but were counter to the way that some poor had regarded their right to parish relief.[2]

The evidence for charity in rural and urban areas largely comes from information gathered during the Charity Commissioners' surveys of the 1830s. The charities investigated by the Commissioners were the formal charities supported by a bequest. Evidence for informal charity remains extremely sparse. The fact that so many clothing charities and societies were established around 1819 and 1820[3] suggests that the depression and economic downturn after the end of the Napoleonic Wars had a profound effect on the lower classes, particularly in urban areas; or at least, that the poverty had become so pronounced by this date that the elite could no longer ignore it. For example, it was affecting attendance at institutions where they too were present, such as the church. On a visit to Bridport in Worcester, in around 1819, the Methodist Susannah Knapp observed, 'two poor women were so badly clothed, that they could scarcely think of coming [to pray], therefore, there appears a necessity for getting a little fund to assist such persons as are in extreme destitution'.[4] As Alannah Tomkins has pointed out, charity has been overlooked by historians studying the economy of makeshifts, being probably at least as significant as poor relief in helping to make ends meet. It was far more wide ranging, reaching a bigger social group of people, but much as poor relief was defined by its specific locality and needs, so too was charity.[5]

This chapter will therefore firstly analyse and compare the different types of charity bequests that existed in rural and urban localities in Herefordshire and Worcestershire. By examining the number of items that were distributed to the local population, it will shed light on the usefulness of formal charities as a method of obtaining clothing for the working-class population at various stages of their life cycle. The chapter will also investigate the clothing children were given when attending charity schools and will consider a specific Herefordshire charity, the Jarvis Charity. Whether there was a role that the people had to play to obtain such clothing will be questioned and the relationship between charity and local parish relief will be examined. The chapter will then move on to investigate the development of the ethos of self-help and how this was manifested in the expansion of clothing clubs.

Rural Charity

People living in rural areas in Herefordshire and Worcestershire did not have access to a wide range of charitable clothing. Bequests often specified similar clothing, usually coats and gowns, with seventeenth- and eighteenth-century bequests frequently needing updating. For example, the seventeenth century costume specified for old soldiers receiving alms at the Coningsby Hospital, Hereford, had disappeared by the 1830s, replaced by contemporary outfits.[6] Pugh's Charity, centred on the Chapelry of Preston Wynne, Withington, Herefordshire, provided men with 'a good and warm great coat made of stout coarse cloth ... for women, with a gown made of dark brown stuff'. If the recipients sold or disposed of any article, they would 'never again ... be entitled to receive the same'.[7] 'Stout', 'strong', 'warm' and 'decent' clothing were common descriptions in bequests for clothing for the 'respectable' poor. There had been a long-term understanding dating back to the Medieval period that the gift of clothing needed to be appropriate in quality, colour and the type of the garment, in the eyes of the benefactor. Particular types of garments were considered correct for certain groups, often linked to a stage in the lifecycle, for example, warm wool coats for the elderly.[8] However, the provision of clothing made of 'stuff' or 'cloth', although durable and warm, was not always the most practical. The woollen fabric was difficult to wash, dry and keep clean, particularly in comparison to cotton. Thus in Kentchurch, Miss Sarah Scudamore's Charity was slightly more up to date, stipulating the purchase of material to make up fourteen printed calico gowns every Christmas. The gowns were to be made up by people in the village who would receive a shilling for this, echoing the paternalistic creation of employment under the Old Poor Law.[9]

Such charitable bequests were also rigid in their choice of suitable recipients. There were stipulations about who could receive such clothing, for example, the 'poor, aged and laborious ... such as did not receive parish pay and maintained themselves without filching and stealing from their neighbours, and were frequenters of the church'.[10] In addition, lists of 'deserving' parishioners were drawn up by trustees or relations of the benefactors. Names on lists were commonly changed every year, with a two- or three-year gap between people receiving the same item again being most usual. Undoubtedly, if a person lived in a village where there was a bequest and was able to fit the criteria, official charity could be an important means for survival. The poorest person in the village of Edvin Ralph, for instance, was annually given 10 shillings for a coat by the Phineaus Jackson Charity.[11]

The Commissioners, with some reservations, saw clothing as an acceptable bequest that would help the poor. For example, Joan Lingen's Charity in Marden was criticized by the Commissioners, as no accounts were kept and small sums of money were distributed in the summer to over a hundred families. With the spectre of pauper fecklessness rising, the Commissioners suggested that these monetary payments stop and in the future, fuel or clothing be given instead.[12]

The majority of charities which gave out clothing listed in the Commissioners' survey detailed the number of garments supplied. In Herefordshire, excluding the city of Hereford and any relating specifically to children, around 350 people could receive an item per year, not always complete outfits. Of course this is not the total number of clothing gifts, but compared to the overall population outside Hereford (around 100,000), and the number of individuals who sought parish relief even in small villages, this seems a very small number. Therefore, despite the Commissioners promoting clothing as a suitable bequest, overall, it was a peripheral method of acquiring clothing for the general populace.

The same is true for Worcestershire, where the same count brings a figure of 646 individual garments distributed yearly. Again, some charities did not specify the number of people given to, and the above number is mainly comprised of the 500 people who received 'something' from Lilley's Charity in Bromsgrove. This charity distributed linen via a ticket system. The linen was to be used for making shirts or shifts.[13] One charity not included in the Commissioners' survey was Mr Brecknell's charity in Belbroughton, probably as it had only recently been established. This charity also distributed 'cloth' annually on 20 December at the school house. The cloth was given in 3, 4½ and 7½ yard lengths, the most common being the 4½ yard length. Three yards was enough to make a man's shirt,[14] seven yards a gown.[15] Between 1834–6, between a third and a half of all Mr Brecknell's charitable distributions were in cloth, although this declined into the 1840s, stopping entirely in 1846.[16] The status of those who received gifts was not recorded, but given the volume of cloth distributed, this charity seems to have offered an alternative to parish relief. Perhaps it is significant that the surviving accounts date from the period when the New Poor Law was being introduced.

Casual relief in kind, which under the Old Poor Law would include clothing, was being phased out, replaced by concentration on workhouse provision. Those who needed extra clothing to maintain a living outside the workhouse may now have turned to local charity instead, before this provision too was discontinued in the 1840s.

Urban Charity

Urban charities operated in a similar way to rural charities. Charitable bequests had specific qualifying terms and were often linked to organizations such as schools and almshouses. The following section will investigate such urban charity, before moving on to examine how charity clothing was supplied.

There seems to have been even less formal charity available to the urban lower classes in comparison to rural areas. Longstanding bequests were perhaps not able to keep up with the recent population growth in cities such as Worcester, Hereford and industrial areas, for example Dudley. Peter Jones's gift, for instance, was distributed in the parish of All Saints, Hereford, annually to five poor men or women who were resident in Weavers' Hospital. This amounted to a woollen gown of the value of 10 shillings given out on St Peter's day. The Commissioners remarked that:

> The five women are supplied with an order by the churchwardens for 10 shillings worth of wearing apparel, which order they take to Mr Gibbs, a draper, and select such clothes as they happen to want. It was formerly customary to give them a woollen gown each, but it has been thought a greater charity to leave the matter to their own choice.[17]

The charity gave the recipients a certain amount of choice in selecting the clothing. However, the women who received the gift had already been chosen as 'deserving poor' by being members of the almshouse. They were also restricted to obtaining clothing from one draper, albeit one of the largest drapers in Hereford. Out of a total population of over 10,000 people, helping five did not amount to much. Charitable bequests which gave out clothing in Hereford were either connected to almshouses or hospitals, or provided for children.

Bishop Hall's Charity had funds for clothing the poor in Kidderminster and Bromsgrove, as long as they did not receive alms or weekly parish relief. Around £5 a year was allowed for clothing by the trustees of Bishop Hall's Charity, with a limit of 10 shillings a person.[18] Compared to the sums associated with Jarvis Charity,[19] this represented a very small amount, providing for only around twenty people annually. In 1812, the charity gave out sixteen pieces of cloth for coats and 'eleven stuff pieces for gounds [*sic*]', which were purchased by John Richardson of Hayford, near Worcester, probably at Worcester and then sent onto Bromsgrove for distribution at Christmas.[20] The control of the purchase was again in official hands, the clothing presumably being made up locally for a cheaper price than by a city tailor or draper. Apart from Lilley's Charity previously mentioned, other charities which gave out clothing in Kidderminster and Bromsgrove were connected to schools.

Individuals who were part of the church establishment became increasingly concerned about the appearance of the poor who lived in the urban slums over the course of the first half of the nineteenth century. For example, in Dudley, the Cartwright Charity was established in 1819. Fifteen pounds was left in trust by a local vicar to clothe six poor men of the parish on the first day of November. These men were nominated by Mr Cartwright's widow and the trustees, the great majority of the recipients being aged seventy and above.[21] The contract to supply the clothing was put out to tender, with Mr Benson, a local draper, winning the first contract in 1822. He supplied a coat, waistcoat, breeches, shirt, stockings and hat for each man at a cost of £2 4s., the badge of the charity being fixed to a conspicuous part of each coat.[22] After the men were given the clothes they had to appear before the board of trustees for their approval, and then go to church dressed in the clothes. In 1822, the trustees noted that the clothing was 'entirely to our satisfaction and we highly approve of the cleanliness and general appearance of the poor men'.[23] The poor were made to look decent to enable them to go to church. The deserving aged that had fallen on hard times were seen as most worthy of Cartwright's charity, although age was not specified in the bequest. The individuals who organized this charity no doubt had compassion at the heart of their gift. However, a Christian way of life was fundamental and influenced who finally received the charity.

Local retailers also supplied clothing for charitable bequests in the parish of St Andrew's, Worcester. From the late eighteenth century through to the second quarter of the nineteenth century, the charities' trustees relied on two retailers to supply the clothing for the three clothing bequests that they had to distribute: Ann Hall's gift, Alderman Sherwin's gift and Robert Veller's gift. William and later Martha Knight held the contract from 1794 until 1810, and then William Spriggs supplied the clothing from 1817 into the 1820s.[24] Spriggs took over Martha Knight's business, calling himself 'W. Spriggs (Late Knight's)'.[25] Martha Knight was described as a mercer[26] while Spriggs had a clothing warehouse catering for the lower end of the market.[27] In 1820 Spriggs supplied clothing for six poor widows at 30 shillings each; three gowns at 9s. 6d. each; another ten gowns at the same price; sixty-six women's linen shifts at 4s. 3d. each; and twenty-three men's cloth coats at 16 shillings each; the total being £47 13s. 1d.[28] The prices charged suggest it was of a reasonable quality, as it was probably not the cheapest available. For example, James Walter, a Worcester clothes dealer and pawnbroker, charged 3 shillings for gowns and 1s. 6d. for shifts in 1833.[29] Overseers tended not to supply coats, favouring practical working garments such as smock frocks and jackets,[30] so it is difficult to judge their price in comparison to Poor Law provision. The supply of a quantity of items, such as the sixty-six linen shifts at the same time, would have meant the organization of some sort of manufacturing process. It is not clear whether this was arranged by the retailer to be made up locally or bought in ready-made from a larger wholesaler outside the city. For a retailer, it was a worthwhile contract to be awarded. Perhaps Spriggs used Knight's contracts for ready-made charity clothing as the basis for developing his own clothing warehouse, making such clothing available to all working-class consumers.

Charity officials and overseers were recognized as valuable customers by some city tradesmen. Sidney and Dickinson, situated on Worcester High Street, advertised goods suitable for charities in 1835.[31] Scotland House, a drapers' shop owned by James Pitt in Hereford, also advertised that he had a special section for the 'poor and charities', which included cloth cloaks, check, gingham, chambray, Russia Duck and black worsted stockings.[32] It is impossible to tell the quality of goods that were being advertised. However, items such as check, gingham and Russia Duck, were used in working-class clothing in general. The volume of goods actually needed by charity officials was not great in comparison to that required by some overseers or to general sales. Retailers such as Sidney and Dickinson and James Pitt were located on the main streets of the cities. They did not otherwise advertise, certainly in the newspapers, that they could provide low-status clothing. Perhaps this was a way to indirectly advertise such stock more widely to the general population.

The Jarvis Charity

One of the few clothing charities to come under censure from the Charity Commissioners was the Jarvis Charity, established in Herefordshire at the turn of the nineteenth century. The charity's trustees were criticized for laxity in the distribution of their charitable clothing. It was an exceptional charity in the breadth of its clothing provision and as such it was atypical of contemporary charities. However, it shows what resources were required to run a charity that actually seemed to make a difference to working people, and alleviated any reliance on parish clothing relief.

George Jarvis, a farmer's son, lived in Bredwardine, Herefordshire, during his childhood. He made his fortune in London over the course of the eighteenth century as a leather currier and through various business dealings.[33] Jarvis fell out with his only surviving daughter and grandchildren and left the majority of his fortune, £30,000 in Government securities, the interest to be paid out annually in money and provisions as the trustees saw fit, to the poor of the villages of Bredwardine, Staunton upon Wye and Letton.[34] Unsurprisingly, the will was contested by his daughter Mary, who argued that these sums of interest would amount to more than £500 annually, the poor rate for the villages amounting to less than £150 per year. Her plea was rejected, and the charity became active after 1800, when the court action was completed.[35]

When the charity began to dispense funds, Bredwardine had a population of 405, with 253 being identified as poor in need, presumably by the trustees. The annual interest it received from the fund was around £1,003. Staunton had a population of 545 with 281 being identified as needy. It received around £848 in interest annually. The smallest village, Letton, had a population of 230 with 44 needy poor, receiving £432 annually.[36] The sums available to spend on clothing, specified as part of the provision in Jarvis's will, were therefore quite substantial. In figures collated by the Charity Commissioners from the 1820s and 30s, in Bredwardine the highest annual spending on clothing was in 1831, £535 7s. 6d., the lowest in 1827, £421 6s. 9d. In Staunton, the highest was in 1823, £535 16s. 1d, the lowest in 1834, £311. In Letton, the highest was in 1832, £252 10s. 7d, the lowest in 1829, £202 6s.[37] These figures equate to the entire poor relief budget of other similar parishes.[38]

As with other charities, there were strict rules governing who could receive gifts. Recipients should not be receiving parish relief, nor have resided less than two years in the villages, no single woman with illegitimate children would be considered, and if there was any 'misconduct' a name could be removed from the list.[39] The charitable regime, at least for the first thirty years of its existence, unsurprisingly seems to have been popular with those able to receive the gifts. Reports by the Charity Commissioners suggested that recipients had been allowed a certain amount of leeway in their choice of clothing. Each eligible person could claim annually a complete set of clothes, for example a coat, waistcoat, breeches, two shirts, stock, shoes and hat. The cost exceeded the annual amount that the Commissioners suggested should be specified for clothing. They recommended an annual allowance of 50 shillings per claimant, effectively reining in clothing expenditure.[40] In the context of local wages and casual payments from parish relief, the amount spent on charity clothes still seems generous.[41] Claimants of successive parish clothing relief, such as Mary Gay and Thomas Poney in Droitwich, were generally given less than 20 shillings worth of items per year.[42]

As well as cutting back on the amount of clothing available, the Charity Commissioners also sought to limit the type of garments distributed, commenting on the improper methods pursued in the clothing department:

> The parties receiving clothes, after procuring an order from the clerk of the trustees, were allowed to select articles at their own discretion, without any restriction as to description or colour, by means of which all control over the disposal of the clothes was lost.[43]

The Commissioners tightened up procedures, and from 1836, the trustees began to advertise tenders to supply clothing in specific fabrics, in the manner of a workhouse tender. New rules for the Charity came into force from 1837, which included continuing to advertise by tender. Misconduct rules for those receiving charity were to be strictly enforced, and thenceforth clothing for men and women was to be of one uniform colour.[44]

No records survive that detail what clothing was offered and how it was distributed by the Charity in the first half of the nineteenth century. The tenders asked for a range of fabrics, the implication therefore being that the clothing was to be made up locally, possibly to some extent by the schools that had also been established as part of the bequest.[45] Tailors such as William Pritchard and Luke Edwards[46] may have supplied ready-made male clothing in the early nineteenth century, although from the mid-1830s onwards only material was required from tradesmen.

Changes to the Jarvis Charity suggest that the moral censure and discipline of the poor by their social superiors was to be achieved by making clothing functional and practical, and by removing anything associated with personal identity and pleasure. It was to amount to a uniform, with the deference and subordination that this implied.[47] As with all charity clothing, the Commissioners were ambivalent about its value. On the one hand: '... to the want of warm and decent clothing, many evils not only physical, but even moral, among the poor might be ascribed'.[48] It was a gift in kind and, unlike money, could not be spent directly on items disapproved of by the Commissioners, most notably alcohol. On the other hand, the Commissioners believed that those receiving charity clothes should look as if they were wearing charity clothes and not be able to choose clothing that they wanted, which would contribute to idleness and improvidence, the fruits of an 'ill-considered and unnatural bequest'.[49] By the 1830s, it was acceptable to give out charity clothing to the proven deserving, as long as it looked like a uniform, not too far removed from workhouse clothing. However, in the 1830s and 40s, workhouse clothing was derived from and was often very similar to ordinary working-class clothing. How much distinction there actually was between charity clothing, workhouse uniform and the clothing of the 'independent' poor is therefore debatable, certainly in the early years of the New Poor Law.[50]

Indeed, the clothing given out by the Jarvis charity seems to have been accepted by the local population, both before and after the Commission, as a valuable part of their clothing provision. This is demonstrated by the development of the local parishes and their welfare structures. The overseers' accounts survive for Staunton from spring 1820 to 1821. In just over 150 entries, there are only two for clothes, a total of 14 shillings spent for two girls.[51] Likewise, Letton's Churchwardens' accounts survive for the period 1769–1887. Between

1800 and 1850, there were only nine entries for clothing in the accounts, seven of which were for one family, the Murrells. For whatever reason, they appear to have been in the rare situation of not using the Jarvis Charity. The total spent on clothing for fifty years was £6 8s. 9d.[52] The overseers' accounts that survive for both parishes show that they provided little clothing in comparison to other rural parishes such as Abbey Dore.[53] It seems that the overseers had no need to provide clothing via the parish when those in want could apply to the Jarvis Charity. For at least the first thirty years of its existence, the Jarvis Charity seems to have represented the best way to procure free clothing for the working population in the local area, with much independence in the choice of garments.

The popularity of the Jarvis charity is emphasized by the growth of the hamlet of Crafta Webb in Bredwardine parish. By the mid-nineteenth century, it had expanded to some twenty households from seven in 1841, most inhabitants born in Herefordshire but not always locally. Villages within a ten-mile radius such as Eardisley, Wormley, Vowchurch and Peterchurch lost inhabitants to Crafta Webb, and a few people from Oxford and Shropshire. If settlement could be gained there, then charity gifts from the Jarvis Charity in some form might be forthcoming.[54] As Tomkins has remarked where charity was munificent, the poor went to some lengths to become eligible.[55] However, this type of continuous charity that could be relied upon, in contrast to customary giving by the elite which will be examined in the next section, was perhaps ultimately detrimental to other welfare structures in the local area. There was increasing unease voiced by commentators into the nineteenth century, that any fund with a reliable income would be subject to abuse, and the poor relying on it would become recalcitrant and idle.[56]

By 1842, such concerns about the Jarvis Charity had led to local disputes. The annual accounts of the Charity were published in the *Hereford Journal*. In the year 1841–2, expenditure on clothing had fallen by about a half from the lowest figures prior to the Charity Commission report in the late 1830s, in line with the Commissioner's guidance.[57] However, there were a series of letters published in the newspaper by 'C. W.' who described himself as the 'Officiating Clergyman of Staunton'. The Rev. Charles Webber accused the Charity of mismanagement and not being true to the founder's aims and rules of provision. He accused the charity of no longer supporting the indigenous poor who often ended up in the workhouse, while food and clothing were handed out to the illegitimate, those who were up dancing all night and Irish tramps. Webber complained about the high number of illegitimate children in the school and the fact that the charity supported a carpenter and his family with food, clothing and apprenticeships, while they had a good living, renting a house for £12 per year, employing a workman and keeping animals. In his eyes, deserving widows and labourers from the parish who had worked hard for thirty-five years were ignored in favour of out-parishioners from over forty different parishes. According to his count, by 1842 there were equal numbers of poor in-parishioners and out-parishioners. He claimed that the hovels in the village would not lead an outsider to expect that so much was spent on the poor in the village. Webber also asserted that the funds mainly went to those undeserving of them either as incomers or those who had exhibited indecent behaviour. He was therefore petitioning the Lord Chancellor with his complaints, which led ultimately to Jarvis's Charity Act of 1852.[58] Richard Pantall sees this as part of a concerted campaign during the 1840s by the local church, which in effect had lost control over the parish community and had no say in the administration of the Charity.[59] As overseers of the poor they had controlled who received items such as clothing. This control had now been lost and clothing was given by the Charity to those seen as undeserving, at least by one clergyman.

Charity Schools

Under the Old Poor Law, clothing was most commonly given to children and the elderly, and this seems equally true of charity. As noted, formal charitable bequests often gave out clothing to elderly people. Provision for children was focused through schools, offering education and supposedly moral improvement, as well as sartorial benefits. The first half of the nineteenth century saw a huge increase in the number of schools open to all social classes and many of these in Herefordshire and Worcestershire had specific bequests relating to clothing. A survey of the free schools of Worcestershire was carried out by George Griffith in the mid-nineteenth century and included details of their clothing provision.[60] He was critical of such schools giving places intended for poor children to 'the sons of opulent people [who were] absorbing the school funds belonging to the poor'.[61] Tomkins too, in her survey of Oxford charity schools, found that paupers were actually excluded from such schools, their places more likely to be taken by tradesmen's children.[62]

Much of the clothing given out in charity schools was uniform. For example, the Blue Coat Schools gave out blue clothing and a badge making their pupils immediately identifiable. Walter Scott's Charity donated uniform for the Blue Coat School in Ross on Wye, the boys supplied with blue coats with red collars, blue waistcoats, and leather breeches, lighter blue stockings, hats and black ribbon round the neck, with a white metal or tin badge inscribed 'Walter Scott's Charity'.[63] Jennifer Craik notes the contradiction inherent in this uniform. She states that although destitute charity school children were generally a problem that had to be removed from public gaze, the distinctive blue dress of Blue Coat schools also meant that their benefactors could see the results of their gift when pupils were allowed out in public. Such children were therefore very public objects of charity and visibly classed as such.[64] These schools gave clothing to a relatively large number of pupils. In 1835, the Blue Coat School at Ross provided clothing for thirty boys and thirty girls at a cost of £95 7s. 6d.[65] In 1832, Dudley Blue Coat School clothed 100 boys at a cost of £166 7s. 6d, out of a total of 114 pupils. They had to have been at school for two years with their parents not receiving relief to qualify. Children who received clothing had to pay fees at 2d. a week, less if they did not.[66] The clothes provided, with approximately 30 shillings allowed for clothing each pupil both in Dudley and in Ross, appear to have been of a decent standard and would have enabled several different garments to be acquired.[67] However, no other member of the family could obtain any parish relief. As has been shown in Chapter 4, obtaining children's clothing through parish relief was a strategy often employed to support general family economies. There was a consequently a choice between which system would best clothe the children, dependent on the number of other family members receiving regular parish relief.

The use of a charity school was a pragmatic decision based on individual family circumstances. The receipt of clothing was probably a major incentive for sending children to a school. There was also the possibility of a longer-term gain of apprenticeship opportunities for pupils, unavailable to those who did not attend. However, uniforms could also be seen as a disadvantage, conveying a mark of poverty, a stigma not a sign of status. Some families would therefore prefer to pay the few pennies for school when possible rather than submit to enrolment at a charity school which would have influence on the behaviour of parents and could impose restrictions on what they might do. This also left open the channel of applying for relief for clothing children, if necessary, claims which were generally looked upon favourably. In the end, charity schooling was likely to benefit most those who did not have to rely on parish relief and therefore did not have to choose between the two welfare channels: in other words, not the paupers the school founders had initially set out to help.[68]

The aristocracy also sometimes maintained their own schools. For example, Lady Lyttleton had established a School of Ancient Industry in Malvern by 1825, which was detailed in a local guide book. Children were taught:

> ... every kind of common needle-work; such as making and mending coarse garments, jackets, and linen, for the use of their parents and themselves. In this manner they may learn to produce their own garments of a cheap and substantial kind, suitable to their condition in life, as in former ages. In order to preserve to society, a useful hardy peasantry, it is intended to encourage field-work.[69]

This clothing may have been helpful to local families and the author, Southall, assured the reader 'that the parents and the friends of the children, greatly desired to purchase the articles made by them'.[70] The comments about the school by Southall, part of the Malvern elite, underlined its perceived function in maintaining social control. It also promoted the use of respectable and acceptable clothing for the 'peasantry' as deemed by their social superiors. The emphasis was on educating the next generation to be self-sufficient. How this idea was taken up by clothing societies and clubs will be examined in the next section.

Annual Gifts and Self-Help Clubs

Aside from the Jarvis Charity, clothing bequests were not particularly extensive. More generous clothing provision was made through seasonal gifts. This section will examine such customary provision and the number of garments given out in comparison to the figures for charitable bequests. It will then move on to investigate the development of the self-help ethos and how this was manifested in the nascent clothing societies. How useful such societies were for acquiring clothing, the type of garments obtained and how recipients were regarded by those running these organizations, will be ascertained.

Charitable gifts, both formal bequests and those of a customary nature, for example from employers to estate workers, were generally associated with particular times of the year. This was usually Christmas and New Year and not necessarily when the gifts were needed.[71] The custom of local aristocrats and landowners giving seasonal gifts was reported successively in *Berrow's Worcester Journal.* For example, in 1845, Lord Southwell gave money and bread to the villagers of Hindlip, and to each of the men and boys a smock frock.[72] In 1850, he gave garments to 300 poor people of Hindlip and the surrounding area, including some for Worcester. These garments included clothes for children and flannel petticoats for women.[73] His annual New Year gift appears to have been a substantial part of the clothing provision for the poor in the area around Hindlip. Lord Southwell also gave the poor of nearby Hallow and Broadheath winter clothing, including several flannel jackets.[74]

At Stoke Edith, Herefordshire, the local landowner, E. T. Foley, gave warm clothing to the poor of the parish, whilst in Wribbenhall, Worcestershire, Miss Skey of Warshill Wood, gave blankets, flannel and clothing to 140 poor women of the parish.[75] This type of customary gifting by the fortunate was not guaranteed charity in the nature of an annual bequest. However, when it was undertaken, it was more substantial and reached a greater proportion of the immediate population than the charity bequests generally did. It was not meant to alleviate poverty entirely, but to help out tenants and employees while ensuring, at least outwardly, deference was due to the donor by the recipients of such gifts.[76] The examples noted above date from after the introduction of the New Poor Law, which stopped the provision of clothing as outdoor relief. Customary charity may have assumed a greater significance from the 1830s onwards.

The growth of self-help movements from the second quarter of the century onwards led to the spread of organizations such as clothing societies, particularly in rural areas. These too were heavily dependent on local elite enthusiasm for charity work. For example, the Foley family, particularly Lady Foley, were instrumental in expanding rural clothing societies. Their estate included the parishes of Tarrington, Weston Beggard, Woolhope and Yarkhill near Hereford, where Lady Foley established clothing societies in 1833. Seventy articles were distributed at Tarrington, £40 worth at Woolhope where a Sunday School was established by the Foleys which also gave apparel to sixty boys and girls.[77] These new organizations complemented the customary donation of clothing. A newspaper report about one such organization summed up the ethos:

> We have ever been of opinion [*sic*] that nothing tends more to draw out the energies of the poor than that of affording them an opportunity of assisting to help themselves; we are therefore most favourable to those Clothing Societies where they contribute a portion in the purchase of those articles provided for them.[78]

Many of these societies appear to have been under the control of the Anglican clergy. A clothing fund was established in Aymestrey, Herefordshire, under the guidance of the vicar during the 1840s. It was limited to forty members who paid a weekly subscription, supplemented by the committee with half a crown, equivalent to two and half shillings.[79] By the 1840s, the parish church may have felt it was losing control of local clothing provision, with the introduction of the New Poor Law and the diminution of parish relief in kind. Thus for parish clergy, clothing societies were perhaps a way to maintain a hold on clothing provision and by implication, the 'respectable' appearance of a parish.

In urban areas, Dorcas Societies were set up, for example Worcester and Bromsgrove.[80] The name derived from the biblical story of Tabitha or Dorcas, who made coats and garments for charity with the widows of Joppa.[81] The rules of the Douglas branch of the society stated that their aim was to provide 'plain' and 'necessary' articles of clothing for the poor. Provision was limited to subscribers, who could be vetted to make sure they were respectable.[82] The Dorcas Society in Worcester was established in 1819.[83] In 1825, for the sum of £27 3s. 3d, the ladies made between 300 and 400 articles of clothing, uniting 'economy with charity'.[84] At their annual sale in 1840, 300 people purchased clothing at half price and 'forty-six subscribers received the value of their subscriptions in garments for private distribution'.[85] One of the aims of the society was to encourage independence in the poor. If able to afford a subscription and deemed respectable enough to receive one, there appears to have been a certain amount of freedom in the way that clothes could be used or passed on once given to a subscriber. By its twenty-fifth annual report in 1845, the society was distributing nearly 800 articles of clothing at half cost price.[86]

Commentary in the *Hereford Journal* about the Ross Clothing Society, founded in late 1831 as a Dorcas Society, provides an insight into how the organizers regarded the recipients.[87] By their third sale in 1832, clothes were distributed 'to poor individuals ... at less than half the original cost and of a better and more suitable quality than they usually purchase'. Everyone who received clothing appeared 'grateful' at the start of the inclement season of winter.[88] Such statements of thankfulness by the recipients concluded all the reports about the society. In 1839, there was a description of how the clothing was distributed. Recipients were 'all seated in regular order and each packet according to its number and the subscriber's name affixed, was handed to the indigent recipients on their giving in their ticket with half a crown'.[89] It was an orderly process. In 1842 the poor were again noted as being seated in regular order around the room, the 'Blue Coat' children now handing out the packets which contained the articles they had requested.[90] The following year, it was commented that the girls' school was now making up the clothing and that their parents were often the beneficiaries of it.[91] The recipients contributed to the cost and apparently requested particular items. Whether they actually thought the garments they received were of a 'more suitable quality' than those they purchased themselves and if this was the only new clothing they acquired, is open to conjecture.

Apart from the necessity of helping the poor to help themselves, the theme of education for future self-help was also strong in the commentary in the local newspapers. In Ross, the clothing was given out ready-made as this 'makes them of double value to the needy recipients; as few are equal to the task of doing it themselves'.[92] Two years later in 1843, the Society started to help educate girls in sewing clothing so the next generation would be self-sufficient and not need to rely on poor quality ready-made items. This sweeping generalization about a lack of sewing skills amongst the poor somewhat contradicts the evidence from the poor law and other sources. Although some women had limited sewing abilities, a large proportion of the manufacture of such women's clothing was still being undertaken within the home, by their social peers or by the local community dressmaker. It was still a skill that could earn women money. The situation was more complex than 'few' women being able to sew or vice-versa. Perhaps it was more an attempt to justify the Society's existence and commitment shown by the elite organizers to originally sew the clothes themselves.

Such charitable concerns would also appear to be part of the formation of a domestic ideology which came to fore in the 1820s and 30s for middle-class women in particular. With the help of educating literature, the way forward was shown for tasteful, decent consumption, recognizing quality while keeping economy. Guides, exemplified by the *Workwomen's Guide* of 1838, detailed how to make basic garments such as petticoats and shirts, to save the expense of dressmakers.[93] These middle-class views, avoiding luxury and unnecessary buying, were inculcated into working-class women and girls through mediums such as clothing clubs.[94] The organizers of such clubs and societies gained an outlet to display their organizing skills outside the home, as well as passing on their knowledge to working-class females, educating them both in practical skills and in decent frugal consumption practices.[95] How far the hegemonic values of decency, cleanliness and economy were accepted by those they sought to educate is a point that will be returned to in the final chapter.

The clothing societies proved popular however the underlying moral tone was perceived (of course it may have been ignored). Their practical nature in both teaching sewing and the useful garments they gave out remained appealing. In December 1845, Ross Clothing Society issued 250 tickets to individuals, which enabled the distribution of 500–600 articles of underclothing and bed linen.[96] This was a reasonable amount of clothing, the total population of Ross being around 3,700. This clothing distribution therefore affected about 7 per cent of the population as well as their associated families.[97] By 1848, the Clothing Society had become an employer, with twenty poor women 'paid liberally' for making up clothing and thus also helping themselves and facilitating their purchases at the Society.[98] The organization had subsumed another role of the parish by becoming employers of the poor, enabling further self-sufficiency to take place.

The success of the Ross society led to the founding of a similar society in Hereford in 1833. The Hereford Clothing Society claimed to provide clothing for around a hundred poor women every six months.[99] As in Ross, the moral point of the provision was also emphasized in the society reports. The poor contributed about 1d a week or about half the value of the material and the 'ladies' made up the clothing. The poor thus learnt 'that in providently assisting themselves they truly '"have their reward"'.[100] In 1835, nearly 100 articles of clothing were given out to 'indigent and distressed families ... [including] flannel and other petticoats, chemises, shirts, frocks, sheets and other articles ... [the] mildness of season induced some subscribers to withhold tickets or more might have been given'.[101] The weather was seen to directly affect the quantity of clothing necessary for the poor.

The association with elite scrutiny and control probably created ambiguous attitudes towards clothing societies for some beneficiaries. This idea was reflected in an advertisement placed in the *Hereford Journal* in 1843 by Edward Jones, a tailor and draper of Broad Street, Hereford:

NB: Persons wishing to avail themselves of the opportunity of having a SUIT OF CLOTHES and to avoid spending Money and [the] procrastination of Clothing Clubs, may have is [*sic*] at this Establishment by paying so much per week or every alternate week, by means of a respectable householder to guarantee the payment of the amount.[102]

When buying from a shop, there was an immediate supply of clothes against the 'procrastination' of the 'clothing club' organizers who distributed clothing bi-annually. Clothing societies were evidently becoming common enough that shopkeepers could perceive them as competition, certainly in the ready-made sector. The use of credit rather than ready money was seen as a viable alternative to the clothing society and similar to the service offered by travelling drapers, albeit with the necessity of a guarantor of credit-worthiness.

By 1840, the cost of clothing had fallen since earlier in the century.[103] This lowering of price meant that clothing was more affordable, possibly reflected in the expansion of clothing societies from the second quarter of the nineteenth century. It was perhaps now easier for the working-class consumer to save small amounts of money which could purchase clothing, especially through the often subsidized clubs and societies. The Charity Commissioners remarked that Samuel Parkes Charity in Great Shelsley was now able to provide three or four people coats or gowns rather than the original two specified in the bequest due to the fall in the cost of clothing.[104] As Vivienne Richmond has suggested, working-class consumers seem to have obtained practical and useful clothing through clothing societies. Clothing was vetted to some degree, but because there was a contribution to the gift, maybe there was felt by the recipients to be less deference due in comparison to traditional charitable bequests. Clothing societies were a tried method to acquire practical, respectable clothing. 'Finery' could be obtained from other sources such as shops and travelling drapers, out of the control of the organizers of the clothing clubs and societies.[105] Although records are often not clear about the specific clothing given out, the emphasis is towards female clothing or undergarments, as in the case of Ross, or fabric lengths which could be made up locally.[106] Aside from customary bequests to tenants or estate workers, or gifts to elderly men, male clothing seems to have been more or less absent, to be sought elsewhere.

Conclusion

Included within the definition of 'charity' were many different sources from which clothing could be obtained. During the first half of the nineteenth century, there was no guaranteed system of provision or study of the practical needs of the poor. As Margaret Hanly has suggested, most charity was intermittent and came in a form that was not particularly helpful or generous. She suggests that those who controlled the charities 'often employed moral judgements in deciding who to relieve and what relief to give'.[107] Formal charity bequests were always under the control of elite society. The supply of charity clothing was thus not consistent across Herefordshire and Worcestershire or for all the population. The depth of provision depended on local middle- and upper-class enthusiasm and contributions. This was also the case with clothing societies and clubs. These too had clear rules of conduct and direction as to where and how items might be acquired. Recipients of such provision maintained the social order of deference by accepting the rules and the supervision of their social superiors.[108] However, the guiding principles of decency and respectability could be ignored completely when acquiring other clothing from different sources.

Alan Kidd has shown that by the mid-nineteenth century, nationally, the emphasis of formal charity bequests had shifted away from able-bodied adults who could help themselves to the less able: children, the sick and infirm.[109] Charitable bequests in Herefordshire and Worcestershire were already quite specific about recipients by the 1830s, usually the young or elderly, particularly in urban environments. Clothing bequests were also often very exact about the garments to be distributed, with items such as woollen gowns and coats given out. These were warm and durable and perhaps more suitable for the elderly, not useful working garments for the labouring population, who used washable cotton textiles such as fustian.

Clothing could be obtained either through charity or poor relief, but these were generally mutually exclusive strategies. It was very difficult to combine both sources of provision with the exclusions set by some charities along with the often partial and unreliable nature of some bequests. With local knowledge of what was available and how to access it, people could piece together welfare from the most advantageous sources for them.[110] This is demonstrated by the Jarvis Charity, which had enough wealth to supply clothing that made a difference to the local community. Clothing provided through this charity precluded claimants from applying for parish relief. There was therefore little call for clothing in the local overseers' accounts, particularly in comparison to the rest of the county. No other charities in the area had the same depth of clothing provision necessary to halt application to the Old Poor Law for clothing. Until the 1830s, apart from the communities covered by the Jarvis Charity, parish relief was generally used more often than charitable bequests to claim clothing, which often had very specific eligibility criteria for recipients.[111]

The development of self-help ideologies from the second quarter of the nineteenth century, running in parallel to changing theological attitudes, for example Evangelicalism and need for believers to demonstrate spirituality by working for others, was reflected in the rise of clothing societies. In the numbers of applicants they dealt with and the amount of garments distributed, clothing societies to a certain extent took over the role of the Old Poor Law from the 1830s.[112] They provided essential, functional garments for local communities. Recipients had a limited amount of control, but in some societies, could request particular garments. Where such clothing societies were established, they could have a large impact on working-class family economies.

Overall, casual or informal charity between kin and communities was doubtless of greater importance for the majority of the working population than regulated charities.[113] Unfortunately, this type of charity leaves little or no evidence behind. Charity from close kin had fewer social obligations than receiving donations from charity benefactors. It could also provide a gateway to other welfare avenues, such as being able to appear in decent clothing to ask for parish relief.[114] Those with no kin had to rely on regulated charity and the social deference that this entailed.[115] Local customary provision in the form of annual seasonal gifts of clothing from the local elite appears to have provided essential garments in quantity for working adults, without direct stipulations about the suitability of the recipients. This type of provision may have helped family members unable to claim clothing from either poor relief or charitable bequests, but it was not guaranteed.

Heavily dependent on local knowledge and local elite largesse, charity could be patchy, intermittent or virtually non-existent in some places, all encompassing in others. This web of aid had to be negotiated by individuals and their households in order to gain help with their clothing provision. Reactions to both giving and receiving clothing reflect the complex nature of charity. Undoubtedly charity was an important clothing provisioning strand in its various guises, particularly for clothing children and the elderly, but it also left large sections of the adult population, especially working-age men, virtually untouched and needing to seek other supply channels for their garments.

6 FASHION AND THE WORKING-CLASS CONSUMER

Fashion: Themes and Debates

So far, this book has shown that working-class consumers could obtain clothing from a variety of sources. This chapter will focus on what clothing such consumers wore and what influenced this choice beyond retail availability. It will examine the effect of fashion on working-class clothing in relation to both gender and age, and will question whether fashion was a gendered construct.

'Fashion' is a notoriously difficult term to define. It can refer to material possessions and the way that they are used, as well as manners and habits. Fashion can also be linked exclusively to clothing and a rapid continuous change in styles.[1] This constant alteration in the manner of dress, allied to knowledge about what style was current and up-to-date, will be examined in the context of provincial working-class clothing. This chapter will question whether working-class clothing had any connection with fashion, or whether practicality and durability were more important.[2] Whilst the elite looked to London for guidance, particularly in matters of fashion, there were regional differences, a localism, associated with plebeian culture, which underscored social hierarchies.[3] Beverly Lemire has noted how inexpensive garments and accessories which could be cheaply purchased and easily changed created fast-changing fashions amongst the lower social orders.[4] These had little connection to elite fashion and formed small distinctive fashions only within peer groups, a practice noted by Francis Place.[5] This chapter will investigate whether such characteristic localized plebeian styles existed in a provincial context, particularly in rural areas.

Clothing was a basic necessity, vitally important in many ways for the lower strata of society. Dennis Frey has pointed out that the working classes devoted proportionally more of their income than the wealthy to items such as clothing as an investment in social capital. It could always be liquidated on the second-hand market if cash was required quickly. By dressing in the latest fashions, with the social and cultural capital which came with this, access might be given to employment and social networks, such clothing becoming an important strategy for survival.[6] The maintenance of appearance, even if not of the latest fashions, displayed outwardly a certain financial security, although Sunday best clothing may have been pawned during the week to ensure economic survival.[7] Margot Finn has also commented that tradesmen often tried to judge a person's credit worthiness by assessing their clothing. Clothing was one way to position people in a hierarchy of social relations and so to give out varied credit terms. For the working-class consumer who could successfully self-fashion an identity approved of by a shopkeeper, whether based on economic reality or not, credit and thus goods would be forthcoming.[8]

A protest ballad printed, probably during the 1830s, by Thomas Ward, a book-seller and printer in Ledbury, rails against the luxurious and elaborate clothing of farmers' wives.[9] Entitled 'My Old Hat', it lamented the low wages of labour-ers, enclosures of common land and the decline of living-in farm hands. It states: 'There's velvet bonnet and silk veils, lace caps on their heads. But O the misery of the poor, they scarcely can get bread ... This cruelty did ne'er abound when this old hat was new'.[10] This type of 'moral' complaint has been seen as indicating that such frivolous dressing was an anathema to working-class people who only desired decent, plain, hardwearing clothing.[11] However, the authors of the ballads did not condemn frivolity in dress *per se*. They were being critical of ostentation in farmers' wives dress when farmers were paying labourers such low wages that the work-ers were unable to afford even plain and simple clothes. Such luxuries were only demoralizing if they were exclusive and, it seems, female. According to the Rev. Henry Bellows, if they were more diffusive, through methods such as ready-made production, then happiness could be possible for the masses too.[12] This chapter will investigate whether or not working-class men and women wanted to dress for more than utility. It will question if the idea of sobriety and longevity in dress was more popular with the middle classes in their role as overseers and clothing-club organizers than with the intended recipients of such clothing.[13]

For this chapter, a variety of sources have been examined to obtain evi-dence for the dress of individual working-class consumers. Firstly, the clothing of working-class men will be discussed, using newspaper reports of runaway men and court reports, before turning briefly to examine male servants' cloth-ing. The chapter will test if there was a 'typical' dress for a working-class male, before moving on to discuss if any men deviated from this and why. Secondly, the chapter will consider the clothing of female labourers, using a group of sur-viving sketches. After a discussion about the type of dress represented in these works and how this varied between sitters, the chapter will examine the clothing of female servants. It will then investigate female 'best' dress in the context of four surviving wedding dresses from Herefordshire. Unfortunately, there are far fewer descriptions of female runaways, and only one sketch of a male labourer with no comparable surviving male garments to allow a broader analysis across the range of sources. Finally, the chapter will draw together conclusions concerning the relationship of the working-class consumer to fashion and will assess whether there is evidence of distinctive 'working-class fashions'.

Men

In working-class society, where literacy was not widespread or perhaps required, there was therefore a greater reliance on visual symbols.[14] Clothing was one of the most basic of these, giving an idea to onlookers about the wearer's status, occupation, age and personal preferences, although this was not always accurate.[15] For instance, a tailor who escaped from the House of Correction in Worcester was described as wearing a short brown jacket, a pair of cotton plaid trousers and a round hat, with the 'appearance of a sailor'.[16]

A picture can be gained of what everyday clothing was worn by working-class males from such descriptions of absconders. The newspapers highlighted clothing details to aid the identification of individuals and help return them to those who paid for the advertisement, generally overseers or employers. This evidence is somewhat skewed by the fact that many accounts of absconded persons published in the newspapers were of apprentices, and therefore single young men. It is not certain whether the clothing apprentices and servants took when they left was stolen from their master's shop or house, although they were very rarely accused of clothing theft in the advertisements.[17] If the clothes that they were wearing belonged to their employer, they would have reflected his or her status rather than the personal tastes of the absconder. However, a large number of descriptions of missing persons in Herefordshire and Worcestershire relate to men absconding and leaving their families chargeable to parish welfare. These men were often described with their occupation and age also noted. Their listed clothing therefore seems to be of a less contested ownership than that of apprentices. By the 1820s, descriptions of absconders had become infrequent, perhaps due to the changes in the apprenticeship system and the Old Poor Law.[18] Detailed evidence about what working-class men were wearing in the second quarter of the nineteenth century in the two counties is therefore difficult to find.

The majority of descriptions of absconders in *Berrow's Worcester Journal* and the *Hereford Journal* were for everyday clothing in muted colours, such as brown corduroy breeches, blue coats and smock frocks. The customary wear of the labourer, the majority of male working-class consumers in Herefordshire and Worcestershire, seems to have been a smock frock, breeches, often enlivened with a colourful waistcoat, along with a coloured handkerchief and striped stockings. For example, Ben Powell, a labourer, deserted his family at Ullingswick, Herefordshire, in 1812. He was wearing a smock frock, light coloured breeches, fustian jacket, yellow striped waistcoat and a red silk handkerchief.[19] This style of dress was representative of the majority of descriptions of missing persons found in the two newspapers. Up until 1820, there were between five and ten such descriptions annually in the *Worcester Journal* and between four and six in the *Hereford Journal*. Clothing which did not conform to this was unusual but certainly not unheard of; for example, two out of seven cases in 1800; and one out of six cases in 1805, both from the *Worcester Journal*. For instance, in 1814, Samuel Cooper from Kidderminster, described as a 'rogue and vagabond', aged twenty-one, escaped from jail. He was wearing a jean jacket with covered buttons, a silk handkerchief round his neck, a striped waistcoat trimmed with black thickset and leather buskins. He carried a smock frock with him to use as a disguise.[20] His subversion of the norms of dress was reflected in his role as a subverter of social rules and alleged criminal behaviour. He was working outside the conventions of labouring represented by the smock frock, although he sought to use them to prevent detection. The seemingly ubiquitous use of the smock frock in Herefordshire and Worcestershire to some extent obscured the clothing worn underneath in surviving descriptions.

Colourful waistcoats were often noted in descriptions of missing persons, perhaps as they provided a simple way to identify an individual. In 1805 in Herefordshire, two waistcoats with yellow spots were worn by two different men leaving their families behind.[21] Charles Gregge from Norton Canon was thirty-seven years old and wearing a green linsey frock coat, velveret waistcoat with black and yellow spots, velveteen breeches and ribbed worsted stockings when he disappeared.[22] Likewise, Thomas Morgan of St Martin's parish, Hereford, left his wife and family chargeable to the parish, so the overseers offered a reward of 5 guineas for information which would lead to his return. He was thirty years old and when he disappeared was wearing a thickset coat, swansdown waistcoat with yellow spots and gilt buttons, corduroy breeches, round hat and red handkerchief round his neck with yellow spots. He was usually employed in 'farming' or working on the roads.[23] Both these men were married and in their thirties. Thus it was not just single young men who sought a colourful appearance.

There are no comparable references to spotted waistcoats in *Berrow's Worcester Journal* for the same date, although there is an earlier example from 1801. James Thomas, aged twenty-seven, was accused of stealing from the Shakespeare Tavern in Worcester. He had come from Leeds and was a cabinet-maker by trade. His waistcoat was of brown swansdown with yellow spots and stripes.[24] Striped waistcoats in bright colours were also popular with some men. For instance, two members of what was described as a 'desperate gang', led by a person known as 'Jack of the Green' in Knighton-upon-Teme, both wore striped waistcoats when apprehended, one of blue and red stripes. Neither had shoes or a hat, but had kept their striped waistcoats, perhaps as some sort of symbol of the 'gang'.[25] This distinctive clothing was described by those who placed the advertisements as a way of readily identifying the runaway, although as seen previously, more mundane clothing was also noted. The fact that the men chose to take distinguishing clothing when a more sober outfit may have made them more anonymous and less traceable suggests that this clothing was important to the men, perhaps because it represented their most fashionable items, reflecting the importance of fashion for men. Maybe such garments would also retain their value in the event of selling or pawning. Possibly they were the clothes that the men thought would best establish their identity when they reached their new life. As seen in chapter 4, clothing could be easily and quickly sold on to raise money or exchanged for a new set of clothes. The garments that runaways took with them were not necessarily the ones they would still be wearing at a later date but would fulfil a particular need when required.

Alongside agricultural labour, service either on an estate or in a household was an important source of work for men. An examination of household accounts reveals how male servants' acquired their clothing. Usually, this was bought ready-made by their employer. This was the case at Northwick Park, near Blockley, the country seat of Lord Northwick, son of the Earl of Coventry. A focus for elite Cotswold society, Northwick Park had a deer park and waterfall, with a picture gallery added in 1832.[26] It was an affluent household, and clothing such as liveries displayed that status to visitors.[27] The clothing male servants were given by the estate was recorded in the estate records, along with their annual wages. For example, in 1818, George Dolphin was taken into service with wages of 18 guineas per year. He was to find his own hat, boots and leather breeches, but was to receive two grooms' livery coats, waistcoats and breeches every year, as well as one pair of overalls, two working jackets with sleeves and a great coat every three years. If he left service before the end of his first year, he had to leave the clothing behind. The assumption was, therefore, that the clothes became his property after a year.[28]

The distinction between livery and working clothes continued into the 1830s, with employees being given up to three separate sets of clothes, full dress livery, small livery and working clothes, with some disparity depending on their position, from coachman down to page. This array of clothing indicated the wealth of the estate but the use of ready-made clothing reflected broader trends in male clothing provision. In general, men took a position in service and accepted ready-made clothes as part of this contract. They were already used to wearing ready-made clothing obtained from a variety of other sources. For example, Mrs Nott, who had houses in Rock and Yardley, seems to have used clothing as incentives to keep her male staff loyal to her. A bill from 1835 details a ready-made blue broadcloth frock coat, twice-striped nankeen jacket and pair of fustian gaiters, bought for one of her male servants from William Spriggs, presumably from his clothing warehouse in Broad Street, Worcester[29].

Such ready-made clothes were similar to those described as being worn by the runaways, suggesting that many men might buy ready-made garments from clothing warehouses. However, in the descriptions of some absconders, several young adult apprentices were wearing something different either to the usual labouring or service dress. Perhaps they were trying to make a statement about their individuality through their clothing, although as apprentices, the clothes may not have actually belonged to them.[30] In 1800, a glover's apprentice absconded in Worcester. He was eighteen years old and dressed in a dark mixed bottle-green coat, striped spotted muslin waistcoat, dark olive corduroy breeches with wide stripes and a round hat.[31] Although the colour palette was muted, the wide stripes on the breeches were unusual and would presumably differentiate him from the everyday clothing worn by his contemporaries. Correspondingly co-ordinated and focused on the breeches was another runaway apprentice, Thomas Stinton. He was apprenticed to Samuel Nicholls, a tailor of Droitwich. He was fourteen years old and wearing a 'blue coat with white metal buttons, a yellow plaided waistcoat, dark coloured corduroy breeches with yellow buttons at the knees' when he ran away in 1805.[32]

Some working-class men thus used cheap but colourful or elaborate items such as buttons to self-fashion an unique style. For example, Francis Williams left his wife chargeable to the parish of Martley. Aged twenty-six, his leather breeches had metal buttons engraved with a fox, his light drab coloured coat had metal buttons engraved with a plough and he was also wearing a smock frock.[33] Using brightly coloured buttons, ribbons and stockings, as noted by Francis Place in a late eighteenth century metropolitan context, was a quick and relatively cheap way of making clothing stand out from the norm.[34]

Unfortunately, descriptions of runaway men diminish both in quantity and in detail from the 1820s onwards. In the few that were published, the style of dress appears similar to that from the first two decades of the century, although trousers were also becoming more common. For instance, in 1831, 'advice' was published about a man asking for employment who was thought to be a machine breaker. He was described as wearing a fustian jacket with red worsted cuffs, dark cord breeches and blue and white striped stockings.[35]

In elite fashion plates of the late 1830s, colourful patterned waistcoats and checked and striped trousers were now being worn, echoing the dress popular with low-status men for at least the first three decades of the century.[36] Although it is not possible to link these fashions directly, the similarities between high fashion and popular fashions by the 1830s, particularly in the use of colour and pattern, illustrate the complex relationship that could occur between various contemporaneous fashion systems. In the second half of the eighteenth century, male fashions had also taken elements of working dress such as trousers and natural unpowdered hair, with commentators noting it was difficult to tell a master from a servant in terms of clothing. This became politically expedient in the era of the French Revolution, although such sober clothing underwent a process of 'gentrification'. There is therefore the possibility that there was some elite appropriation of popular fashions that were worn by both metropolitan and provincial working men.[37]

Clothing was important to at least some working-class men on more than a practical level. They had a sartorial confidence, seeking out the right garments or accessories to create the correct appearance, particularly for peer group recognition. Purchasing such clothing would seem to have been a notable way for some men to spend any surplus cash they had and brought its own benefits. This concept has perhaps been less recognized in terms of male fashion than for women, whose relationship to fashion will be examined in the following section.

Women

Whether female working-class clothing could be considered fashionable is a question that is addressed by examining the sketches of the artist Joshua Cristall depicting working women in a small rural community.[38] This visual evidence is valuable, as women feature very infrequently in descriptions of absconders.

When studying an area of history where there is little direct surviving evidence, here working-class dress, the visual evidence should not be over-looked, despite the methodological problems with it.[39] The reason why Cristall sketched the mainly women workers is unknown. He was a well-respected water-colourist and president of the Watercolour Society before he left London and moved to Herefordshire in 1823, living there for the last twenty years of his life.[40] Cristall lived in the village of Goodrich, close to the river Wye and the viewpoint of Symonds Yat famed for its picturesque outlook as part of the Wye Tour. In an era of perceived rapid industrialization and urbanization, Herefordshire was held out as a lost land, a pastoral haven, where the old rural way of life was preserved.[41] Its labourers and peasants were thought to be happy, industrious and prosperous, deriving their income from the county's fertile soil, although the reality was not that simple. Cristall sometimes sketched the same person more than once. Julian Mitchell speculates that he was perhaps intending to incorporate the figures into one of his major neo-classical works but he never seems to have got round to it.[42] Instead, he has left a visual record of the people he knew in his village, along with local landscapes.

The depiction of rural scenes in particular, is fraught with difficulties during this period. The hard-working, morally deserving peasant, sanitized enough to hang on a middle-class wall, has been well documented.[43] There is, of course, a need to be concerned with the degree of reliability of these drawings: how idealized was Cristall's vision and what was his opinion about the people he sketched?[44] As Peter Burke notes, sketches drawn directly from life, 'in the field', literally in Cristall's case, are perhaps more trustworthy and freed from artistic constraints than paintings worked up in a studio at a later date.[45] However, the artist is still sketching their subject for a particular reason and their view is still highly subjective, possibly omitting or changing what they see, coloured by their own artistic process and intent.[46] Did Cristall admire and respect the women's hard-labour in order to survive, reflected by the patches he drew on their clothing? How much social distance was there between them: did he know them personally as friends or were they perhaps employees in some context, implying a different sort of relationship? Or did he see them as feckless and undeserving poor? Maybe it was a mixture depending on individual people.[47]

When younger, Cristall had drawn and painted classically influenced scenes, featuring, for example, Arcadian nymphs. Perhaps some of these influences can be seen in his drawings of workers around Coppett Hill. Mitchell has suggested that the workers have been turned into Arcadian peasants, reflecting the view of Herefordshire as a rural idyll.[48] However, some sketches seem to have been done in the field with realistic features maintained, such as patches and hob nailed boots. Thus Basil Taylor suggests that Cristall's work was more directly related to contemporary ideas about artistic sincerity and truth, which strove for the identification of an authentic, than the merely conventional, expression of pastoral ideology.[49] The importance of visual evidence is particularly valuable in the re-construction of everyday items for ordinary people which do not otherwise survive in the written historical record. These drawings show how different people might have dressed within a small community and the type of dress this actually was.[50]

The setting for these studies was Coppett Hill, which overlooked the village. This was common land, which by the early nineteenth century had been settled by workers. Those who lived there had certain rights over the land, such as grazing, gathering fern and cutting wood.[51] It was noted by diarist, Sarah Wilmot, on the Wye Tour in 1795 which passed along the river nearby, that the fern was burnt to ash which was then wet and mixed into a paste, worked into a ball and sold for washing and whitening blankets and flannel. It was a principal occupation for the 'industrious' poor in the area.[52] The production of lime was also a significant activity and areas of the hill were covered in lime kilns, making it an industrial as well as a rural area, much to the dismay of Wye Valley tourists. In 1841, the village had a population of about 500 people. Dew and Southan were recorded names of Cristall's sitters, but also common family names in the village, making identification of their extended families difficult.[53] In the overseers' accounts that survive for the parish in the first quarter of the century, people with both surnames claimed clothing from the parish. Between 1815 and 1817, for instance, the parish set up James Dew as a shoemaker, subsidizing his purchase of leather and also paying him 3 shillings to buy leather so he could make shoes for his son.[54] An Elizabeth Dew was given '£1 5s' to 'clothe herself' in 1817, an amount commonly associated with providing clothes for service.[55] The parish was an important source of clothing into the early 1820s, although after 1822 casual payments for clothing petered out. The parish registers record the baptism of Cristall's sitters Elizabeth Dew in 1813, William Dew in 1817 and Rachel Dew in 1819. They were from two families where both fathers were labourers.[56] Thus, while the subjects of Cristall's studies were probably not wearing parish clothing in the late 1820s, they were likely to belong to families that had turned to the overseers in the recent past as a way of gaining additional garments. They were typical of the working-class population; some members of a family, especially the old and young, might rely on poor relief, while others who could work would use other methods for acquiring clothing.

Cristall's sketches show that the older women and children wore clothing that was practical and did not follow current fashions. Young girls wore voluminous pinafores to protect their dresses. Protective narrow lower sleeves, which may have been detachable from the short-sleeved dresses commonly worn, were also sketched by Cristall on both young and older women.[57] Older women generally wore an all-encompassing apron instead of a pinafore and were depicted without headwear or with simple sun bonnets. However, older girls and young women seem to have been more aware of current fashions. A watercolour from 1830 shows a young woman carrying a bundle of bracken. She wore a brown patched petticoat but appears to have worn a printed cotton dress over this, tied up for practicality's sake. The blue kerchief tucked into her apron emphasized the fashionable line of a high waist and puffed sleeves. It seems that she was trying to be fashionable even in her work clothes, tempered by practical difficulties and economic restraints represented by the patch on her petticoat.[58]

Likewise, in 'Fern burners reposing' of 1828, the two young women facing the artist both had puffed sleeves (see Figure 6.1) One also wore a turban style head-dress, rather than the usual bonnet which would have offered more protection from the weather. Both elements were fashionable during the first half of the decade. Thus, the women demonstrated an awareness of such fashions, although the style achieved in their working clothes was out of date in relation to contemporary elite modes.

Figure 6.1: 'On Coppet Hill Goodrich 1828 Fern burners reposing', pen and ink with watercolour, courtesy of the Dyer Collection, photograph courtesy of Chepstow Museum.

In addition to the examples mentioned above, in the collection of Hereford Museum there are six sketches of young women working on Coppett Hill from 1826 and 1827. Some are more detailed than others, but they appear to have been sketched *in situ*, and all the women wear similar clothing, for example, the woman holding a pitchfork (see Figure 6.2). The skirt of the woman in this drawing does not quite seem to work as an actual item of clothing, showing some confusion in its depiction. From the other more successful sketches, it appears that she was holding the skirt of a pinafore, worn over a chemise, kerchief and petticoat, her striped stockings visible beneath the hoiked-up skirt. The pinafore in the sketches follows the fashionable high-waisted line, a garment that would wrap around the body, crossing over at the front, fastening with ties, visible in two of the sketches.[59] This echoed contemporary bodice construction. In another sketch, a girl holding a scythe wears an elaborate pelerine over her shoulders, trimmed with fashionable ruching. She also has a distinctive collar to her high-waisted dress, a reference to the revival of the sixteenth-century ruff collar, fashionable during the 1820s.[60] However, a patch is clearly visible near the hem of her skirts, suggesting this was a much-worn piece of clothing.

Figure 6.2: 'J. Cristall, Goodrich 1827', drawing, Hereford Museum, catalogue number 3028, courtesy of Hereford Museum and Art Gallery, Herefordshire Heritage Services.

For some young women, it seems to have been important to wear stylish clothing, even when labouring outside, or perhaps when being sketched by an artist. These clothes were not always up to date with current elite fashion and the fashion plate ideal. However, the styles had been fashionable within the previous few years, with the depiction of similar clothing in dated fashion plates. The context for the display of such clothes demonstrates that practicality was not always the primary consideration for the female labourer when choosing garments. Also, such clothing was not just kept for 'best', but worn everyday. Although the sitters may have conceivably dressed up for Cristall, the patching visible on some of the garments would suggest they were not 'best' clothes but usually worn for work. The town of Ross was only about three miles away from Goodrich and, as noted, offered a wide availability of shops from which to obtain articles and information about the latest fashions.[61] Some of the young adult female labourers depicted by Cristall certainly appear to have tried to dress fashionably even while working.

Domestic service was the other major source of employment after agricultural work for women in Herefordshire and Worcestershire. Maintaining a correct appearance was a delicate balance for women thus employed. Employers who engaged domestic servants expected a certain standard of dress from them, as they were a reflection of the status of the household overall. Even quite humble households could employ servants to help with washing and cleaning.[62] For example, in an undated letter, seemingly relating to the Old Poor Law and therefore pre-1830s, Sarah Brown wrote to her mother. She had just taken up her first post as a servant and asked her mother to request clothing for her from the parish:

> ... still it is necessary for fear I should lose my place that I should appear a little better than I am at present, and as this is my first place I have not the means of doing it myself.[63]

Brown obviously felt that her current outfit did not meet what was expected and needed to augment it through whatever channel was possible, without yet having accumulated wages. As Pamela Sharpe comments, society was 'ferociously appearance-conscious' and a servant needed new clothing to both search for work and to take up a position. Humble households were probably not wealthy enough to supply clothing, even cast offs, and it was necessary to apply to the parish instead, as in the case of Sarah Brown.[64] The clothing distributed under Poor Law provision was probably the kind of clothing that employers sought for their servants, plain, durable and decent, not 'finery'.

At Northwick Park in Worcestershire, the various housemaids earned less than the men at around 10 guineas per year and although some received odd cash gifts, none received any clothing.[65] As no separate 'working' clothing was required for indoor work, acquisition was probably left to individuals.[66] As clothing was not part of female servants' wages or given as an additional incentive for good behaviour, this might suggest that clothing was a more personal choice for female servants in comparison to men. It may also reflect their status as less obviously visible members of the household, certainly to outsiders. Presumably, if an employer had felt a servant's clothing was not up to standard, there would have been intervention. The relationship between female servants and the lady of the house could also have been more informal with regard to clothing in contrast to male servants. For example, borrowing may have taken place in smaller households. In 1828, a note in Thomas Wheeler's diary suggests that a servant had stolen some clothing, perhaps with the defence of borrowing it: 'I discharg'd Mary Gardener from service she had made free with some of my wifes wearing apparrel [sic]'.[67] The informal disposal of cast offs to servants was unlikely to be recorded in the household accounts and no examples have yet been found of this type of gift. This might also suggest that such practices were not widespread for this area or period, mistresses clothing not usually being passed on to servants.

In a way, women employed as servants may have had less freedom to dress fashionably, as opposed to 'decently' and 'acceptably', than their peers working in the fields. However, female servants were seen as one of the sections of working-class society most aware of fashion. Their role in passing on fashionable cast-offs and observations about current styles to their families back in the country has been widely documented.[68] Female servants were perhaps the most readily visible young women for social commentators to focus upon, especially in urban areas. As noted in the introduction to this book, a letter to the editor of the *Hereford Journal* in 1835 criticized the consumption patterns of local female domestic servants.[69] The evidence from Goodrich would suggest that young women who laboured outdoors also sought to dress fashionably. They dressed in a style of clothing which would need to be frequently changed to be fashionable, the fall in the cost of clothing perhaps helping them to maintain such an appearance.[70] Unlike servants, they did not have the constraints of an employer vetting clothing. Fashionable clothing was thus important for at least some working-class women and was worn within an everyday context.

'Best' Dress

Surviving wedding dresses provide additional evidence for female clothing. It was not until the second half of the nineteenth century that white wedding dresses became customary, and then only for the upper classes. The nineteenth-century wedding dress was generally used on successive occasions as best dress, when attending church or associated community activities. Presumably it made sense to show social status through clothing to the greatest degree possible on such occasions.[71] Hereford Museum has four wedding dresses from this period.

It should be noted that the fact that these dresses have survived means that they were not worn out as 'best', and as such they may have been atypical. However, they are rare examples of surviving female non-elite dress, and illustrate what the standard of a 'best' dress was. Two of the dresses were worn by women connected to the clothing trades, which may also make them uncharacteristic of those worn by the majority of female working-class consumers. Like the Cristall sketches, differences in style between these dresses demonstrate distinctive ways of dressing within a local area.

The first wedding dress dates from about 1805 and was made and worn by Miss Mercy Butler of Hurst Manceaux. It is a very simple dress of monochrome floral brown printed cotton, with an apron skirt and cross-over front at the bodice, a common construction of that date. The only decoration comes from a ruffle around the bodice collar and the cuffs of the long sleeves, which are gathered at the end[72] (see Figure 6.3). There is no documentary evidence about the status of the family, but the plainness of the dress, both in the decoration and the choice of the cotton print, would suggest that it was not particularly high. Both the material and the style were some way off the contemporary fashion plate ideal of neo-classical-inspired white muslin drapery.[73]

Mary Bufton was a smock maker in Hereford who married in 1834. As a smock maker, she probably made her own wedding outfit. Her dress was made from printed cotton, with principally blue and brown floral stripes on a seaweed ground. This was a popular design at the time for printed cottons.[74] What made the dress modish were the large gigot sleeves, which had been fashionable since the late 1820s, continuing in various styles for a decade (see Figure 6.4). Sleeve supports were needed to maintain the puff for full effect so the surviving garment was not an everyday dress and unsuitable for manual labour. Judging from the style, Bufton's dress would be dated to the first half of the 1830s. Although in a fashionable shape, it was not an elite dress. It was made of cotton not silk, the bodice was un-boned, the pintuck around the hem has been let down at some stage, and the skirt was unlined apart from a panel at the hem. It was perhaps an approximation of what Mary Bufton thought was fashionable, and what her means allowed. By the 1840s, it would have appeared very out of date, the large puffed sleeves immediately marking it out as clothing from earlier in the 1830s.

In contrast, the wedding dress of Elizabeth Wright, who married the tailor James Powell in the village of Marden in 1839, was made from a plum-coloured satin silk, a less obviously dateable textile. Elements from contemporary fashions are evident, such as the pointed waist and off the shoulder full gathered sleeves. The ruching and pin tucking used as decoration on what was otherwise a fairly plain dress were also fashionable (see Figure 6.5).[75] The dress seems to represent the aspirations of someone who wanted to appear respectable as the wife of a village artisan. It was made of silk, the bodice was boned and the skirt was lined

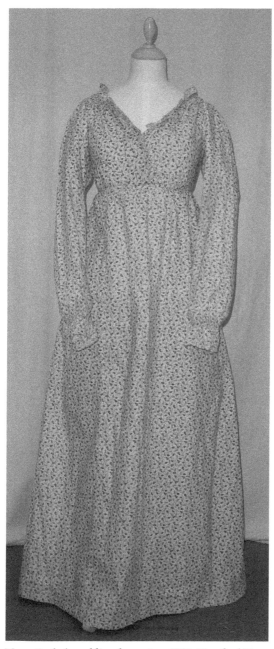

Figure 6.3: Mercy Butler's wedding dress, circa 1805, Hereford Museum, accession number 2728, courtesy of Hereford Museum and Art Gallery, Herefordshire Heritage Services.

Figure 6.4: Mary Bufton's wedding dress, 1834, Hereford Museum, accession number 1048, courtesy of Hereford Museum and Art Gallery, Herefordshire Heritage Services.

Figure 6.5: Elizabeth Wright's wedding dress, 1839, Hereford Museum, accession number 4209, courtesy of Hereford Museum and Art Gallery, Herefordshire Heritage Services.

with glazed cotton, making it of a higher quality and probably more expensive than Mary Bufton's. Arguably, it was also less immediately fashionable, mainly due the fabric's sober colouring. This was in contrast to Mary Bufton's printed cotton, which made an explicit statement about the date when it was made. Elizabeth Wright still had all the fashionable elements in place, but they were presented in a more subtle manner, perhaps reflecting the potential prosperity of a respectable tradesman's wife in a small village.

James Powell, her husband, was originally from Hereford, apprenticed in 1822 to Edward Francis, a tailor.[76] Sometime after his seven-year apprenticeship ended, he moved to Marden, a village to the north of Hereford, and accepted a parish apprentice himself in 1843. William Price, aged eleven, was apprenticed for seven years, the £9 premium paid by Smith's Charity, Powell providing his 'Meat, Drink, Apparel, Lodging & Washing'.[77] This would appear to have been his first help with the business. In the 1841 census, James Powell was listed as living at Berrington Cottage, Litmarsh, Marden, aged twenty-nine, with his wife Elizabeth, aged thirty and James, their son, aged eight months.[78] His age in 1841 would mean he was apprenticed himself when about ten years old, a standard age to do so. Elizabeth's wedding dress therefore represented the aspirations of the couple at the time of their marriage, to be respected trades people within their local community. The evidence would suggest that in 1839, this in the main remained hoped for, rather than actually achieved. By constructing a model of appropriate appearance and behaviour through dress, Elizabeth may well have helped James on the way to his aims and his business certainly seems to have prospered into the 1840s.

The final surviving wedding dress dates from about 1840, and is thought to have belonged to Annie Mitchell when she married Thomas Cooke in Much Marcle.[79] However, it is clearly a much earlier dress from around 1815, which has been substantially altered to try and bring it up to date with later fashions. The floral printed cotton dates from the early nineteenth century. By 1840, the back had been altered and the crossover front removed from the bodice, although it still had an apron-front skirt, the construction most commonly found on dresses from 1815. The way the skirt was gathered so it was full at the back was also a survival from the earlier date. The dress was remade in an attempt to make it like a front-closing dress of a simple plain style, fashionable in 1840. The cotton print and the details of previous construction, reveal its earlier origins (see Figure 6.6). Again, there is no documentary evidence about the status of Thomas Cooke or Annie Mitchell. It could be that this was a dress used and altered for a second marriage, perhaps it was a dress passed through the family or maybe acquired as a cast-off. Even here, where there appears to have been limited means, an awareness of current fashions is visible and an attempt was made to copy these.

Figure 6.6: Annie Mitchell's wedding dress, circa 1840, Hereford Museum, accession number 1999–22, courtesy of Hereford Museum and Art Gallery, Herefordshire Heritage Services.

The importance of status in dress for working-class women is emphasized in all these examples. The value of the clothes lay not in their cost but in their ability to highlight the role the wearer was, or wished to be able, to play within a community hierarchy. The appearance of a 'best dress', whether at a wedding or on a Sunday, showed financial acumen and a certain amount of financial security, even if only short-term.[80] The respectability which came with being able to dress 'well' at least one day a week was an important indicator of place within the working-class hierarchy, as well as a demonstration of fiscal independence for the community to witness. The materiality of the actual clothing formed the basis for social comparison and distinction within a community. What a woman chose to wear for her wedding, when her dress was self-consciously displayed, did, and still does, make a strong statement about how she regarded herself and her new role as a wife, as well as being indicative of her new husband's social status, or at least how she perceived that standing to be.[81]

The Influence of Fashion on the Working-Class Consumer

'Fashion' was not an alien concept to the working-class consumer. Outside the constraints of clothing required by employers, some working-class people dressed in fashionable clothing, as shown by the wedding dresses and the descriptions of certain male runaways. Before they had children, young adults had arguably the greatest disposable income available. They perhaps also had the most exposure to fashionable clothes, frequently changing location to seek employment.[82] Both agricultural workers and servants often changed jobs and so gained mobility, suggested, for example, by the settlement examination of Sarah Boulton in 1822 by Kingsland parish. She was twenty-two years old, born in Presteigne, but hired in about 1817 for a year to Mrs Palmer of St Martins, Worcester for £6 per year. She left after this to return to Leominster to be with her parents and to learn the art of finishing gloves, which became her trade.[83] Such movement was of economic benefit to the parish. If parish officers could find places away from the home parish for apprentices or servants, their place of settlement could often be transferred. This would save any potential expense of relief in the future. Many young people were therefore apprenticed outside their own locality, both by the parish and independently, some in London, perhaps meaning that they would gain wider experience of different methods of clothing acquisition and a broader spectrum of fashion. For example, Richard Belcher, born in Banbury, was the son of a tailor and apprenticed himself to a draper at Stratford-upon-Avon, working in various drapers in Birmingham, Coventry and London, before setting up by himself in Kidderminster.[84] This was often a life-cycle stage, when young adults, particularly female domestic servants and male apprentices, lived away from home and perhaps had some wages to spend on non-essential goods.[85] It is difficult to calculate what effect this period in their lives had both on the shops that some established later in their careers and the influence of their clothing on their social peers if they returned home. Presumably, both could be considerable.

Young adults were probably the most likely to be able to enhance their status and standing though fashionable dress, or at least by wearing dress recognized as such by their immediate peer group. Such clothing would have a value in succeeding years and was not just an improvident purchase, as some social commentators believed.[86] Dressing up and spending freely for holidays were acceptable means of winning approval amongst peer groups, not irresponsible and extravagant as deemed by the middle classes.[87] This material self-advancement, to impress peers and perhaps to attract sexual attention, could also bring economic benefits, particularly for women, who found it difficult to survive economically without marriage.[88] This acquisition of portable material goods has been called 'thrift in reverse' by Paul Johnson, writing about the late nineteenth century. He sees such possessions as a substitute for a savings account, bought during the summer when wages were plentiful, to be sold off during the winter when necessary.[89] As previously noted, this showing off was criticized in correspondence to the editor of the *Hereford Journal* in 1835:

> It is on Sunday and especially on Sunday Wake days that young women of this class come forth decked in a style so far superior to their relatives at home and of even to their betters ... they feel themselves inflated by the vanity of dress and the amount of outdoor attention which ... [they] received ... [to go] anywhere to show off.[90]

Perhaps it was also an enjoyable pastime and a pleasurable release from ordinary life for the working man or woman. Certainly, the desire to dress up for particular events, either personal events such as weddings or social events such as fairs or holidays, was recognized. Sarah Jones planned to wear a muslin dress, bought for the 'express object of adorning her person at the late Worcester Steeple chase', before she was charged with theft of the same dress.[91] Although she was discharged as her identity could not be proved, this perhaps emphasizes the lengths that people would go to obtain suitable garments for the right occasion. Thus the examples discussed in this chapter have indicated that functionality was not always the primary issue when choosing clothing. The long-term needs of a household were sometimes subjugated to the desires an individual to dress up and enjoy themselves, particularly young adults without children earning independent wages.[92]

A year before Mary Bufton was married in her printed cotton gigot sleeved dress, Cristall sketched a young woman carrying a bundle of fern leaves. The waistline of her dress followed the same fashionable line but the puffed gigot sleeves so noticeable in Bufton's dress were not even hinted at (see Figure 6.7).

There were possible patches on her sleeves and under the arm. Bufton's choice of wedding dress, with its modish gigot sleeves, made a statement about an interest in fashion. It was a dress for display rather than for manual labour and demonstrated an income that was high enough to spend on impractical clothing, even if not of the highest quality. Cristall shows the working clothes of a young woman, with a protective handkerchief around the neck and low crowned bonnet. However, the lines of contemporary fashion were still present, making the image dateable to the 1830s. Although this was a working dress rather than a 'best' dress, even within a small village setting, some individuals attempted to be more fashionable than others, for example by wearing a turban headdress or pelerine, with their working clothes.

Figure 6.7: 'J. Cristall 1833 Coppet Hill Goodrich', drawing, Hereford Museum, catalogue number 1795a, courtesy of Hereford Museum and Art Gallery, Herefordshire Heritage Services.

The lack of evidence of clothing belonging to one individual across a period of time means that it is difficult to calculate how fast fashions were taken up and how often clothing was changed to be in fashion. Nevertheless, the fact that some consumers such as Bufton dressed in clothing that followed the fashionable style at a specific date, suggests that when circumstances allowed, fashion might be followed. This clothing was not necessarily right up to the minute in seasonal changes or of the highest quality, but it reflected the broad chronology of change in elite fashion. This material evidence backs up the claim of both the writer of the letter to the newspaper and other social commentators, that working-class women would buy fashionable clothing when possible, perhaps also giving them a sense of independence and freedom from the constraints of normality.[93]

Working-class men tended not to follow the fashion plate ideal, which would generally have been impractical for labour. No male 'best' clothes survive, to offer a contrast to everyday dress, as the female wedding dresses do. The clothing that they acquired was usually dependent on what could be obtained ready-made, either new or second-hand.[94] These garments might be adapted to follow fashions, perhaps set by their peers and often very localized. Their general appearance was not fast-changing and seems to have remained static, certainly over the first three decades of the nineteenth century. The deficiency in information about the way individuals dressed over a period of time means that small changes in dress and the popularizing of particular styles, patterns or colours, especially within a localized area, may not be evident. Nonetheless, some working-class men were also buying clothing that was not particularly practical or necessary, for example, coloured waistcoats or striped stockings. This was a working-class style, not derived from metropolitan or elite modes, but popular in the provinces, including the countryside. As Christina Fowler has noted in her study of a rural Hampshire tailor and his customers, 'apparel was more than mere utility' to many men, with some, particularly young adults, spending up to 40 per cent of their wages on clothes.[95]

Certainly, purchasing clothing was an important part of many working people's lives: not all of this was utilitarian and may have been of a reasonable quality, with some people owning a considerable quantity. How much they spent and how related this was to fashion was usually contingent on the age of the wearer and if they had other dependents to support.

Conclusion

Despite the pre-conception that provincial working-class people were only interested in durable and practical clothing, this chapter has shown that a broad range of clothing was worn by working-class consumers, including garments which could be regarded as fashionable. There was familiarity with the broad trends of fashion, but clothing could also be adapted, according to taste and circumstances.[96] For instance, much male clothing was bought ready-made so could be easily customized to reflect popular taste with items such as buttons and ribbons. Such additions would make an outfit stand out, along with cheap accessories such as stockings. Many women bought material to make up themselves or often, to give to the local dressmaker to do so, allowing them to choose which style they wanted made up. This reliance on professional workers rather than home sewing reflected the significance of clothing for working-class women.[97] The importance of achieving the correct finished style by using skilled workmanship was emphasized, especially as the sewing abilities of some women may have been limited.[98] As shown by Mary Bufton, depending on an individual's aptitude for sewing and their facility for obtaining the necessary resources, the finished garment could be quite close to a fashion plate ideal.

Fashionable clothing was important to both male and female working-class consumers. Fashion, by its very nature, is elitist in its purest form, being a continuous search to differentiate between individuals. However, this process can potentially function within any social group, whether low- or high-status. As Lemire states: fashion 'has multiple expressions among a range of social groups' which have different motivations and stimuli for the individuals involved.[99] Particularly for some young adults of both sexes, where economic circumstances would allow, it appears to have been essential to spend money on fashionable clothing both for everyday and 'best' wear. The clothing working-class people chose to wear was a complex mixture of practicality, protection, display, showmanship, emulation of the elite, emulation of peers, social differentiation and affordability. Being able to routinely change this clothing, for whatever reason, by accessing a variety of clothing supply networks, played a significant role in the lives of many working-class consumers.

CONCLUSION

This book has explored how the provincial clothing trade operated during the first half of the nineteenth century, examining the interlocking supply networks that were used by working-class consumers. Rarely was one network used in isolation. Boundaries were crossed between first- and second-hand markets, ready-made and home-made, parish relief clothing or school uniform, to weave a complex provisioning process, both by individuals and those within the same household. Retailers also operated across fluid boundaries, some shops selling new and second-hand clothing side by side, as well as providing clothing for parish relief, or employing itinerant sellers to take stock further afield.

Shops which sold clothes to working-class consumers were scattered over the countryside, not just in the cities, towns or even larger villages. The importance of the rural market should not be underestimated.[1] Up to 90 per cent of the population of Herefordshire and Worcestershire lived outside the large cities and either needed to journey into them to buy clothes or purchase them locally in small towns, village shops or from other networks. Buying clothes from shops in urban and rural areas was a normal practice by the early nineteenth century. Such shops could be the centre of communities, a place to meet and find out information, both news and about stock, a diversion from normal routine, as well as a source of good quality, well-priced goods.[2]

By the early nineteenth century, there appears to have been a rising rural demand for garments, such as smock frocks in the Midlands, needed as protective clothing for agricultural work. This stimulated trade locally, with local urban ready-made clothing shops acting as middlemen, selling on stock, often of their own manufacture, to shopkeepers in the countryside. These supply networks were independent of metropolitan control, focused on meeting particular resident markets.[3] For example, in 1800, an auction of stock, including scarlet cloaks, was advertised as 'worthy of the attention of country shopkeepers'.[4] Such cloaks were traditional wear for country women and were often made-up by drapers to sell ready-made.[5] Although the out-workers who made up the clothing in the first place may have lived in rural areas, clothes retailers in local towns and cities would sell wholesale to smaller shopkeepers, especially those in the surrounding countryside.[6] Small village shops, which often combined the stock of trades such as grocers or hardware too, took a small supply of clothing which needed to be ready-made as they often did not have the capacity, skills or desire to get it made up themselves. The rural trade was thus important to the large urban retailers too. This was reflected in their advertisements, promoting their clothing as worthy of the attention of country shopkeepers. For example, some city drapers such as Daniel Patrick of Hereford advertised themselves as whole-salers for country shopkeepers.[7] Charles Anthony of the Manchester Warehouse in Hereford stated at the end of his advertisement, 'charities, tailors, country shopkeepers and all wholesale dealers served on liberal terms.'[8] The rural hinter-land acted both as a stimulus to urban manufacture with the need for necessary 'country' items such as scarlet cloaks and smock frocks, and as an important mar-ket, the home of the majority of the population who needed to purchase routine items as quickly and as cheaply as possible.[9]

The connection between production and distribution was thus very close in this sector. Clothing manufacturers were often retailers, or became retailers, or vice-versa, an efficient way both to sell their product and to gauge local demand.[10] Where local supply networks did come into conflict with London trade net-works, for example, the sale of Myers-and-Hyam-manufactured male clothing in Hereford, the autonomy of the local trade was strongly fought for by resident manufacturers and retailers. This successful blending of manufacturing and sell-ing focused on localized supply networks, helped change the nature of retailing in the second quarter of the nineteenth century. There was an increased concen-tration on retailing specific working clothing to working-class consumers, both in rural and urban areas. Shops now advertised that they sold ready-made work-ing garments such as smock frocks, some even using them in their shop name to emphasize the importance of the market.[11] Many provincial shops stocking clothing and textiles had sold goods to all social classes during the eighteenth century, but by the second quarter of the nineteenth century, the significance of the working-class market, particularly for men's ready-made clothing, was more frequently acknowledged and promoted, especially in urban areas.[12]

The provincial retail environment for male ready-made clothing had devel-oped some complexity, allowing men to show up and buy the clothing they needed, giving them choice in both retailers and also in products and prices once inside a shop. In Worcester, the choice of retailers selling cheap clothing, particularly for men, seems to have drawn in male consumers from other areas of the county, especially when clothing was needed quickly or in an emergency. According to his wife, Isaac Cook, a down-on-his-luck weaver from Kidder-minster, travelled to Worcester in 1834: 'His only intention in doing so was to Endeavour to Obtain some Apparel for himself and some shoes for the Chil-dren'. Having returned home newly outfitted, he then set off for Macclesfield to look for work, leaving his wife and children chargeable to the parish.[13] In 1833, the Carter brothers robbed a shopkeeper near Bewdley in the north-west of Worcestershire. Afterwards, they headed straight for the city of Worcester and purchased smock frocks from the clothes dealer Richard Skeat of Broad Street.[14] Working-class men in these cases were shown to be active shoppers, frequenting clothes dealers and cheap tailors, to a much greater degree than working-class women.[15] Male clothing of a certain standard seems to have been an absolute necessity to be able to work and was sought through whatever means possible, usually actively by men themselves. Cheap ready-made clothing offered by an increasing variety of shops was the most important method of acquisition, parish relief and clothing charities giving little help to adult working men. In contrast, women's clothing often required some personal direction in its making up, whether this was done within the household or by a local dressmaker. The female ready-made clothing sector was yet to develop the complexity of the male garment trade, although there are signs that ready-made dresses were becoming more widely available from the 1840s onwards, particularly from drapers.

In rural areas, the retail infrastructure was almost as complex and diverse as that of urban districts, with networks of pedlars and travelling drapers as well as shops selling clothing.[16] Itinerant selling remained essential for distributing goods to working-class people in both rural and urban areas throughout the first half of the nineteenth century. Pedlars and hawkers were particularly important for supplying female clothing and fabric, perhaps filling in gaps not covered by fixed-shop retailers so effectively. Many pedlars and hawkers appear to have lived in larger towns and cities, travelling out into the surrounding countryside to sell their goods. The amount of itinerant selling in rural locations does not seem to have declined between 1800 and 1850, as suggested by some commentators.[17] However, the majority now travelled out from towns and cities into rural areas, a practice continued by travelling drapers from the second quarter of the nineteenth century onwards. The rapid expansion of travelling drapers, as noted in the contemporary trade directories, seems to indicate that they were a popular way to acquire clothing for working-class people, especially, although not exclusively, for women.

The 'economy of makeshifts' and the recourse to various types of clothing provision within this, including the informal second-hand market, was also important for many households. With parish relief or charitable donations, there was little choice about what garments would be received and considerations such as warmth, durability and the cost of clothing were perhaps more important than any focus on style.[18] As recipients were usually very young or very old, this was perhaps less of an issue than for working-age adults. A garment given out by the parish would be regarded as essentially different to one obtained independently from a choice of stock in a city clothing warehouse. Both were important clothing provisioning strands and likely to be used by many people at particular points in their life-cycle, especially in the first quarter of the nineteenth century. Independent purchase of clothing from shops and itinerant sellers was perhaps more significant for the adult majority, but as part of household economies, receiving garments via poor relief or charity could be important for other family members.

Although social commentators may have wished that all working-class people would dress in decent sober clothing, fashion was important for some. It influenced the selection of garments, which were becoming increasingly affordable into the 1830s.[19] Often the desired outfit was made fashionable with minimum financial outlay, with the use of cheap accessories such as ribbons and buttons, or by remaking old dresses into a more fashionable style as with the wedding dress of Annie Mitchell.[20] Nevertheless, for some, spending a significant amount of money on clothing was important. The reasons were manifold: for example, it was an area of life which was not subject to outside controls; also, any cost could be subsequently justified by a resale value when pecuniary circumstances demanded. Although it was generally young adults who probably had the time and economic means to engage in such dressing, some older adults also tried to maintain a 'fashionable' appearance, showing how popular such clothing was across the spectrum of the working-class population. Many working-class people were active and wily consumers of clothing, which was both a necessity, visually and materially, and often a statement of fashion too, indicating status within a peer group or community.

The studies of different clothing acquisition methods from various areas undertaken in this book has shown the importance of local context when investigating routine consumption patterns. Each district had circumstances unique to that place, from the poverty visible in Bromyard to the respectability of Malvern. By focussing on specific locations, links and relations between different sectors of the trade and various consumers become apparent, linkages which may be missed in a general survey. It is a picture that could be played out across the whole country. Herefordshire and Worcestershire were neither ordinary nor extra-ordinary in comparison to the rest of the country. Outside the large and growing cities of the era, the supply networks in the two counties show how working-class people sought to clothe themselves, sometimes with ease, other times with a great struggle. By connecting evidence such as poor law material, with its wealth of surviving retailers' bills, to newspaper advertising and trade directory evidence, an idea is gained both about the extent of certain businesses and what their 'bread and butter' stock might have been. Parish expenditure on items such as clothing could be of considerable benefit to local shopkeepers and should not be overlooked in studies of retailing. Whilst pauper dress is in itself an important study, with many of the working-class population experiencing poverty at some point in their lives, examining poor law material for particular communities also reveals evidence about the wider retailing environment for other working-class people in that locality. The diversity of local clothing supply networks suggests that there was no hierarchy as such as to which was the most favoured method overall. It very much depended on individual or household circumstances, and where that household was located. Presumably economic considerations and autonomy in choice would have been two of the most important, if sometimes opposing, factors for an individual deciding which method to use.

The evidence which has emerged from this study is sometimes surprising and perhaps at odds with previous notions of how working-class people both purchased and regarded their clothing. There were many different types of retailer selling clothing to working-class consumers and that clothing varied in style, price and whether or not it was ready-made. The clothing trade in provincial England was already vibrant, commercially important and an expanding sector, before the era of mass manufacturing later that same century. Working-class people did not produce textiles at home and only some made up clothing, so both men and women were necessarily active consumers. The expansion of provincial clothes retailing was evident by the second quarter of the nineteenth century and was integral to the way that working-class people acquired their dress and ultimately the clothing that they wore.

This book has shown the complex supply networks that working-class consumers had to negotiate and could sometimes exploit to their advantage, to obtain their clothing. Gathering evidence from all these sectors of the trade is necessary to gain a full picture of the commerce involved in clothing the working-class population. Working-class people used clothing for display, investment and income. How clothing was obtained influenced who wore that clothing and in what way. It was an important commodity in its own right, and one increasingly purchased new and ready-made from an ever-widening range of shops.

GLOSSARY

Baragon	a type of fustian, a heavy woven cotton, practical for working jackets.[1]
Broad cloth	a fine woollen cloth in plain twill weave, heavily milled with dress face finish.
Buskins	high boots reaching sometimes to the knee, mainly riding boots.
Cambric	a fine quality of linen.
Cassimere	a fine woollen cloth made out of merino wool, sometimes with a diagonal ribbed weave.
Chambray	a thick, coarse, chequered cotton fabric.
Chemise	a female undergarment: a long, loose, low-necked, short-sleeved shirt, worn next to the skin, made usually of cotton or linen.
Cloth	a woollen fabric.
Clothier	by the nineteenth century, a clothier was an outfitter commonly of ready-made clothing, associated with fixed prices and money back guarantees.[2]
Coburg	a thin, soft, wool and cotton twilled cloth, produced from the 1840s.
Corduroys (cords)	a thick corded cotton fabric, giving a ribbed effect with a pile-like velvet.
Drab/drabbett	a thick strong fabric, of linen and cotton, usually twilled, of a dull brown or grey colour.
Duck/Russia Duck	a coarse white linen or cotton canvas, using a double weft and warp. Russia duck is a finer version of the same.
Fustian	originally a coarse twilled textile with a linen warp and cotton weft, the surface resembling velvet. By the nineteenth century, it was normally made from just cotton. It was usually cut loosely, used without a lining and available in several colours. By the second quarter of the nineteenth

century, it had developed political connotations associated with radicalism.[3]

Gigot	'leg-of-mutton' sleeves, with full puffed shoulders tapering to the wrist.
Grogram	a thick, coarse taffeta, a plain glossy silk, sometimes watered, and often mixed with wool or worsted.
Gros de Naples	a corded silk.
Habit clothes	a female riding outfit.
Hurden	a coarse linen fabric made from hurds, the coarsest part of flax or hemp.
Jean	a twilled cotton fabric.
Kersey	a coarse narrow cloth, usually ribbed.
Kerseymere	a fine twilled woollen cloth, woven so textured, similar to cassimere.
Linsey	a coarse linen fabric.
Linsey Woolsey	a coarse linen and wool mixed fabric.
Moleskin	a coarse, strong fustian.
Nankeen	a cotton fabric of yellowish/brown colour, originally from Nankin.
Narrow cloth	woollen cloth woven on a loom worked by one operator, hence cheaper than broad cloth which was woven by two operators.
Orleans	similar to Coburg, but not twilled.
Paletôt	a French term for overcoat, applied to short loose coats, usually without a waist seam.
Pelerine	a very wide, cape-like collar.
Pelisse	a woman's fitted overcoat.
Plush	a shaggy, hairy cotton velvet, resembling fur.
Salesman	or saleswoman, a term used from at least the second half of the seventeenth century to denote clothes dealers and brokers. Some were also manufacturers and they retailed both old and new ready-made clothing. They often dealt in new and second-hand clothing at the same time, relying partly on the exchange of old clothes for acquiring new stock.[4]
Shift	the traditional word for chemise.
Skeleton dress	a boy's outfit comprising a tight jacket and trousers buttoned together around the waist.
Stuff	a cloth made from worsted wool, with no nap or pile.
Swansdown	a material made from wool and cotton.
Thicksett	a coarse fustian.

Twill	a weave producing a diagonal pattern.
Velveret	a fustian with a velvet like finish.
Velveteen	a cotton imitation of velvet.
Worsted	a cloth made of long stapled combed wool, producing a hard woollen cloth with a smooth finish, originally from East Anglia.

General References

C. W. and P. E. Cunnington and C. Beard, *A Dictionary of English Costume 900–1900* (London: A. and C. Black, 1960), pp. 241–80.

V. Foster, *A Visual History of Costume, The Nineteenth Century* (London: Batsford, 1992), pp. 142–4.

P. Hamilton, 'Haberdashery for Use in Dress 1550–1800' (PhD dissertation, University of Wolverhampton, 2007), glossary, pp. 290–324.

Notes
1. See E. E. Perkins, *A Treatise on Haberdashery &c.* (London: T. Hurst, 1834), p. 84.
2. See J. Tozer and S. Levitt, *Fabric of Society, A Century of People and their Clothes, 1770–1870* (Carno: Laura Ashley, 1983), p. 14.
3. See S. Levitt, 'Cheap Mass-Produced Men's Clothing in the Nineteenth and early Twentieth Centuries', *Textile History*, 22:2 (1991), p. 179. Also P. Pickering, 'Class Without Words; Symbolic Communication in the Chartist Movement', *Past and Present*, 112 (1986), pp. 144–62, and F. Engels, *The Condition of the Working Class in England* (London: Penguin, 1987), pp. 102–3.
4. B. Lemire, *Dress, Culture and Commerce, The English Clothing Trade before the Factory, 1660–1800* (Basingstoke: Macmillan, 1997), p. 57.

NOTES

Introduction

1. *Hereford Journal*, 15 April 1835. Italics in original.
2. See, for example, Anne Buck, who details similar contemporary comments relating to the eighteenth century. A. Buck, *Dress in Eighteenth-Century England* (London: Batsford, 1979), pp. 109–12.
3. *Hereford Journal*, 29 April 1835.
4. J. de Vries, *The Industrious Revolution, Consumer Behaviour and the Household Economy, 1650 to the Present* (Cambridge: Cambridge University Press, 2008), pp. 116, 178–9, who notes that the commentaries about working people which pointed out their fecklessness and irresponsibility, were part of an ideology that defined working people as having no capacity for self-governance. He quotes very similar commentary to the Hereford letter from Austria, dating to 1839, see idem, p. 178.
5. G. Elson, *The Last of the Climbing Boys* (London: John Long, 1900), p. 259, comment relating to the mid-nineteenth century.
6. L. Fontaine and J. Schlumbohm, 'Household Strategies for Survival: An Introduction', in L. Fontaine and J. Schlumbohm (eds), *Household Strategies for Survival 1600–2000: Fission, Faction and Cooperation* (Cambridge: Cambridge University Press, International Review of Social History supplement, 2000), pp. 11–12.
7. J. White, cited in J. Benson, *The Working Class in Britain 1850–1939* (Harlow: Longman, 1989), p. 3.
8. P. J. Corfield, *The Impact of English Towns 1700–1800* (Oxford: Oxford University Press, 1982), p. 138.
9. A. Clark, *The Struggle for the Breeches. Gender and the Making of the British Working Class* (London: University of California Press, 1997), particularly pp. 7, 177 and 267.
10. J. Benson, *The Rise of Consumer Society in Britain, 1880–1980* (London: Longman, 1994), p. 26, who considers 86 per cent of the population to be working class from 1801 and 1851 census data.
11. Defined as such in L. Davidoff and C. Hall, *Family Fortunes, Men and Women of the English Middle Class, 1780–1850* (London: Routledge, 1992), p. 463. See also, H. R. French, *The Middle Sort of People in Provincial England, 1600–1750* (Oxford: Oxford University Press, 2007), particularly chapter 2.
12. F. Trentmann, 'Beyond Consumerism: New Historical Perspectives on Consumption', *Journal of Contemporary History*, 39:3 (2004), pp. 374–5.
13. Benson, *The Working Class in Britain*, pp. 207–8.

14. See Trentmann, 'Beyond Consumerism', pp. 373–401.
15. For example, see N. McKendrick, J. Brewer and J. H. Plumb, *The Birth of a Consumer Society: The Commercialization of Eighteenth Century England* (London: Europa, 1982), Benson, *The Rise of Consumer Society*, and C. Breward, *The Hidden Consumer: Masculinities, Fashion and City Life 1860–1914* (Manchester: Manchester University Press, 1999).
16. For instance, see A. Adburgham, *Shops and Shopping, 1800–1914* (London: George Allen and Unwin Ltd, 1981), ch. 5.
17. For example, see W. Hamish Fraser, *The Coming of the Mass Market* (Basingstoke: Macmillan, 1981), pp. 59–61, who sees only a small proportion of the working class as being able to buy new clothing before the 1870s. He argues that they were dependent on the second-hand market, hand-me-downs and charity. He does not see a market for cheap new clothing for the masses until the 1880s and 1890s.
18. Namely, J. Styles, *The Dress of the People. Everyday Fashion in Eighteenth-Century England* (London: Yale University Press, 2007); B. Lemire, *Fashion's Favourite, The Cotton Trade and the Consumer in Britain, 1660–1800* (Oxford: Oxford University Press, Pasold Research Fund, 1991); B. Lemire, *Dress, Culture and Commerce, The English Clothing Trade before the Factory, 1660–1800* (Basingstoke: Macmillan, 1997).
19. See J. Styles, 'Clothing the North; the Supply of Non-Elite Clothing in the Eighteenth Century North of England', *Textile History*, 25:2 (1994), pp. 139–66, and Lemire, *Fashion's Favourite*, chs 4 and 5.
20. The main exception to this is Christina Fowler and her work on Hampshire, summarized in her article, C. Fowler, 'Robert Mansbridge, A Rural Tailor and his Customers 1811–15', *Textile History*, 28:1 (1997), pp. 29–38.
21. B. Blondé, P. Stabel, I. Van Damme and J. Stobart, 'Retail Circuits and Practices in Medieval and Early Modern Europe: An Introduction', in B. Blondé, P. Stabel, I. Van Damme and J. Stobart (eds), *Buyers and Sellers: Retail Circuits and Practices in Medieval and Early Modern Europe* (Turnhout: Brepols Publishers, Studies in European Urban History, 2006), p. 7.
22. V. Richmond, '"No Finery": The Dress of the Poor in Nineteenth Century England' (PhD dissertation, Goldsmiths, University of London, 2004), p. 148. See also B. Lemire, *The Business of Everyday Life, Gender, Practice and Social Politics in England, c. 1600–1900* (Manchester: Manchester University Press, 2006), p. 133, who writes about 'thousands of clothes dealers scattered through the urban landscape'.
23. Styles, *The Dress of the People*, pp. 161, 164.
24. D. Alexander, *Retailing in England during the Industrial Revolution* (London: Athlone, 1970).
25. For example, H. C. Mui and L. H. Mui, *Shops and Shopkeeping in Eighteenth Century England* (London: Routledge, 1989), particularly ch. 1, and M. J. Winstanley, *The Shopkeeper's World, 1830–1914* (Manchester: Manchester University Press, 1983), ch. 1.
26. N. Cox, *The Complete Tradesman, A Study of Retailing, 1550–1820* (Aldershot: Ashgate, 2000).
27. For example, see Mui and Mui, *Shops and Shopkeeping*, and Cox, *The Complete Tradesman*. See also Blondé *et al.*, 'Retail Circuits', p. 8, for a summary of early modern research into retailing.
28. J. Stobart, *Spend Spend Spend! A History of Shopping* (Stroud: The History Press, 2008), pp. 102–3, 105–8.

29. See G. Riello, *A Foot in the Past, Consumers, Producers and Footwear in the Long Eighteenth Century* (Oxford: Oxford University Press, Pasold Research Fund, 2006), p. 129, for comments about shoe retailers for lower class consumers between 1750 and 1850.

30. See P. Sharpe, *Adapting to Capitalism, Working Women in the English Economy, 1700–1850* (Basingstoke: Macmillan, 2000), p. 65, who notes mass clothes production developed out of retailing as did mass shoe manufacturing.

31. N. Sleigh-Johnson, 'Aspects of the Tailoring Trade in the City of London in the Late Sixteenth and Earlier Seventeenth Centuries', *Costume*, 37 (2003), p. 28.

32. A. Ribeiro, 'Provision of Ready-Made and Second-Hand Clothing in the Eighteenth Century in England', in *Per Una Storia della Moda Pronta, Problemi e Richerchi, Atti del v Convegno Internazionale del CISST, Milano, 26–28 Febbraio 1990* (Florence: Edifir Edizioni,1991), p. 86.

33. M. Charpy, 'The Scope and Structure of the Nineteenth-Century Second-Hand Trade in the Parisian Clothes Market', in L. Fontaine (ed.), *Alternative Exchanges, Second-hand Circulations from the Sixteenth Century to the Present* (Oxford: Berghahn Books, 2008), p. 139.

34. For example, see J. Z. Seidel, 'Ready-to-Wear Clothing in Germany in the Sixteenth and Seventeenth Centuries: New Ready-Made Garments and Second-Hand Clothes Trade', in *Per Una Storia della Moda Pronta,* pp. 9–10, who has found woollen ready-made trousers bought at Frankfurt fair at the turn of the fifteenth century. See also J. Arnold, 'Smocks, Shirts, Falling Bands and Mantuas: Evidence of Loosely-Fitting Garments and Neckwear produced for the Ready-to Wear Market, *c*. 1560–1700', in *Per Una Storia della Moda Pronta,* p. 18, for ready-made accessories imported into sixteenth century London; and M. Ginsberg, 'The Tailoring and Dressmaking Trades, 1700–1850', *Costume*, 6 (1972), pp. 64–71, p. 67.

35. See J. Thirsk, *Economic Policy and Projects, The Development of a Consumer Society in Early Modern England* (Oxford: Clarendon Press, 1978), pp. 5–6, 45–6, for the stocking industry. M. Spufford, *The Great Re-clothing of Rural England; Petty Chapmen and their Wares in the Seventeenth Century* (London: Hambledon, 1984), p. 33, for ready-made accessories carried by itinerant sellers.

36. Seidel, 'Ready-to-Wear Clothing', p. 10.

37. H. Deceulaer, 'Entrepreneurs in the Guilds: Ready-to-wear Clothing and Subcontracting in late Sixteenth and early Seventeenth-century Antwerp', *Textile History*, 31:2 (2000), pp. 133–49.

38. B. Lemire, 'Redressing the History of the Clothing Trade in England: Ready-made Clothing, Guilds, and Women Workers, 1650–1800', *Dress*, 21 (1994), pp. 62–3.

39. Seidel, 'Ready-to-Wear Clothing', pp. 12–13, and Arnold, 'Smocks, Shirts', p. 26, for charity clothing; See Lemire , *Dress, Culture and Commerce,* ch. 1, for a detailed study of the seventeenth and eighteenth century government contracts for naval and army slop uniforms.

40. Arnold, 'Smocks, Shirts', p. 26.

41. J. Craik, *Uniforms Exposed, From Conformity to Transgression* (Oxford: Berg, 2005), pp. 25–7.

42. Riello, *A Foot in the Past*, pp. 46–50. He also notes standardization in the ready-made shoe market during the eighteenth century through the adoption of a scale of measures for accurate sizing.

43. J. Styles, 'Product Innovation in Early Modern London', *Past and Present*, 168 (2000), pp. 124–69, on p. 161. Also Lemire, *Dress, Culture and Commerce*, pp. 11, 22; C. Sham-

mas, *The Pre-Industrial Consumer in England and America* (Los Angeles, CA: Figueroa Press, 2008) p. 310, n. 33.

44. See for example, M. J. Becker, 'Match Coats and the Military: Mass-Produced Clothing for Native Americans as Parallel Markets in the Seventeenth Century', *Textile History*, 41:1 Supplement (2010), pp. 153–81; Lemire, *Dress, Culture and Commerce*, pp. 32–8 for the colonial trade and pp. 12–13 for navy figures.

45. A. Miller, *Dressed to Kill, British Naval Uniform, Masculinity and Contemporary Fashions, 1748–1857* (London: National Maritime Museum, 2007), p. 14.

46. Ibid., p. 15.

47. Lemire, *Fashion's Favourite*, p. 180. Also, McKendrick, Brewer and Plumb, *The Birth of a Consumer Society*. Styles, however, notes that this order failed to sell with no further orders or uptake for the shirts, see Styles, 'Product Innovation', pp. 136–9.

48. Arnold, 'Smocks, Shirts', pp. 22–3.

49. Ribeiro, 'Provision of Ready-Made and Second-Hand Clothing', p. 86.

50. See M. Zakim, *Ready-Made Democracy, A History of Men's Dress in the American Republic, 1760–1860* (London: University of Chicago Press, 2003), pp. 41–7, for the process in America.

51. Lemire, 'Redressing', p. 63, footnote 25. See also Styles, 'Product Innovation', p. 160 for complaints against salesmen from Tailors Companies.

52. See below pp. 32, 105, for workhouse sizing in the early nineteenth century and p. 23 for smock-frock sizing.

53. Miller, *Dressed to Kill*, p. 14.

54. Styles, 'Product Innovation', pp. 161–2.

55. See satirical cartoons, for example, 'Snip's Warehouse for Ready made Cloaths', published 1791, Robert Sayer, British Museum, illustrated as plate 9, Styles, 'Product Innovation', p. 163.

56. Riello, *A Foot in the Past*, pp. 8–9.

57. J. A. Schmiechen, *Sweated Industries and Sweated Labor, The London Clothing Trades, 1860–1914* (London: Croom Helm, 1984), p. 9. See also K. Honeyman, *Well Suited, A History of the Leeds Clothing Industry, 1850–1990* (Oxford: Oxford University Press, Pasold Research Fund, 2000), p. 11.

58. Schmiechen, *Sweated Industries*, pp. 12–17.

59. B. Lemire, '"In the Hands of Work Women", English Markets, Cheap Clothing and Female Labour, 1650–1800', *Costume*, 33 (1999), pp. 23–35.

60. C. B. Kidwell, *Suiting Everyone, The Democratization of Clothing in Amercia* (Washington D. C.: Smithsonian Institution Press, 1974), pp. 53 and 63. M. Zakim, 'Sartorial Ideologies: From Homespun to Ready-Made', *American History Review*, 106:5 (2001), pp. 1553–86, on p. 1575, notes there was no mass production of female ready-made clothing before the American Civil War. P. Perrot, *Fashioning the Bourgeoisie, A History of Clothing in the Nineteenth Century* (Chichester: Princeton University Press, 1994), p. 54, traces the development of female ready-made clothes in France from 1845 onwards.

61. See Mercy Butler's dress, Chapter 6, pp. 140–1, below, for an example of this type of dress.

62. B. Lemire, 'Developing Consumerism and the Ready-Made Clothing Trade in Britain, 1750–1800', *Textile History*, 15:1 (1984), pp. 21–44, on pp. 36–8, 41. Cotton gowns sold for 8 or 9 shillings in the 1760s and 1770s.

63. A. J. Kershen, *Uniting the Tailors, Trade Unionism Amongst the Tailors of London and Leeds, 1870–1939* (Ilford: Frank Cass & Co. Ltd, 1995), p. 54, n. 10, notes that John

Barran's company did not manufacture female ready-made tailored garments until 1927, see also idem, pp. 100–2.

64. See Perrot, *Fashioning the Bourgeoisie*, pp. 74–5, for a contrasting French view, where the civilizing mission of ready-made clothing was also noted in that it might improve the morals of the working class as they could aspire to be bourgeois by appearing close in dress, thus increasing social integration as well as hygiene, sobriety, self-respect, family values and thrift.

65. H. Mayhew, *Mayhew's London, being selections from 'London Labour and the London Poor'* (1851; London: Spring Books, n.d.), p. 218; C. Kingsley, 'Cheap Clothes and Nasty', in *Novels, Poems & Letters of Charles Kingsley, Alton Locke* (1898; London: Kessinger Publishing, 2003); A. Smith, *The Natural History of the Gent* (London: D. Bogue, 1847), especially pp. 94–5,100–1.

66. Sharpe, *Adapting to Capitalism*, p. 67; there is a large literature on seamstresses and labour conditions during this period. See Zakim, *Ready-Made Democracy*, ch. 6, for American criticism of the sweated trades.

67. Lemire, 'In the Hands of Work Women', pp. 29–34.

68. See Kershen, *Uniting the Tailors*, pp. 6–8.

69. Francis Place Papers, Volume XXXIX, 'Manners, Morals, Improvement of the People and its Causes ... , 1646–1836', Volume III, British Library, Manuscript Collection, Add. 27827, pp. 51, 144–5.

70. Kershen, *Uniting the Tailors*, p. 27. See also Honeyman, *Well Suited*, pp. 21–2, 260–1, for developments under John Barran, leading to the development of the wholesale made-to-measure suit around the turn of the twentieth century, the forerunner to the famous Burton's suit.

71. A. Godley, 'Singer in Britain: the Diffusion of Sewing Machine Technology and its Impact of the Clothing Industry in the United Kingdom, 1860–1905', *Textile History*, 27:1 (1996), p. 65.

72. Sharpe, *Adapting to Capitalism*, pp. 151–2.

73. See J. Benson and L. Ugolini, 'Introduction: Historians and the Nation of Shopkeepers', in J. Benson and L. Ugolini (eds), *A Nation of Shopkeepers: Retailing in Britain, 1550–2000* (London: IB Tauris, 2003), pp. 11–14; and B. Reay, *Microhistories, Demography, Society and Culture in Rural England, 1800–1930* (Cambridge: Cambridge University Press, 2002), pp. 260–2.

74. Sharpe, *Adapting to Capitalism*, pp. viii, 4–5.

75. As termed by Steven King, along with Gloucestershire. See S. King, *Poverty and Welfare in England, 1700–1850, A Regional Perspective* (Manchester: Manchester University Press, 2000), p. 188.

76. Indeed parts of modern Birmingham, for example, Sellyoak, Deritend and Yardley, were part of Worcestershire at this date.

77. See P. Burke, *Eyewitnessing: The Uses of Images as Historical Evidence* (London: Reaktion Books Ltd, 2001), p. 9, who suggests 'new fields', such as the history of the everyday, need to use a broader range of evidence including images.

78. C. L. Fowler, 'Satisfying Popular Consumer Demand 1775–1815 with Specific Reference to the Dress Trades in Hampshire' (PhD dissertation, University of Portsmouth, 1998), pp. 4–6. See also V. C. E. Morgan, 'Producing Consumer Space in Eighteenth Century England: Shops, Shopping and the Provincial Town' (PhD dissertation, Coventry University, 2003), p. 84, for a study of retailing in eighteenth century Warwickshire.

79. Styles, *The Dress of the People*, p. 136.

80. For example, see the business of Edward Passey, pawnbroker and salesman, Ludlow, *Hereford Journal*, 16 November 1808, 11 November 1818; James Murrell, milliner and grocer, Alcester, *Berrow's Worcester Journal*, 30 November 1820.

81. See *Bentley's History and Guide and Alphabetical and Classified Directory of Worcester ..., Evesham ..., Dudley ..., Stourbridge ..., and Bentley's History, Gazetteer, Directory and Statistics of Worcestershire* (Birmingham: Bull & Turner, 1840–2), 3 vols, entries for Dudley, Martley, Badsey, Broadway, Bellbroughton, Pershore and Upton-upon-Severn.

82. Riello, *A Foot in the Past*, pp. 17–18, 38, citing Miller.

83. L. Taylor, *The Study of Dress History* (Manchester: Manchester University Press, 2002), p. 84; and B. Burman, and C. Turbin, 'Introduction: Material Strategies Engendered' *Gender and History*, 14:3 (2002), p. 376.

84. Riello, *A Foot in the Past*, p. 6. However as Prown notes, this means developing a methodology for their examination, using as a basis, those developed in archaeology and art history. See J. D. Prown, *Art as Evidence, Writings on Art and Material Culture* (London: Yale University Press, 2001), pp. 78–92, 224, 232, 239. Also, J. Attfield, *Wild Things: The Material Culture of Everyday Life* (Oxford: Berg, 2000), p. 40 and ch. 5.

85. B. Burman and J. White, 'Fanny's Pockets: Cotton, Consumption and Domestic Economy, 1780–1850', in J. Batchelor and C. Kaplan (eds), *Women and Material Culture, 1660–1830* (Basingstoke: Palgrave Macmillan, 2007), pp. 31–51.

86. J. Styles, 'Dress in History: Reflections on a Contested Terrain', *Fashion Theory, The Journal of Dress, Body and Culture, Methodology Special Issue,* 2:4 (1998), pp. 383–9, on pp. 387–8, and Taylor, *The Study of Dress History*, pp. 70–3, who question Fine and Leopold's criticism to object-based dress history in their study *The World of Consumption* (London: Routledge, 1993), pp. 93–4. See also A. D. Hood, 'Material Culture and Textiles: An Overview', in *Material History Bulletin*, 31 (1990), p. 9, who also makes the point that historians need to read and evaluate artefacts as much as they would do with written evidence.

87. L. Baumgarten, *What Clothes Reveal, The Language of Clothing in Colonial and Federal America* (Williamsburg, VA: The Colonial Williamsburg Foundation and Yale Press, 2002), p. 135.

1 Clothing Shops and Working-Class Consumers

1. Fowler, 'Robert Mansbridge'; Styles, 'Clothing the North'. See also M. Lambert, '"Cast-off Wearing Apparel": The Consumption and Distribution of Second-hand Clothing in Northern England during the Long Eighteenth Century', *Textile History*, 35:1 (2004), pp. 1–26, for a regional survey focussing on the second-hand trade.

2. J. Stobart, 'Leisure and Shopping in the Small Towns of Georgian England, A Regional Approach', *Journal of Urban History*, 31:4 (2005), p. 495.

3. B. Gwilliam, *Old Worcester: People and Places* (Bromsgrove: Halfshire Books, 1993), p. 69.

4. The *Worcester Postman*, from which the *Worcester Journal* derived, had been published irregularly since 1690. The *Worcester Herald*, a competitor, had a circulation of approximately 2,000, giving some idea of the numbers circulated. *Hereford Journal*, 3 June 1840.

5. Gwilliam, *Old Worcester*, p.132.

6. Richard Sanders, Bills and Receipts, 3 February 1837, Worcestershire Record Office [hereafter WRO], 2193/77 iv.

7. For example, see entries in *Holden's Annual Directory, 1st Edition for the Years 1816 & 1817* (London: Thomas Underhill, 1817), where lists of traders are a similar length for the three towns, Nottingham (population 40,000 in 1821), York (population 31,000 in 1821) and Worcester (population 16,000 in 1821).

8. See P. Large, 'Urban Growth and Agricultural Change in the West Midlands during the Seventeenth and Eighteenth Centuries', in P. Clark (ed.), *The Transformation of English Provincial Towns 1600–1800* (London: Hutchinson, 1984), p. 169.

9. T. C. Turberville, *Worcestershire in the Nineteenth Century, A Complete Digest of the Facts Occurring in the County since the Commencement of the Year 1800* (London: Longman, Brown, Green and Longmans, 1852), p. 150.

10. T. Bridges and C. Mundy, *Worcester, A Pictorial History* (Chichester: Phillimore, 1996), p. xxix.

11. *National and Commercial Directory and Topography ... for Worcestershire ...* (London: James Pigot and Co., 1828), p. 883.

12. See J. Bentley, *Ancient and Modern History of Worcestershire ...* (Birmingham: Bull & Turner, 1840–2), pp. 104–5.

13. Turberville, *Worcestershire*, p. 328, appendix 1.

14. Ibid., p. 189.

15. Ibid., pp. 190–6.

16. *Berrow's Worcester Journal*, 7 May 1835.

17. Ibid., 30 April 1835.

18. Bridges and Mundy, *Worcester*, p. xxvii.

19. *Berrow's Worcester Journal*, 17 July 1845.

20. E. Berridge (ed.), *The Barrett's at Hope End, The Early Diary of Elizabeth Barrett Browning* (London: J. Murray, 1974), pp. 83, 124 and 180.

21. M. Spevack, (ed.), *A Victorian Chronicle, the Diary of Henrietta Halliwell–Phillipps* (Hildesheim: Georg Olms Verlag AG, 1999), pp. 9, 32, and 49 for examples including shopping at Howitts, Holborn in 1841, Swan and Edgars and Strattons in 1847 and Waterloo House in 1850. For gentry shopping by proxy in an earlier period see C. Walsh, 'Shops, Shopping and the Art of Decision Making in Eighteenth Century England', in J. Styles and A. Vickery (eds), *Gender, Taste and Material Culture in Britain and North America, 1700–1830* (London: Yale University Press, 2007), pp. 170–1.

22. *Berrow's Worcester Journal*, 19 November 1835 and 21 September 1837.

23. Ibid., 23 February 1837, 6 April 1837, 26 October 1837.

24. Ibid., 5 June 1816. See S. Chapman, *Merchant Enterprise in Britain, From the Industrial Revolution to World War I* (Cambridge: Cambridge University Press, 1999), pp. 175–81 for further discussion about the history and selling practices of Morrison, Dillon & Co.

25. The County Court was occupied from 1838, the museum from 1836, the station opening after the railway to Malvern and Hereford was built in 1860. See Bridges and Mundy, *Worcester*, pp. xxix–x and plate no. 137.

26. Gwilliam, *Old Worcester*, p. 69.

27. Bridges and Mundy, *Worcester*, see plate number 52.

28. Eleven directories were examined ranging in date from 1809 to 1847. See Works Cited for full listings.

29. J. Stobart and A. Hann, 'Retailing Revolution in the Eighteenth Century? Evidence from North–west England', *Business History*, 46:2 (2004), pp. 171–94, on p. 190.

30. Lemire, *Dress, Culture and Commerce*, p. 57.

31. Blondé *et al.*, 'Retail Circuits', p. 18.

32. Gwilliam, *Old Worcester*, pp. 89–90.
33. *Berrow's Worcester Journal*, 17 August 1837. Ann Whewell was listed as a clothes dealer in Pigot's Directory of 1828.
34. *Worcestershire General and Commercial Directory for 1820* (Worcester: S. Lewis, 1820), pp. 67 and 100.
35. The street numbering for Worcester in the city centre runs concurrently up one side of the street and down the other. Many of the shops today have a late eighteenth-century foundation, and this is still visible to the rear, only the fronts and the actual shop being modernized.
36. *Berrow's Worcester Journal*, 14 July 1831.
37. Mrs H. Wood, 'A Tragedy II – In the Buttery', *Johnny Ludlow*, 6th ser. (London: Macmillan, 1901), p. 219.
38. *Worcestershire ... Directory for 1820* (Lewis); *Pigot and Co.'s ... for Worcestershire ... 1828 and 1835* (London: James Pigot and Co.); *Guide and Directory to the City and Suburbs of Worcester for 1837 ...* (Worcester: T. Stratford, 1837).
39. Richard Sanders, Bills and Receipts, 3 February 1837, WRO, 2193/77, p. iv. See ch. 2, pp. 47–8 for further details of Sanders's business.
40. See T. Fawcett, 'Bath's Georgian Warehouses', *Costume*, 26 (1992), pp. 32–9.
41. *Berrow's Worcester Journal*, 2 February 1837.
42. Richard Sanders, Bills and Receipts, 8 May 1837, WRO, 2193/77 iv.
43. Alexander, *Retailing in England*, pp. 214–17.
44. W. Ablett, *Reminiscences of an Old Draper* (London: Sampson Low, Marston, Searle and Rivington, 1876), p. 94.
45. See Chapter 2, p. 47, for more details.
46. Parish of St Nicholas, Receipts, Accounts and Financial Papers relating to the Churchwardens, Overseers and Officials, Bills from John Sanders, 10 June 1778 and 22 November 1778, WRO, 3696/9. *The Worcester Royal Directory* (Worcester: J. Grundy, Worcester, 1790).
47. Turberville, *Worcestershire*, p. 328, appendix 1.
48. Shammas, *The Pre-Industrial Consumer*, p. 277.
49. L. D. Smith, 'Industrial Organization in the Kidderminster Carpet Trade 1780–1850', *Textile History*, 15:1 (1984), pp. 75–100.
50. *Holden's Triennial Directory (Fifth Edition) for 1809, 1810, 1811*, vol. 2 (London: John Davenport, 1811). Queen Street was in the centre of Dudley, the market place formed in 1848–9, when houses between Queen Street and the High Street were pulled down. See W. Page and J. W. Willis-Bund (eds), *The Victoria History of the County of Worcester* (Folkestone: Dawsons, 1971), Vol. 3, p. 99. See glossary, p. 157, for a definition of a clothier.
51. For example in Evesham, there were six drapers noted in 1820, one of whom was also a clothier, with only one further clothier. See *Worcestershire ... Directory for 1820* (Lewis).
52. Between 1820 and 1841, fourteen different clothes dealers or salesmen, and likewise, three clothiers and eleven pawnbrokers, were listed.
53. *Worcestershire ... Directory for 1820* (Lewis), p. 252.
54. R. E. Palmer, 'The Funny Rigs of Good and Tender–hearted Masters in the Happy Town of Kidderminster. Anno 1828', *Transactions of the Worcestershire Archaeological Society*, 3 (1970–2), pp. 105–13 p. 109 in particular.

55. See Lemire, *Dress, Culture and Commerce*, pp. 14–16. See also S. Levitt, 'Cheap Mass-Produced Men's Clothing in the Nineteenth and early Twentieth Centuries', *Textile History*, 22:2 (1991), p. 182.

56. A. Buck, 'The Countryman's Smock', *Folk Life*, 1 (1963), p. 18, n. 6. See also M. Hall, *Smocks* (Princes Risborough: Shire Publications, 1979), p. 3, who notes that the word 'slop' was still used in parts of rural Herefordshire as a term for an overall.

57. Buck, 'The Countryman's Smock', p. 23; R. Worth, 'Rural Working-Class Dress, 1850–1900: A Peculiarly English Tradition?', in C. Breward, B. Conekin and C. Cox (eds), *The Englishness of English Dress* (Oxford: Berg, 2002), p. 109; S. Payne, *The Gurteens of Haverhill, Two Hundred Years of Suffolk Textiles* (Cambridge: Woodhead–Faulkner, 1984), p. 22. See A. Toplis, 'The Manufacture and Provision of Rural Garments, 1800–1850: a Case Study of Herefordshire and Worcestershire', *Textile History*, 40:2 (2009), pp. 153–4, 162–3, for further discussion about smock frocks.

58. Account Book of William Baker, 59 Parsons Street, Banbury, 1813–22, Bodleian Library, MS.Top.Oxon.c.453.

59. See Lambert, 'Cast–off Wearing Apparel', pp. 3–8, for trade directory evidence for northern urban centres.

60. *Worcestershire ... Directory for 1820* (Lewis), p. 293, and *Pigot's ... Directory, 1828*, p. 881.

61. J. E. Norton, *Guide to the National and Provincial Directories of England and Wales* (London: Offices of the Royal Historical Society, 1984), p. 16. See pp. 16–19, idem, for an examination of collation methods.

62. *Bentley's History, Guide and Alphabetical and Classified Directory of the Borough of Evesham ... and Seventy-Eight Parishes South of the City of Worcester* (Birmingham: Bull & Turner, 1841), p. iv.

63. D. Page, 'Commercial Directories and Market Towns', *Local Historian*, 11:2 (1974), pp. 86–7.

64. G. Shaw, *British Directories as Sources in Historical Geography* (Norwich: Geo Abstracts, Historical Geography Research Series, Number 8, 1982), pp. 32–40. See also N. Raven, 'The Trade Directory: A Source for the Study of Early Nineteenth Century Urban Economies', *Business Archives, Sources and History*, 74 (1997), pp. 16–25, for further discussion of trade directories as a source.

65. Barker estimates that only between 3 and 13 per cent of the population were included in directories during the nineteenth century. See H. Barker, *Business of Women: Female Enterprize and Urban Development in Northern England 1760–1830* (Oxford: Oxford University Press, 2006), pp. 51, 53–4.

66. *Berrow's Worcester Journal*, 5 April 1810.

67. *Worcestershire ... Directory for 1820* (Lewis); *Pigot's ... Directory*, 1835.

68. St Peter's Parish Records, Droitwich, bills, 1804–31, WRO, 5476/13. See Chapter 4, pp. 101–4, for the clothing of paupers.

69. St Peter's Parish Records, Droitwich, bills, 1813, 1820, 1822, 1823, WRO, 5476/13.

70. *Pigot's Directory, 1828, 1835*; *Robson's Commercial Directory of the Western Counties, viz. ... Hereford ... Worcester* (London: William Robson, 1838); *Bentley's History and Guide*, 1840–2.

71. St Peter's Parish Records, Droitwich, bills, bill from Pumfrey to the Overseers for 1830, WRO, 5476/13.

72. Levitt, 'Cheap Mass–Produced Men's Clothing', pp. 184–5; B. Lemire, '"A Good Stock of Cloathes": The Changing Market for Cotton Clothing in Britain 1750–1800', *Textile History*, 22:2 (1991), pp. 311–28, on p. 316.
73. St Peter's Parish Records, Droitwich, bills, 1830, 1831, WRO, 5476/13.
74. Collection of George Marshall Bills, no. 494, 1805, WRO, 9937/2/280. Pumfrey also sold shirts and shifts to the overseers in 1804, WRO 5476/13. George Marshall was listed as a farmer, from Himbleton near Droitwich, in *Worcestershire ... Directory for 1820* (Lewis), p. 412.
75. In 1810, Henry Langford provided two pairs of breeches for overseers in Droitwich, priced 4 and 7 shillings. St Peter's Parish Records, Droitwich, papers and accounts, 1810, WRO, 5476/12.
76. Barker, *Business of Women*, pp. 57–60, 76.
77. *Berrow's Worcester Journal*, 30 December 1830.
78. Collection of George Marshall Bills, 1844, WRO, 9937/2(iii) – 1.
79. *Berrow's Worcester Journal*, 9 November 1843. In 1844, John Pumfrey was listed as the mayor of Droitwich, see Turberville, *Worcestershire*, p. 326.
80. *Berrow's Worcester Journal*, 12 May 1836.
81. Styles, 'Clothing the North', p. 146.
82. B. Didsbury, 'Cheshire Saltworkers', in R. Samuel (ed.), *Miners, Quarrymen and Saltworkers* (London: Routledge and Kegan Paul, 1977), pp. 137–203, who also looks briefly at the salt industry in Worcestershire.
83. F. C. Laird, *Worcestershire or Original Delineations, Topographical, Historical and Descriptive of that County, The Result of Personal Survey* (London: J. Hams, 1818), p. 174.
84. *Robson's Commercial Directory, 1838*, p. 43. By 1840, it was claimed the baths attracted many visitors to enjoy sea bathing in the heart of the country, *Bentley's History and Guide*, vol. 2 (1840–2), p. 62.
85. M. Gillet, 'Supply of Shopkeepers in Besançon in the First Part of the Nineteenth Century: Novelties between 'Old' and 'New', in B. Blondé, N. Coquery, J. Stobart and I. Van Damme (eds), *Fashioning Old and New: Changing Consumer Preferences in Europe (Seventeenth – Nineteenth Centuries)* (Turnhout: Brepols, Studies in Urban History, 2009), pp. 159, 162–3.
86. For example, see J. Stobart and N. Raven, 'Introduction: Industrialization and Urbanization in a Regional Context', in J. Stobart and N. Raven (eds), *Towns, Regions and Industries, Urban and Industrial Change in the Midlands c. 1700–1840* (Manchester: Manchester University Press, 2005), p. 11, who exclude Herefordshire from their survey of the Midlands because of its proximity to and associations with central and southern Wales.
87. H. Barker, 'Catering for Provincial Tastes? Newspapers, Readers and Profit in Late Eighteenth-Century England', *Historical Research*, 69:168 (1996), pp. 55–7 for reasons for the dominance of the *Hereford Journal* in south Wales.
88. For instance, Thomas Freame opened a branch of his furniture manufactory in Hereford in 1817, after running a successful business in Worcester. He noted that his father had already previously served the neighbourhood, presumably from his Worcester shop. *Hereford Journal*, 28 May 1817.
89. By the mid-nineteenth century, Mingay notes that Herefordshire had the greatest number of gentry estates (£1,000–10,000 per annum) in England, along with Shropshire and Oxfordshire. G. E. Mingay (ed.), *The Agrarian History of England and Wales, Vol. VI, 1750–1850* (Cambridge: Cambridge University Press, 1989), p. 839.

90. G. Roberts, *The Shaping of Modern Hereford* (Almeley: Logaston Press, 2001), pp. 45, 47.
91. Ibid., pp. 48–50.
92. Ibid., pp. 105, 133.
93. *Pigot and Co.'s, National and Commercial Directory and Topography ... for Herefordshire, 1822* (London: James Pigot and Co., 1822), p. 72.
94. *Hunt & Co.'s Commercial Directory; for the Cities of Gloucester, Hereford, and Worcester ...* (London: E. Hunt & Co., 1847).
95. K. Coburn (ed.), *The Letters of Sarah Hutchinson from 1800 to 1835* (London: Routledge & Kegan Paul, 1954), pp. 284 and 364.
96. See J. Thirsk, 'Popular Consumption and the Mass Market in the Sixteenth to Eighteenth Centuries', *Material History Bulletin*, 31 (1990), pp. 51–8, p. 56, who speculates that if gentry were resident in a local area, the population in general would enjoy a better service from shopkeepers and pedlars.
97. Cox, *The Complete Tradesman*, pp. 67–70.
98. Hereford City Quarter Session Papers, Mayors Court, 24 February 1812[?], Herefordshire Record Office [hereafter HRO].
99. For example, see Herefordshire Quarter Session Minute Book, vol. 17, 1803, p. 58, HRO. At Easter 1803, Peter Williams, prison tailor, was awarded a bill for £2 8 0 for 'making prisoners cloaths [*sic*]', Richard Barrol, being awarded a bill for £6 6 5 for cloth for the prisoners' dresses.
100. Hereford City Quarter Session Papers, Mayors Court, 12 November 1804, HRO. For another salesman, see Richard Baldwyn, Herefordshire Quarter Session Minute Book, vol. 20, 1814, p. 118.
101. *Hereford Journal*, 30 April 1828. Bishop was noted as a salesman in Pigot's *Directory* of 1822, Turner as a tailor in the same directory.
102. *Hereford Journal*, 30 April 1828.
103. Ibid., 21 October 1840.
104. Ibid., 7 May 1845 and 15 October 1845.
105. Ibid., 5 March 1845.
106. See M. Tebbutt, *Making Ends Meet, Pawnbroking and Working-Class Credit* (London: Methuen, 1984), p. 123. There had been a Jewish community in Hereford during the medieval period. In the seventeenth and eighteenth centuries, the Jewish quarter was near Blue School Lane and the City Walls Road. See Roberts, *The Shaping of Modern Hereford*, pp. 18 and 66. However, both Exon and Myer were not born in Herefordshire, having settled their recently. See HRO, 1841 Census. No census listing was found for Lazarus, although it was noted in the *Hereford Journal*, 30 July 1834, that he had been in Hereford for twenty-three years. Myer stated that his business was founded in 1812. See *Hereford Journal*, 3 March 1847.
107. *Hereford Journal*, 20 May 1846.
108. *Hunt & Co.'s Commercial Directory*, 1847.
109. *Hereford Journal*, 29 May 1816.
110. See A. Backhouse, *The Worm-Eaten Waistcoat* (York: A R Backhouse, 2003), p. 25, for Fettes, where she notes that 75 per cent of all pledges were for adult clothing. See also A. Tomkins, *The Experience of Urban Poverty, 1723–82, Parish, Charity and Credit* (Manchester: Manchester University Press, 2007), pp. 213– 29; and A. Ribeiro, 'Provision of Ready-Made and Second-Hand Clothing ', p. 88 and figure 21, for London examples.

111. See *Pigot's Directory,* 1835, p. 86, where the figures for the 1831 census are cited. The approximate population of the county was 110,000, of whom just over 10,000 lived in Hereford.
112. *Hereford Journal,* 15 March 1837.
113. For example, in Ledbury, Levi Hooper is noted in *Holden's Annual Directory* (1817), as a pawnbroker. In Pigot's *Directory* of 1835 he is listed as a clothes and furniture broker.
114. See C. Roth, *The Rise of the Provincial Jewry. The Early History of the Jewish Communities in the English Countryside, 1740–1840* (London: The Jewish Monthly, 1950), pp. 67–70.
115. See Mingay, *Agrarian History,* pp. 696–8 and 1092–4 for Herefordshire. See J. Burnett, *A History of the Cost of Living* (Harmondsworth: Pelican, 1969), pp. 250–1; and E. Hopkins, *Birmingham: The First Manufacturing Town in the World, 1760–1840* (London: Weidenfeld & Nicholson, 1989), p. 152, for general wages.
116. For the tourist trade along the Wye Valley see J. Mitchell, *The Wye Tour and its Artists* (Almeley: Logaston Press, 2010).
117. Mitchell, *The Wye Tour,* pp. 36–8.
118. *Hereford Journal,* 13 January 1830.
119. Ibid., 4 October 1815 and 16 March 1814. The partnership between James Morgan and his son Nathaniel was dissolved in 1812, James having been in business for upwards of fifty years. *Hereford Journal,* 15 January 1812.
120. Levitt, 'Cheap Mass-Produced Men's Clothing', p. 185.
121. Herefordshire Quarter Session Minute Book, Vol. 24, 1842, no page number, HRO.
122. 'Calendar of the Prisoners to be tried at the Michelmas ... Sessions', 1845, HRO.
123. *Hereford Journal,* 22 August 1827.
124. *Berrow's Worcester Journal,* 13 April 1820.
125. B. Lemire, 'Developing Consumerism and the Ready-made Clothing Trade', pp. 36–8, 41. 'Day Book of 'G', a Manchester firm ... 1773–79', GB127.MS ff 657 D43, Greater Manchester County Record Office, details the ready-made dresses sold, including cotton and silk ones in a variety of colours, for example, pink and white, blue and white, 'straw', red and purple, ranging in price from 8*s.* to 26*s.* They supplied drapers nationally and internationally although none were noted in Herefordshire and Worcestershire in the surviving pages of the day book.
126. R. Newman, a draper from the High Street, Worcester, advertised in 1845 along with his usual goods, 'About 250 mousseline de laine and cashmere dresses, 100 printed cambric dresses ...', *Berrow's Worcester Journal,* 3 April 1845.
127. *Pigot's Directories,* 1830 and 1844.
128. Board of Health Report, 1850, cited in B. Reay, *Rural Englands* (Basingstoke: Palgrave Macmillan, 2004), p. 107. See also *Hereford Journal,* 7 August 1850, for reportage on the same.
129. J. McCulloch, 'Some Aspects of Victorian Bromyard from the 1851 Census', in J. G. Hillaby and E. D. Pearson (eds), *Bromyard: A Local History* (Worcester: Bromyard and District Local History Society, 1970), p. 135.
130. Pigot's *Directory,* 1842, p. 2.
131. Mary Grice, clothes broker, 1822; Edward Hays, clothes dealer and tailor, 1822–50; Martha Hayes, clothes dealer, 1822–30; Sarah Hays, clothes dealer, 1830–35; Edward Jones, clothes dealer, tailor and draper, 1822–50; John Lane, clothes dealer, 1830–35; Martha Lane, clothes dealer and tailor, 1838–44; John Thorn, clothes dealer and tailor,

1842–44; Samuel Wil[l]cox, tailor and draper, salesman, 1822–44; Lucy Wilcox, tailor and clothes dealer, 1850. Source: Pigot's *Directories* 1822–50, Robson's *Directory* 1838.

132. This contrasts with one for every 1,800 people in the city of Worcester for 1820–1, although this may, of course, reflect the differences in the way that directory entries were compiled in various places, with Worcester clothes dealers under-represented and under counted in reality.

133. *Berrow's Worcester Journal*, 17 August 1837.

134. The Minute Book of the Bromyard Union 1836–38, p. 122, HRO, K42/1.

135. 'ATK Vale's bankruptcy, Bromyard, linen draper, hosier and haberdasher – sold by tender in 4 lots, stock sold subject to lowest discount from book price and payment in cash on delivery. Lot 1 – general assortment of drapery, £123 13s. 2d., Lot 2, ditto, £116 11s. 8d., Lot 3, ditto, £113 15s. 10d., Lot 4, ditto, £110 3s 3d'. *Berrow's Worcester Journal*, 8 June 1837. Unfortunately, the advertisement did not mention the items of ready-made clothing that he was meant to be producing.

136. *The Minute Book of the Bromyard Union 1836–8*, pp. 246–7, HRO, K42/1.

137. *Berrow's Worcester Journal*, 10 April 1834.

138. For example, see Lemire, *The Business of Everyday Life*, p. 133. The main exception to this is Fowler, 'Robert Mansbridge'.

139. F. M. Eden, *The State of the Poor. A History of the Labouring Classes in England with Parochial Reports,* A. G. L. Rogers, (ed.), (London: George Routledge & Sons Ltd, 1928), p. 108. See also Styles, 'Clothing the North', pp. 139–40, for comment on Eden's survey.

140. See Shammas, *The Pre-Industrial Consumer*, p. 127, who sees market accessibility effecting consumer expenditure, rural areas being more self-sufficient in the early modern period.

141. This is also the case in an early period. See Shammas, *The Pre-Industrial Consumer*, p. 240, who notes there were tailors in 80 per cent of all villages, the most common trade represented.

142. Evidence from the account books suggests that this may have been the business of Edward Steadman from Leintwardine. See Tailors Account Books, Brampton Bryan, 1834–50, HRO, E61/2/1–2. However, James Steadman was listed as a tailor in Leintwardine in Lascelles Survey of 1851. See *Directory and Gazetteer of Herefordshire* (Birmingham: Lascelles & Co., 1851).

143. Places were customers lived included: Obley, Hagley, Hopton Castle, Clungunford, Heath House, Bedstone, Buckton and Coxall, New Park, Brampton Bryan, Brampton Bryan Park, Brampton Bryan Heath, Wigmore, Stanage Castle, Weston, Stow, Leintwardine and Knighton.

144. Tailors Account Books, Brampton Bryan, 1834–50, HRO, E61/2/1–2.

145. A. Buck, 'Buying Clothes in Bedfordshire: Customers and Tradesmen, 1700–1800', *Textile History*, 22:2 (1991), p. 218.

146. Tailor's Accounts, Brampton Bryan, HRO, E61/2/2, no page number.

147. Fowler, 'Robert Mansbridge', p. 34, also notes this in her study.

148. *Lascelles Directory*, 1851, William Morgan was listed as a tailor and farmer in Lower Kinsham and likewise, Joseph Etherington in Luston, both in Herefordshire.

149. See below pp. 56–7.

150. See P. Clark, *The English Ale House, A Social History, 1200–1830* (Harlow: Longman, 1983), pp. 311–18, for further uses of the pub as a focus for local society and the emphasis on male customers.

151. In Tenbury, Samuel Wilden was noted as a tailor in Pigot's *Directories* of 1828 and 1835, but in *Robson's Commercial Directory* of 1838, also at the Union Tavern. Likewise in *Robson's Commercial Directory* of 1838, Charles Steward was a tailor, beer retailer and assurance agent, again in Tenbury. In Evesham, William Beach was noted as a tailor in 1828 in Pigot's *Directory* and in 1841 in *Bentley's History and Guide* was a beer seller too. Eight further examples have been found in *Bentley's History and Guide,* 1840–2, including some in small villages. In Herefordshire, Samuel Bullen was a tailor and victualler at the Crown & Anchor Inn, Lugwardine, Frederick Seall, a tailor and victualler at the Bullring, Kington, William Thomas, tailor, also a cider retailer and shopkeeper in Madley. All were listed in *Lascelles Directory* of 1851.

152. Reay, *Microhistories,* p. 22.

153. *Hereford Journal,* 4 November 1835 and 25 November 1835.

154. *Berrow's Worcester Journal,* 24 June 1830.

155. Account Book of Joseph Blewitt, 1816–29, WRO, 9600/9iii. See also glossary, p. 157.

156. Fowler, 'Robert Mansbridge', p. 35.

157. Account Book of Joseph Blewitt, 1826, p. 26, WRO 9600/9iii.

158. *Berrow's Worcester Journal,* 13 January 1820.

159. Ibid., 27 April 1820.

160. Ibid., 15 September 1836.

161. Pigot's *Directory,* 1828.

162. Tebbutt, *Making Ends Meet,* p. 22.

163. Mui and Mui, *Shops and Shopkeeping,* particularly pp. 47 and 135–40.

164. Parish of Ombersley, bill to overseers 1828, WRO, 3572/16. Population figure from *Bentley's History and Guide,* 1840–2.

165. Buck, 'Buying Clothes', pp. 229–33. Smock frocks in Bedfordshire were also priced starting at 4 shillings in the 1780s.

166. *Hereford Journal,* 2 November 1825.

167. For example, *Berrow's Worcester Journal,* 21 November 1816.

168. *Hereford Journal,* 16 March 1814.

169. *Berrow's Worcester Journal,* 2 May 1850.

170. For Stewkley see *The Aylesbury News,* 29 April 1843; for Wingrave see *The Aylesbury News,* 2 March 1844.

171. See A. Smart Martin, 'Ribbons of Desire: Gendered Stories in the World of Goods', in J. Styles and A. Vickery (eds), *Gender, Taste and Material Culture in Britain and North America, 1700–1830* (London: Yale University Press, 2007), p. 191, for women exchanging eggs and chickens for textiles and durable goods at rural stores in eighteenth-century America.

172. *Worcestershire ... Directory for 1820* (Lewis), *Bentley's History and Guide, 1840–2.*

173. See K. D. M. Snell, *Annals of the Labouring Poor, Social Change and Agrarian England 1660–1900* (Cambridge: Cambridge University Press, 1985), ch. 1.

174. See above, pp. 23–4, for the limitations of using trade directory evidence.

175. Worcestershire Quarter Session Papers, WRO, 1/650/211–12 and Worcestershire Quarter Session Order Book, Vol. 11, p. 62a, 1822.

176. J. Tozer and S. Levitt, *Fabric of Society, A Century of People and their Clothes, 1770–1870* (Carno: Laura Ashley, 1983), pp. 78–80.

177. See ch. 4, pp. 98 and 99–100, for examples in the villages of Castlemorton and Abbey Dore.

178. For example, Rev. Witts and his wife went shopping in Cheltenham in May 1830. See D. Verey (ed.), *The Diary of a Cotswold Parson, Reverend F. E. Witts, 1783–1854* (Stroud: Sutton Publishing Ltd, 2003), p. 79.
179. Styles, 'Clothing the North', p. 157.
180. *Berrow's Worcester Journal,* 13 December 1849.
181. Ibid., 21 November 1816.
182. See Introduction p. 8.
183. See Introduction, p. 10.
184. This contrasts with the view of A. J. Kershen, 'Morris Cohen and the Origins of the Women's Wholesale Clothing Industry in the East End', *Textile History*, 28:1 (1999), pp. 39, 42, who claims that in the first half of the nineteenth century, working-class females dressed in cast-offs, cobbled together, or second-hand clothes, only the middle classes using dressmakers. She argues that it was not until the early twentieth century that such consumers could concern themselves with fashion and style, not solely price. See Ginsberg, 'The Tailoring and Dressmaking Trades', p. 69, for comments about difficulties of dressmaking in relation to the complex and elaborate fashions of the period.
185. See Smart Martin, 'Ribbons of Desire', pp. 181–2, for an interesting discussion about American rural female shoppers in the eighteenth century. Smart Martin notes the awe shown a shopkeeper by an ordinary customer, recorded in the journal of a wealthy merchant's daughter. She speculates about the control of the shopkeeper over the goods offered for sale to ordinary customers, although notes that these observations were written for comic effect.
186. Styles, 'Clothing the North', p. 150.
187. *Berrow's Worcester Journal*, 14 July and 25 July 1825. Jones was also in court answering other theft charges.
188. T. C. Whitlock, *Crime, Gender and Consumer Culture in Nineteenth Century England* (Aldershot: Ashgate, 2005), particularly pp. 150–70. See also, S. Ticknell, 'The Prevention of Shoplifting in Eighteenth-Century London', *Journal of Historical Research in Marketing*, 2:3 (2010), pp. 300–13.
189. Whitlock, *Crime, Gender and Consumer Culture,* pp. 162–3, for the case of Mrs Winnall.
190. Fowler, 'Robert Mansbridge', p. 31.
191. Riello, *A Foot in the Past*, p. 126.
192. Ibid., p. 127.

2 The Shopkeeper and the Working-Class Consumer

1. For a definition of 'salesmen', see glossary, p. 158.
2. Parish Accounts of St Martins, Worcester, Bill to Overseers from Thomas Freame, 1798, Worcestershire Record Office [hereafter WRO], 5234/14.
3. *Berrow's Worcester Journal*, 13 December 1804, for announcement of his imminent retirement.
4. Ibid., 14 September 1809.
5. Ibid., 5 October 1809.
6. Ibid., 9 April 1807.
7. Ibid., 28 September 1809.
8. Ibid., 10 May 1810.

9. *Worcester Royal Directory for the Year 1794* (Worcester: J. Grundy, 1794), p. 38, the Fraternity of Taylors was instituted in 1504 and incorporated by charter in 1551.
10. *Berrow's Worcester Journal*, 7 June 1810. He does not appear in the list of Master Tailors of Worcester that was published in the same edition of the newspaper.
11. *Berrow's Worcester Journal*, 21 June 1810.
12. C. Walsh, 'Shop Design and the Display of Goods in Eighteenth-Century London', in J. Benson and G. Shaw (eds), *The Retailing Industry Volume 1, Perspectives and the Early Modern Period* (London: IB Tauris, 1999), pp. 380–1.
13. See Riello, *A Foot in the Past*, p. 95.
14. P. J. Corfield, *The Impact of English Towns 1700–1800* (Oxford: Oxford University Press, 1982), pp. 87–90.
15. *Berrow's Worcester Journal*, 28 June 1810.
16. See P. Hudson, 'Proto-industrialization: the Case of the West Riding Wool Textile Industry in the Eighteenth and Early Nineteenth Centuries', *History Workshop Journal*, 12 (1981), pp. 39–40
17. Worcester City Records, Minutes of the Company of Master Tailors, WRO, C9, Shelf 647, Box 1.
18. *Berrow's Worcester Journal*, 30 April 1812, 9 July 1812.
19. Ibid., 9 and 16 February 1815.
20. Ibid., 26 October 1815 and 23 November 1815.
21. Ibid., 4 April 1811.
22. Ibid., 8 June 1820. A billhead from 1817 also described him as a linen and woollen draper, hatter and hosier with no mention of being a salesman. Collection of George Marshall Bills, 1817, WRO, 9937/2/280 no. 189.
23. *Berrow's Worcester Journal*, 21 October 1830.
24. Ibid., 27 October 1831 and 19 January 1832.
25. Ibid., 7 May 1829.
26. Ibid., 23 May 1844.
27. Zakim, *Ready-Made Democracy*, p. 38.
28. *Worcestershire ... Directory for 1820* (Lewis).
29. *Berrow's Worcester Journal*, 9 June 1825.
30. Mui and Mui, *Shops and Shopkeeping*, p. 21. Other drapers in Worcester appealed to country shopkeepers as wholesalers. For example, William Miles, a linen draper and silk mercer sold his stock at 20 per cent off seeking the attention of 'country shopkeepers'. See *Berrow's Worcester Journal*, 13 July 1820.
31. Hindlip Parish Records, Bill from Stephen Burden, 1822, WRO, 8669/6i–70.
32. The Acts were meant to correct abuses of the Poor Law and address concern about high relief expenditure by changing the voting system for rate-payers which determined policy. Poor Law functions were to be transferred to a smaller elected body, a select vestry, enabling close scrutiny of claimants and tighter control of relief budgets. See King, *Poverty and Welfare in England*, pp. 26–7.
33. In a bill to the parish of Hindlip in 1814, Burden has a printed billhead where he describes himself as a 'Woollen & Linen Draper, Hatter, Hosier &c', an elaborate scroll beside, listing the type of stock that he sold, 'executed by an experienced foreman from London'. However, he does not mention his ready-made clothing stocks. See Hindlip Parish Records, WRO, 8669/6iii–25. A bill from Richard Sanders in 1818, in contrast, is completely handwritten and has no further details apart from the ready-made clothing that was sold. See Bill from Richard Sanders to the parish of Hindlip, Hindlip Parish Records, WRO, 8669/6/ii–81.

34. In *Pigot and Co.'s, National and Commercial Directory and Topography for Worcestershire ... 1828* (London: James Pigot and Co.), and thereafter in the Worcester trade directories, Burden was listed as a tailor and woollen draper.

35. Richard Sanders, Bills and Receipts, 3 February 1837, WRO, 2193/77 iv.

36. Bill from John Sanders to the Parish of St. Helen's, Worcester, 1844, WRO, 4426/17.

37. Bill from Richard Sanders to the parish of Hindlip, 1818, Hindlip Parish Records, WRO, 8669/6/ii–81.

38. Richard Sanders, Papers, bill, 1836, WRO, 2193/77 iv.

39. Richard Sanders, Papers, bills 1836 and 1837, WRO, 2193/77 iv. William Anthony and Charles Cross were previously in business together as Cross and Anthony, Manufacturers and Calico Printers, 55 High Street, Manchester, for much of the 1820s. See, for example, *Pigot and Son's General Directory of Manchester, Salford &c.* (Manchester: J. Pigot and Sons, 1830).

40. In *Pigot and Co.'s, National and Commercial Directory and Topography... for Herefordshire ... Worcestershire ... Gloucestershire, 1842* (London: James Pigot and Co., 1842), Stanley Mills were located in Stroud, Gloucestershire, although under different ownership by 1842. Stephens was noted as having depôts in Manchester and Scotland. See J. de L. Mann, *The Cloth Industry in the West of England from 1640 to 1880* (Oxford: Clarendon, 1971), p. 224.

41. Richard Sanders, Papers, bill, 1836, WRO, 2193/77 iv.

42. Richard Sanders was listed as a salesman in Pigot's *Directory,* 1828. During the 1830s he was variously listed as a draper, tailor and silk mercer. John Hawkes Sander was listed as a salesman and clothes dealer in *Hayward's Directory of the City and Borough of Worcester* (Worcester: R. Haywood, 1840).

43. His clothing warehouse was noted on his printed billhead, see Billhead for Richard Sanders, 3 February 1837, WRO, 2193/77 iv.

44. WRO, Worcestershire Census, 1841.

45. See bill from James Walter, Worcester, 1833, to the parish of Hindlip, where clothing sold included gowns for 3 shillings and 3s 6d and stays for 2 shillings, Hindlip, Parish Records, WRO, 8669/6i– 39; William Spriggs sold a blue broadcloth frock coat for a servant for £1 15s, a 'stripe twiced nankeen jackt' for 7s. 6d. and fustian gaitors for 2 shillings. See bill from William Spriggs, Worcester, 1835, WRO, Nott Family Records, 3164/20. Both these bills were completely handwritten, unlike Stephen Burden's. See A. Toplis, 'The Non-Elite Consumer and "Wearing Apparel" in Herefordshire and Worcestershire, 1800–1850' (PhD dissertation, University of Wolverhampton, 2008), figures 2.1–2.4, for reproductions of the bills.

46. 'Particular attention paid to the workmanship of the ready-made article – the lowest price that can be afforded for ready money', *Berrow's Worcester Journal*, 14 July 1831.

47. See *Berrow's Worcester Journal*, 13 September 1849, for a court case where a tramp called James Campbell stole a plaid cotton jacket from Mr Spriggs, the shop ticket that had been hung on the jacket being found in Campbell's possession.

48. In *Berrow's Worcester Journal,* 2 March 1837, Walters was described as 'as one of the most respected citizens of Worcester'.

49. *Hereford Journal*, 19 January 1820.

50. Ibid., 8 November 1820.

51. Ibid., 6 August 1823.

52. Ibid., 23 February 1842 and 12 April 1848, and *Directory and Gazetteer of Herefordshire* (Birmingham: Lascelles & Co., 1851).

53. Captain Nicholas Patershall was listed under the section for 'Gentry, Nobility and Clergy', in the directories of the period, with a house in St Owen Street in the 1830s, moving to Milk Lane and Offa Street in the 1840s and 1850s.

54. Bills of Captain Patershall, 5 March 1825, Herefordshire Record Office, [hereafter HRO], F60/26.

55. Bills of Captain Patershall, 1826–F60/51, 1827–F60/82, 1829–F60/187, 1834–F60/474, 1835–F60/564, HRO.

56. Bills of Captain Patershall, F60/34, 1826 and F60/171, 1829, HRO.

57. See Lemire, *Fashion's Favourite*, p. 69. See also Lambert, 'Cast-off Wearing Apparell', pp. 11–12, who notes James Boswell sold his suit in 1763.

58. See B. Lemire, 'Consumerism in Pre-Industrial and Early Industrial England, The Trade in Second Hand Clothes', *Journal of British Studies*, 27:1 (1988), pp. 1–24, on p. 10.

59. *Hereford Journal*, 24 March 1830 and 21 July 1830.

60. Ibid., 12 October 1831, 14 November 1832.

61. Buck also records the practice of gentry buying from drapers and tailors in their local market towns. See Buck, 'Buying Clothes in Bedfordshire', p. 220.

62. Riello, *A Foot in the Past*, p. 127.

63. *Berrow's Worcester Journal*, 24 April 1817, 6 November 1817, 29 October 1818, 21 January 1819, 21 October 1819, each a different auction. See Charpy, 'The Scope and Structure of the Nineteenth-Century Second-Hand Trade in the Parisian Clothes Market', p. 132, for slightly later similar French auctions, where the uniform was altered and recycled for civilian use.

64. *Hereford Journal*, 15 April 1818.

65. Ibid., 15 March 1820

66. Ibid., 9 July 1823 and 23 July 1823.

67. Ibid., 29 September 1830.

68. Ibid., 5 September 1828.

69. See above, p. 47.

70. *Hereford Journal*, 26 March 1828.

71. Ibid., 29 February 1832 and 26 April 1837.

72. Ibid., 8 May 1839.

73. Ibid., 20 October 1839.

74. Ibid., 15 April 1840.

75. Whitlock, *Crime, Gender and Consumer Culture*, pp. 218–19.

76. *Hereford Journal*, 2 December 1840.

77. Ibid., 19 May 1841.

78. Ibid.

79. For example, St. Peter's, Hereford, Overseers' Accounts, 1827–48, 4 December 1828, 'Bosworth for cloaths for James Morgan, 7/6', HRO, AR77/19.

80. For example:

    'And if my endeavours to please should succeed,
    In my shop you'll just venture to peep,
    My goods then before you I'll cheerfully spread,
    And care not how many you sweep ...
    I've Shoes in which Laplanders trudg'd in the snow,
    French Clogs and old Moorish Slippers,
    I've Archenfield's famous long Arrows and Bows,

And Check Aprons for scolding House-keepers ...
I'm ready to Purchase, to Sell, or Exchange,
Any Article new or antique;
I've Hundreds of Grates from plain bars to the range,
And Books both in Latin and Greek ...
What strange Dresses and Coats do pray come and see 'em,
I've arranged them in different niches,
But the chief curiosity in my museum,
Is the late Parson H – 's Breeches ...

81. *Hereford Journal,* 29 September 1841.
82. Ibid., 6 April 1842.
83. Ibid., 29 March 1843.
84. P. Sharpe, '"Cheapness and Economy": Manufacturing and Retailing Ready-made Clothing in London and Essex, 1830–50', *Textile History*, 26:2 (1995), pp. 203–13, for a history of Hyams. She notes that they had a retail shop in Bristol by 1845. See also Sharpe, *Adapting to Capitalism*, pp. 65–8.
85. S. Chapman, 'The Innovating Entrepreneurs in the British Ready-made Clothing Industry', *Textile History*, 24:1 (1993), pp. 14–22, for Moses. See S. Levitt, 'Bristol Clothing Trades and Exports in the Georgian Period', in *Per Una Storia della Moda Pronta, Problemi e Richerchi, Atti del v Convegno Internazionale del CISST, Milano, 26–28 Febbraio 1990* (Florence: Edifir Edizioni, 1991), pp. 39–40.
86. *Hereford Journal,* 12 April 1843.
87. Kershen, *Uniting the Tailors*, p. 4.
88. *Bucks Herald*, 10 October 1840.
89. *Hereford Journal*, 19 April 1843.
90. Ibid., 26 April 1843.
91. Lemire, 'Redressing the History of the Clothing Trade in England', p. 68, for similar advertising sentiments relating to eighteenth-century petticoat production.
92. Sharpe, 'Cheapness and Economy', p. 211.
93. *Hereford Journal*, 17 May 1843.
94. See Whitlock, *Crime, Gender and Consumer Culture*, p. 73.
95. *Hereford Journal,* 19 July 1843. By 1851, Evans had settled with his family in the High Street, Cheltenham, noted as a draper in the 1851 census. See 1851 Census.
96. Ibid., 14 August 1844 and 20 November 1844.
97. Ibid., 18 October 1848.
98. Ibid., 9 April 1845. John Jones, a tailor, advertised that he was moving 'next door but one to Green Dragon...' in Broad Street in the *Hereford Journal*, 6 June 1825. He was listed in *Hunt & Co.'s Commercial Directory*, as a clothes dealer.
99. *Hereford Journal,* 6 December 1848.
100. Ibid.,28 March 1849.
101. Ibid., 12 September 1849.
102. See also A. Toplis, 'Ready-Made Clothing Advertisements in Two Provincial Newspapers, 1800–1850', *International Journal of Regional and Local Studies*, Series 2, 5:1 (2009), pp. 85–103.
103. Mui and Mui, *Shops and Shopkeeping*, p. 246. Also J. Stobart, 'In and Out of Fashion? Advertising Novel and Second-hand Goods in Georgian England', in Blondé *et al.* (eds), *Fashioning Old and New: Changing Consumer Preferences in Europe (Seventeenth – Nine-*

teenth Centuries) (Turnhout: Brepols, Studies in Urban History, 1100–1800, 18, 2009), pp. 137, 141.

104. V. Morgan, 'Beyond the Boundary of the Shop: Retail Advertising Spaces in Eighteenth Century Provincial England', in J. Benson and L. Ugolini (eds), *Cultures of Selling: Perspectives on Consumption and Society since 1700* (Aldershot: Ashgate, 2006), pp. 59–79, especially pp. 69–74 and 77–8.

105. T. Nevett, 'Advertising and Editorial Integrity in the Nineteenth Century', in M. Harris and A. Lee (eds), *The Press in English Society from the Seventeenth to the Nineteenth Centuries* (London: Rutherford, 1986), p. 152.

106. I. Asquith, 'The Structure, Ownership and Control of the Press, 1780–1855', in G. Boyce, J. Curran and P. Wingate (eds), *Newspaper History from the Seventeenth Century to the Present Day* (London: Constable (etc.) for the Press Group of the Acton Society, 1978), p. 112.

107. Cox, *The Complete Tradesman*, pp. 108–10. See also V. Berridge, 'Content Analysis and Historical Research on Newspapers', in Harris, and Lee, (eds), *The Press in English Society from the Seventeenth to the Nineteenth Centuries* (London: Rutherford, 1986), pp. 201–18, on p. 214.

108. See Barker, *Business of Women*, p. 84, for comment.

109. M. C. Finn, *The Character of Credit, Personal Debt in English Culture 1740–1914* (Cambridge: Cambridge University Press, 2003), pp. 89–91.

110. Asquith, 'The Structure, Ownership and Control of the Press', pp. 100–1,114.

111. See R. C. Gaut, *A History of Worcestershire Agriculture and Rural Evolution* (Worcester: Littlebury, 1939), p. 260, who notes a weekly newspaper was taken by a lawyer in Wribbenhall in 1830 which was then read out every Thursday night by the parish clerk in the local pub. Also, Gwilliam, *Old Worcester*, p. 39, who cite examples of newspapers being read in Worcester pubs in the nineteenth century.

112. *Hereford Journal*, 13 September 1820.

113. Ibid., 8 December 1847.

114. *Berrow's Worcester Journal,* 16 July 1835, 'two glasses of gin a day for a year at 3½d per glass will cost a sum which will purchase [clothing including] two shirts, two pairs of hose, two pairs of shoes, a fustian jacket, a waistcoat, a pair of trowsers [*sic*] ... a flannel waistcoat, a coarse cloth cloak, a neckcloth'.

115. *Berrow's Worcester Journal*, 27 August 1830.

116. For examples, see above, pp. 28 and 53. Also Reay, *Microhistories*, for a discussion about literacy in this period, including mixed literacy within families and the ability to read but not write, pp. 235–53.

117. H. Barker, *Newspapers, Politics and English Society, 1695–1855* (Harlow: Longman, 2000), p. 63. See also pp. 50–4, 61–4, idem, for discussion about working-class accessibility to newspapers during this period.

118. See above, pp. 47–8.

119. See, for example, *Berrow's Worcester Journal,* 8 June 1820.

120. *Hereford Journal,* 28 February 1849, 24 January 1849.

121. See above, pp. 49–50.

122. See above, p. 52–3.

123. *Hereford Journal,* 25 April 1832.

124. See Introduction above, p. 1, for servants as consumers.

125. Smith, *The Natural History of the Gent*, pp. 94–5,

126. *Berrow's Worcester Journal,* 3 January 1850. See also illustration of 'Allins Cheap Clothes & York Shoe Warehouse', Birmingham, illustration 26 in Lemire, *Fashion's Favourite, verso* p. 181.

127. *Berrow's Worcester Journal,* 11 April 1844.

128. *Hereford Journal,* 18 March 1846.

129. See Walsh, 'Shop Design', pp. 378–80.

130. *Worcestershire ... Directory for 1820* (Lewis), inserted between pp. 50–1.

131. See M. Berg, *Luxury and Pleasure in Eighteenth Century Britain* (Oxford: Oxford University Press, 2005), pp. 272–7, for an interesting discussion about trade card advertising.

132. Morgan, 'Beyond the Boundary', pp. 64–5.

133. Whitlock, *Crime, Gender and Consumer Culture,* pp. 35–6, especially n. 80.

134. Ibid., particularly pp. 87–8, 90, 100.

135. A copy of half of the same trade card is in the John Johnson Collection, Bodleian Library. It has been catalogued as belonging to James Barnett Lillington of Birmingham although the address on the sign and the complete double page advertisement (see Figure 2.1) would definitely suggest it was Richard Lillington's from Worcester, at No. 4, Broad Street. See J. A. Lambert, *A Nation of Shopkeepers, Trade Ephemera from 1654 to the 1860s in the John Johnson Collection* (Oxford: Bodleian Library, Exhibition Catalogue, 2001), entry no. 164, pp. 80–1.

136. *Berrow's Worcester Journal,* 22 February 1816. Lillington commenced business in his own account after splitting from a partnership with W. Whitehead, glover, who carried on business separately.

137. *Berrow's Worcester Journal,* 2 November 1837. Charles Mackintosh, a Glasgow born Manchester mill owner, patented the fabric in 1825. Lillington was selling Mackintoshes by 1830, *Berrow's Worcester Journal,* 18 November 1830.

138. *Berrow's Worcester Journal,* 21 May 1840. Zephyr appears to have been a waterproof lightweight checked woollen fabric.

139. For example, see *Berrow's Worcester Journal,* 24 April 1845.

140. *Berrow's Worcester Journal,* 5 November 1846.

141. See S. Chapman, 'The "Revolution" in the Manufacture of Ready-made Clothing 1840–1860', *London Journal,* 29:1 (2004), p. 50 and above p. 53.

142. Chapman, 'The Innovating Entrepreneurs', particularly p. 12, for an illustration of Nicoll's shop.

143. Riello, *A Foot in the Past,* pp. 42–3.

144. Ibid., pp. 56–7.

145. Advertisements first appeared for 'Nicols' Paletôts to be purchased direct from London in 1849 after Lillington had retired. *Berrow's Worcester Journal,* 20 September 1849 and *Hereford Journal,* 19 September 1849.

146. *Hunt & Co.'s Commercial Directory,* pp. 151, 160.

147. Jacob Moses was a clothes dealer with a shop in the Market Place, Ross, by 1847. Israel Moses was listed as a pawnbroker, 199 High St, Cheltenham in 1842 and likewise, Moses Moses & Son [*sic*], pawnbrokers in Gloucester. See *Hunt & Co's Commercial Directory,* 1847 and Pigot's *Directory,* 1842.

148. See Kingsley, 'Cheap Clothes and Nasty', pp. 97–8. See also Chapman, 'The "Revolution" in the Manufacture of Ready-made Clothing', pp. 51–2, for the design of Moses's ostentatious shop building and interior.

149. Winstanley, *The Shopkeeper's World,* p. 10.

150. For example, see Edward Jones, 'Clothing Establishment' in Hereford, *Hereford Journal*, 29 March 1843; also Edward Meates, Worcester, previously a draper, a 'Ready-Made Clothes and Smock Frock Warehouse', bill to overseers, 8 December 1832, Ombersley Parish Accounts, WRO, 3572/16.

151. Deceulaer has linked the development of the ready-made clothing industry in the Low Countries to demand from local rural markets, see H. Deceulaer, 'Second-Hand Dealers in the Early Modern Low Countries, Institutions, Markets and Practices', in L. Fontaine (ed.), *Alternative Exchanges, Second-hand Circulations from the Sixteenth Century to the Present* (Oxford: Berghahn Books, 2008) pp. 28–9.

152. Chapman, *Merchant Enterprise in Britain*, p. 168.

153. Ibid., p. 168.

154. *Hereford Journal*, 12 April 1843 for Evan's prices; Eden, *The State of the Poor*, p. 110.

155. See Chapman, 'The "Revolution" in the Manufacture of Ready-made Clothing', p. 49. See also Chapter 5, p. 124, for local comments.

3 Selling by Non-Fixed Traders

1. Spufford, *The Great Re-clothing of Rural England*.

2. Mui and Mui, *Shops and Shopkeeping*, ch. 4.

3. Blondé *et al.*, 'Retail Circuits', pp. 8 and 11.

4. Shammas, *The Pre-Industrial Consumer in England and America*, pp. 286–7, for figures of Worcestershire licensed pedlars in the seventeenth and eighteenth centuries; Alexander, *Retailing in England*, pp. 63–5. See also J. Benson and L. Ugolini, 'Beyond the Shop: Problems and Possibilities', *Journal of Historical Marketing*, 2:3 (2010), p. 258, for summary of licensed numbers in the eighteenth and nineteenth centuries.

5. H. Deceulaer, 'Dealing with Diversity: Pedlars in the Southern Netherlands in the Eighteenth Century', in B. Blondé, P. Stabel, I. Van Damme and J. Stobart (eds), *Buyers and Sellers: Retail Circuits and Practices in Medieval and Early Modern Europe* (Turnhout: Brepols, 2006) p. 172.

6. D. Brown, 'Persons of Infamous Character' or 'an Honest, Industrious and Useful Description of People'? The Textile Pedlars of Alstonfield and the Role of Peddling in Industrialization', *Textile History*, 31:1 (2000), pp. 1–26, pp. 3 and 24.

7. Ibid., p. 5. See also S. Jaumain, 'Un Métier Oublié: Le Colporteur dans La Belgique du XIXe Siècle', *Belgisch Tijdschrift voor Nieuwste Geschiedenis*, 16: 3–4 (1985), pp. 309–12, for discussion of similar problems of definition.

8. *Berrow's Worcester Journal*, 11 May 1809. See glossary, p. 158, for a definition of habit clothes.

9. *Berrow's Worcester Journal*, 19 May 1803.

10. D. R. Green, 'Street Trading in London: A Case Study of Casual Labour, 1830–1860', and J. Benson, 'Retailing', both in J. Benson and G. Shaw (eds), *The Retailing Industry, Volume 2, The Coming of the Mass Market, 1800–1945* (London: IB Tauris, 1999), pp. 118–21, 134–5. Also J. Benson, *The Penny Capitalists, A Study of Nineteenth-Century Working-Class Entrepreneurs* (Dublin: Gill and Macmillan, 1983), especially pp. 99–102.

11. A letter to the *Hereford Journal* from 4 March 1835 complains about the flood of Irish vagrants into the county.

12. Deceulaer, 'Dealing with Diversity', p. 180.

13. *Berrow's Worcester Journal*, 6 April 1843.

14. Ibid., 4 July 1844.

15. D. Hey, *Packmen, Carriers and Packhorse Roads, Trade and Communications in North Derbyshire and South Yorkshire* (Leicester: Leicester University Press, 1980), p. 210. See also Clark, *The English Ale House*, pp. 306 and 315. Also pp. 36–7, above.

16. See Elson, *The Last of the Climbing Boys*, pp. 10–11. Their emphasis was on stock for female consumers.
17. Alexander, *Retailing in England*, p. 66.
18. Out letter Book of the Board of Stamps, 1831–6, 29 March 1832, National Archives, Kew [hereafter NA], IR51/6, pp. 33–4.
19. See *Hereford Journal*, 2 November 1831.
20. Ann Clements was noted as a staymaker in *Pigot and Co.'s, National and Commercial Directory and Topography ... for Worcestershire ... 1828* (London: James Pigot and Co.) at 62 Broad Street; Bennett and Batchelor were noted as woollen drapers and tailors in *Pigot and Co.'s, National and Commercial Directory and Topography ... for Worcestershire ... 1835* (London: James Pigot and Co.), at the same address, which suggests that McGedy may have been working in the clothing trades.
21. Entry Book of Letters between the Treasury and Board of Stamps, 1831–4, 20 March 1832, p. 29, and 31 March 1832, p. 37, NA, IR51/5. McGedy received the remission of the Crown's part of the penalty, that is £5.
22. *Berrow's Worcester Journal*, 20 May 1830.
23. 'Manchester Men' worked exclusively for one Manchester textile firm, acting as middlemen between the manufacturer and shop, and to a lesser extent pedlars. L. Fontaine, *History of Pedlars in Europe* (Cambridge: Polity, 1996), pp. 79 and 93. Clapham notes that they were disappearing by the 1820s, as selling by sample books took over. See J. H. Clapham, 'The Organization of Commerce', in Benson and Shaw, (eds), *The Retailing Industry, Volume 2*, p. 40. See pp. 77–9, for discussion of 'Scotch' and 'tally' men.
24. See R. B. Westerfield, *Middlemen in English Business Particularly Between 1660–1760* (New Haven, CT: Yale, 1915, reprint Newton Abbot: David and Charles, 1968), p. 316.
25. Worcestershire Quarter Session Papers, Worcestershire Record Office [hereafter WRO], 1821, 1/650/183.
26. *Hereford Journal*, 6 January 1830 and 13 January 1830.
27. See Chapter 2, p. 55.
28. *Hereford Journal*, 19 March 1845.
29. *Hereford Journal*, 1 March 1815. Several hawkers and pedlars were noted as travelling to many parts of Wales claiming to be the son of the late Hyam Barnett [a silversmith and jeweller of Hereford] with no authorization to do so. See also Elson, *The Last of the Climbing Boys*, pp. 257–8, who opened a haberdashers in Hereford in the 1860s. He was also an agent for the sale of maps, selling these in Monmouth, Brecon and 'beyond' Merthyr Tydfil.
30. Mingay (ed.), *The Agrarian History of England and Wales*, p. 246. See also T. Shakesheff, *Rural Conflict, Crime and Protest: Herefordshire 1800–1860* (Woodbridge: Boydell, 2003), p. 188, n. 48, for the 'Welshness' of Herefordshire in the south and west.
31. See example from 1775, I. Mitchell, 'The Development of Urban Retailing 1700–1815', in P. Clark (ed.), *The Transformation of English Provincial Towns 1600–1800* (London: Hutchinson, 1984), p. 262.
32. Quarter Session Papers, 1827, WRO, 1/674/99 and 106, and *Berrow's Worcester Journal*, 26 April 1827. Shopkeepers did not need a licence if they had a permanent shop.
33. See also Deceulaer, 'Dealing with Diversity', p. 176, for examples from the Netherlands.
34. Mui and Mui, *Shops and Shopkeeping*, ch. 4.

35. Alexander, *Retailing in England,* pp. 63–5. He suggests that the country trade declined to become an urban rather than a rural practise during the first half of the nineteenth century.
36. *Berrow's Worcester Journal,* 2 July 1840.
37. Ibid., 22 October 1846.
38. *A Concise History of the City and Suburbs of Worcester* (Worcester: T. Eaton, 1816), pp. 169–71. See Hey, *Packmen, Carriers and Packhorse Roads,* p. 204. This seems in direct contravention to the national acts passed in the 1780s to allow licensed hawkers to trade from shops. Presumably the local act became more difficult to enforce as the apprenticeship and guild system broke down completely after 1814. See p. 67 above and the case of Francis McGedy.
39. *A Concise History of the City and Suburbs of Worcester,* pp. 174–5.
40. Brown, 'Persons of Infamous Character', pp. 17–18.
41. Mingay, *The Agrarian History of England and Wales,* p. 859.
42. The Commissioners for Hawkers and Pedlars Licences were taken over by the Hackney Coach Office from 1 August 1810, see Minute Books of the Hackney Coach Commissioners, 1807–12, 10 October 1810, NA, IR51/2. The Stamp Office took over licences on the 1 August 1832, the start of the new year for issuing licences, see Out-letter Book of the Board of Stamps, 1831–6, 2 July 1832, NA, IR51/6, p. 49.
43. Treasury Letter Books of the Hackney Coach Commissioners, 1820–6, 25 April 1822, NA, IR51/3, p. 240.
44. Instead licence inspectors received a percentage for every licence sold and half the fine of a convicted hawker, usually the statutory £10. See Entry Book of Letters between the Treasury and Board of Stamps, 1831–4, NA, IR51/5, p. 385.
45. In 1834, a petition was made by an inspector asking for payment for any successful prosecution regardless of economic circumstances. It was refused by the Lords of the Treasury, see Entry Book of Letters between the Treasury and Board of Stamps, 1831–4, 24 April 1834, NA, IR51/5, p. 88.
46. Minute Books of the Hackney Coach Commissioners, 1807–12, 10 October 1810 re: Minutes from 18 September 1810, NA, IR51/2.
47. Out-letter Book of the Board of Stamps, 1831–6, 20 January 1832, NA, IR51/6, p. 15. See also 6 August 1833, p. 155.
48. Interestingly, at Flash in Leek, close to Alstonefield, where the evidence for pedlars has been gathered by Brown. Brown, 'Persons of Infamous Character', pp. 5–13.
49. Treasury Letter Books of the Hackney Coach Commissioners, 1820–6, NA, IR51/3, p. 212, approved by Lord Deerhurst, son of the Earl of Coventry, the local M.P. and Lord Lieutenant of Worcestershire, whose ancestral seat was Croome Court, near Severn Stoke.
50. Treasury Letter Books of the Hackney Coach Commissioners, 1820–6, NA, IR51/3, pp. 218–28, which list the names of all hawkers successfully prosecuted for contravening the licensing act between 1817 and 1822, although unfortunately no specification of wares were given.
51. Treasury Letter Books of the Hackney Coach Commissioners, 1820–6, NA, IR51/3, pp. 218–28, and Quarter Session Papers, WRO: Edward Swindley, Kidderminster, flannels, (1/650/179); Patrick Morgan, Lower Mitton, Irish Linen, (1/650/181); John Broadbent, Kidderminster, 'a parcel' of cloths and shawls, (1/650/183); Joseph Williams, Hagley, lace, cotton handkerchiefs and stays, (1/647/132).

52. Treasury Letter Books of the Hackney Coach Commissioners, 1820–6, 31 January 1820, NA, IR51/3, pp. 9–10.
53. See *Berrow's Worcester Journal*, 3 August 1820, for advertisement also highlighting the rules of the statute for licensing hawkers.
54. Quarter Session Papers, 1821, WRO, 1/650/179.
55. Ibid., 1821, WRO, 1/650/183.
56. Ibid., 1822, WRO, 1 /657/83.
57. Ibid., 1828, WRO, 1/679/171.
58. Out-letter Book of the Board of Stamps, 1831–6, 12 March 1836, NA, IR51/6, p. 304.
59. Out-letter Book of the Board of Stamps, 1831–6, 21 December 1831, NA, IR51/6, p. 3.
60. See *Bentley's History and Guide* (1840–2), and pp. 22–3 above.
61. Distributor of stamps were based in Hereford, Kington, Leominster and Ross, Entry Book of Deputations to Distributors of Stamps, 1832–60, 6 January 1832, NA, IR51/7, p. 7. Sub-Distributors were in Bromyard and Ledbury, Book of Deputations to Distributors of Stamps, 1832–60, 18 June 1832, NA, IR51/7, p. 38.
62. E. Pawson, *Transport and Economy: The Turnpike Roads of Eighteenth Century Britain* (London: Academic Press, 1977), pp. 96, 121, 155.
63. *Berrow's Worcester Journal*, 21 July 1825. It now took less than two hours and there was improvement across the county.
64. Spufford, *The Great Re-Clothing of Rural England*, pp. 72, 161–2.
65. *Hereford Journal*, 13 July 1831.
66. Ibid., 24 July 1833.
67. Ibid., 17 May 1826. A similar advertisement was placed by Scotland House run by James Pitt in 1831. See *Hereford Journal*, 16 November 1831.
68. Broadway Parish Records, Examination of William Shorey, 29 October 1810, WRO, 4869/6/iv. He traded for three years before becoming a toll collector on the Hampton and Winchcombe turnpike.
69. Deceulaer, 'Dealing with Diversity', p. 190.
70. See *Worcestershire ... Directory for 1820* (Lewis), and *Bentley's History and Guide, 1840–2*. See also Chapter 1, pp. 33–5.
71. Quarter Session Papers, 1821, WRO, 1/647/132.
72. Ibid., 1826, WRO, 1/672/168.
73. Ibid., 1839, WRO, 1/732/240.
74. Ibid., 1848, WRO, 1/774/702.
75. P. Hurle, *Castlemorton Farmer, John Rayner Lane 1798–1871* (Storridge: P. Hurle, 1996), p. 23.
76. J. Styles, 'Clothing the North', p. 150.
77. *Hereford Journal*, 14 August 1844.
78. I have found only two examples of male clothing, neither from prosecutions of unlicensed hawkers. Lloyd Pugh hawked waistcoat and breeches pieces around Staffordshire and Worcestershire, see Quarter Session Papers, Examination of Lloyd Pugh, 1809, WRO, 1/597/71. Also Bartholomew Connell, a hawker, allegedly sold stockings and trousers in a counterfeit money case in Kidderminster, see *Berrow's Worcester Journal*, 25 July 1850.
79. *Worcestershire ... Directory for 1820* (Lewis) and *Hunt & Co.'s Commercial Directory* (1847).

80. Quarter Session Papers, 1824, WRO, 1/663/143, and *Worcestershire ... Directory for 1820* (Lewis).
81. Mui and Mui, *Shops and Shopkeeping*, p. 41.
82. Such a stick survives in Hereford County Museum, accession number 627, dated to the early nineteenth century.
83. M. Finn, 'Scotch Drapers and the Politics of Modernity: Gender, Class and National Identity in the Victorian Tally Trade', in M. J. Daunton and M. Hilton (eds), *The Politics of Consumption: Material Culture and Citizenship in Europe and America* (Oxford: Berg, 2001), pp. 93–4.
84. Quarter Session Papers, 1848, WRO, 1/774/702. According to the newspaper report about his case, he was only caught when another hawker whom he refused to deal with informed on him. See *Berrow's Worcester Journal*, 21 December 1848.
85. *Hunt & Co.'s Commercial Directory*, 1847, p. 171. Robert Brown's address in the directory was 14 Severn Terrace, next door to another travelling draper. Other popular listed addresses for travelling drapers were Spring Gardens and the Tything, all outside the historic retail centre of Worcester.
86. *Pigot's Directory*, 1835, and *Bentley's History and Guide ... Dudley*, 1840.
87. *Worcestershire ... Directory for 1820* (Lewis).
88. See pp. 67–8.
89. Mui and Mui, *Shops and Shopkeeping*, p. 179.
90. Finn, 'Scotch Drapers', p. 93.
91. *Bentley's History and Guide ... Dudley*, 1840 and Pigot's *Directory*, 1835 and Worcestershire Census, 1841, WRO.
92. *Bentley's History and Guide ... Dudley*, 1840, and Worcestershire Census, 1841, WRO.
93. Robert Keay, draper and tea dealer, Scottish; William McClean [*sic*], draper, Scottish; Terence Burns, draper and clothes dealer, Irish; John Mackown, draper, Irish; John M'Mullen, tea dealer and linen draper, Irish; Herefordshire Census, 1841, Herefordshire Record Office [hereafter HRO].
94. Herefordshire Census, 1841, HRO.
95. *Hereford Journal*, 2 December 1846.
96. Ibid., 29 November 1848.
97. Ibid., 4 April 1849.
98. Deceulaer, 'Dealing with Diversity', p. 190.
99. See Chapman, *Merchant Enterprise in Britain*, p. 113, for the prominence of the Scottish textile trade.
100. V. Reilly, *The Official Illustrated History, The Paisley Pattern* (Glasgow: Richard Drew Publishing Ltd, 1987), particularly pp. 39–40.
101. A. Hann, 'Industrialization and the Service Economy', in J. Stobart and N. Raven (eds), *Towns, Regions and Industries, Urban and Industrial Change in the Midlands, c. 1700–1840* (Manchester: Manchester University Press, 2005), p. 51, table 3.4.
102. Finn, 'Scotch Drapers', pp. 93–4, found there was a disproportionate concentration of Scottish surnames in this sector of the trade in later nineteenth-century trade directories. Robert Brown in Worcester, was also born in Scotland, see Worcestershire Census, 1851, WRO.
103. Shammas, *Pre-Industrial Consumer*, p. 307.
104. British Parliamentary Papers 1833, pp. 625–6, quoted in I. Mitchell, 'Retailing Innovation and Urban Markets, c. 1800–1850', *Journal of Historical Marketing*, 2:3 (2010), pp. 289–90.

105. See J. Woodforde, *The Diary of a Country Parson, Volume V: 1797–1802*, ed. J. Beresford (Oxford: Oxford University Press, 1981), p. 407. The items he purchased from itinerant sellers were those commonly sold by drapers and were generally bought for the female members of his household. For further examples see E. Ewing, *Everyday Dress 1650–1900* (London: Batsford, 1984), pp. 68–9 and Buck, 'Buying Clothes in Bedfordshire', p. 218.

106. Benson and Ugolini, 'Beyond the Shop', pp. 260–4, for the attitudes towards hawkers and pedlars and the value of the goods that they sold. They conclude that it is very difficult to generalize as it was heavily dependent on individual circumstances and also sometimes bound up with notions of poverty and charity.

107. There is some evidence for this, for example, W. H. Maclean in Hereford probably sold male ready-made clothing.

108. Wood, Mrs H., *Mrs Halliburton's Troubles* (London: Collins, undated, original 1862), pp. 157–8. Ellen Wood was born in Worcester in 1814, the daughter of a glove manufacturer. She lived there until her marriage in 1836, when she moved to France.

109. See also G. R. Rubin, 'The County Courts and the Tally Trade, 1846–1914', in G. Rubin and D. Sugarman (eds), *Law, Economy and Society, Essays in the History of English Law 1750–1914* (Abingdon: Professional Books, 1984), p. 346, who cites the economist J. H. Elliot, who in 1845 praised the tallymen for providing credit and clothes where otherwise there would have been none.

110. Finn, 'Scotch Drapers', p. 91. See also Rubin, 'The County Courts', pp. 346–7, and Finn, *The Character of Credit*, pp. 258–9.

111. Wood, Mrs H., *Johnny Ludlow*, 3rd Series (London: Macmillan, 1898), pp. 203–22.

112. See Chapter 2, p. 62.

113. For example, see John MacMullen in Hereford, who held a market stall in the 1820s and John Kirk in Worcester, who was listed as a draper in the trade directories of the 1820s.

114. To counter this, credit drapers began to set up professional associations to protect the name of the trade, one established in Worcester during the 1840s. Finn, 'Scotch Drapers', p. 102.

115. For a discussion of markets and fairs, see Alexander, *Retailing in England*, particularly Part II, II, p. 44, where he notes that shops dominated the retail trade in goods such as clothing by the mid-nineteenth century.

116. See, for example, W. Pitt, *A General View of the Agriculture of the County of Worcester, a Reprint of the Work Drawn Up for the Consideration of the Board of Agriculture and Internal Improvement* (London: Sherwood, Neely and Jones, 1813, reprint Newton Abbot: David and Charles, 1969), p. 275.

117. Fowler, 'Satisfying Popular Consumer Demand', p. 115, found it was unusual for textile goods to be sold at markets by the early nineteenth century. Also D. Hodson, '"The Municipal Store", Adaptation and Development in the Retail Markets of Nineteenth Century Urban Lancashire', *Business History*, 40:4 (1998), pp. 103–5, who suggests that by the 1820s/30s, markets were mainly for perishables except for a few markets known for specific items. This situation was reversed by the end of the nineteenth century, when they sold non-perishable goods again, especially in industrial areas.

118. Roberts, *The Shaping of Modern Hereford*, pp. 7–8. The Butter Market building was opened in 1860.

119. Hereford City Market Account Books, vol. 1, 1810–28, 1821–2, no page number, HRO, BG11/13.

120. Hereford City Market Account Books, Vol. 2, 1829–35, 1829, no page number, HRO, BG11/13.
121. Hereford City Market Account Books, Vol. 2, 1829–35, 1830, 1835, no page number HRO, BG11/13.
122. Hereford City Market Account Books, Vol. 1, 1810–28, and Vol. 2, 1829–35, 1821–2, 1830, 1835, HRO, BG11/13.
123. See *Hunt & Co.'s Commercial Directory,* 1847.
124. *Hereford Journal,* 9 August 1848, and pp. 000 above, for Sillifant's business.
125. Ibid., 28 February 1844.
126. Ibid., 29 April 1846.
127. Letter to the editor, *Hereford Journal*, 21 February 1844.
128. There were similar complaints in the Low Countries from the 1830s and 1840s, see Jaumain, 'Colporteurs', p. 315.
129. *Hereford Journal,* 21 February 1844.
130. *Hereford Journal,* 28 February 1844. See also Deceulaer, 'Dealing with Diversity', who notes a new category of goods sold by itinerants appearing in the late eighteenth century. This consisted of new unused goods which had lost their appeal and become unfashionable and were consequently sold on for low prices.
131. See Deceulaer, 'Dealing with Diversity', pp. 172 and 182–4 for comments about the different reasons that itinerant sellers were opposed.
132. See also Blondé *et al.*, 'Retail Circuits', p. 16.
133. Pigot's *Directory,* 1828, p. 861.
134. See Worcestershire Quarter Session Papers, 1823, WRO, 1/659/172, and *Berrow's Worcester Journal,* 20 January 1825 and 30 September 1830.
135. See *Robson's Commercial Directory,* 1838.
136. Quarter Session Papers, 1817, WRO, 1/629/204, and Quarter Session Order Book, Volume 10, p. 180b.
137. Kidderminster Market Minute and Order Book, 1822–26, WRO, 10470/365.
138. *Hereford Journal,* 9 August 1848. See also the stock in trade of a bankrupt salesman and draper sold at Pershore Fair in 1812, which included coats, waistcoats, striped cotton and Russia Duck trousers and smock frocks, *Berrow's Worcester Journal,* 18 June 1812.
139. Worcester market charged 12d per week for a stall, equivalent to £2 12s per year, for one of sixty-eight in the sundry section of the market. This was up to a third cheaper than Hereford market, where stalls were between £4 and £6 10s per year. Worcester City Records, Market Accounts, 1823–35, WRO, B7, box 2, pp. 17–18, and Hereford City Market Account Books, Vol. 1, 1810–28, 1821–22 HRO.
140. For the importance of market hall buildings see Mitchell, 'Retailing Innovation', pp. 292–4.
141. See also Fontaine, *History,* pp. 162–3.
142. Deceulaer, 'Dealing with Diversity', p. 191, for the economic dynamism of pedlars.
143. S. Williams, 'Earnings, Poor Relief and the Economy of Makeshifts: Bedfordshire in the Early Years of the New Poor Law', *Rural History,* 16:1 (2005), p. 41.
144. See Deceulaer, 'Dealing with Diversity', p. 177, who found pedlars to be more active in less populous areas and where villages were too small to have their own shop.
145. Mui and Mui, *Shops and Shopkeeping,* p. 104.
146. For example, coaches going to the Welsh coast for sea bathing were advertised, *Hereford Journal,* 28 June 1815.

147. Barker, 'Catering for Provincial Tastes?', pp. 55–7 for reasons for the dominance of the *Hereford Journal* in south Wales.

148. P. Borsay, *The English Urban Renaissance, Culture and Society in the Provincial Town 1660–1770* (Oxford: Clarendon, 1989), p. 9.

149. Deceulaer, 'Dealing with Diversity', p. 188.

150. See, for example, C. P. Hosgood, 'The 'Knights of the Road': Commercial Travellers and the Culture of the Commercial Room in Late Victorian and Edwardian England', *Victorian Studies*, 37, 4 (1994), pp. 519–47, for the developing trade of commercial salesmen in the second half of the nineteenth century.

151. Deceulaer, 'Dealing with Diversity', p. 178, who found pedlars sold items not otherwise stocked locally, for example, small fashionable items.

4 Clothing the Poor: Parish Relief

1. For exceptions to this, see M. Reed, 'Gnawing it Out': A New Look at Economic Relations in Nineteenth-Century Rural England', *Rural History*, 1:1 (1990), pp. 83–94, and P. Lane, 'Work on the Margins: Poor Women and the Informal Economy of Eighteenth and Early Nineteenth Century Leicestershire', *Midland History*, 22 (1997), pp. 85–99.

2. S. King and C. Muldrew, 'Cash, Wages and the Economy of Makeshifts in England, 1650–1800', in P. Scholliers and L. Schwarz (eds), *Experiencing Wages: Social and Cultural Aspects of Wage Forms in Europe since 1500* (Oxford: Berghahn Books, 2003), pp. 160–1.

3. S. King and A. Tomkins (eds), *The Poor in England 1700–1850: An Economy of Makeshifts* (Manchester: Manchester University Press, 2003), pp. 1, 14–19.

4. Fontaine and Schlumbohm, 'Household Strategies for Survival' p. 2.

5. See ibid., pp. 10 and 12.

6. B. Lemire, 'Plebeian Commercial Circuits and Everyday Material Exchange in England, *circa* 1600–1900', in Blondé *et al.*, *Buyers and Sellers*, pp. 245–66, on p. 250.

7. See Fontaine and Schlumbohm (eds), *Household Strategies*; Fontaine (ed.), *Alternative Exchanges*, in Blondé, *et al.*, *Fashioning Old and New*; J. Stobart and I. Van Damme (eds), *Modernity and the Second-Hand Trade, European Consumption Cultures and Practices, 1700–1900* (London: Palgrave Macmillan, 2010); J. Benson and L. Ugolini (eds), 'Retailing Beyond the Shop: Britain *c.* 1400–1900', *Journal of Historical Research in Marketing, Special Issue*, 2:3 (2010), and various articles within these collections.

8. N. Gregson and L. Crewe, *Second-Hand Cultures* (Oxford: Berg, 2003), p. 125.

9. Gregson and Crewe, *Second-Hand Cultures*, pp. 2–3.

10. Herefordshire Quarter Session Minute Books, Volumes 22 [labelled 23 though should be 22], 23, 24, 25, 26; Herefordshire Quarter Session Order Books, Vols. 17 and 18, Herefordshire Record Office [hereafter HRO].

11. Worcestershire Quarter Session Papers, 1820, Worcestershire Record Office, [hereafter WRO], (644/184–5) and Quarter Session Order Book, acquitted, Vol. 10, p. 319a, WRO.

12. Worcestershire Quarter Session Papers, 1822, WRO, (653/178) and Quarter Session Order Book, Vol. 11, p. 85b, WRO.

13. See above pp. 36, 66–7.

14. Hereford Assizes Calendar, Lent 1844, HRO, and *Hereford Journal*, 27 March 1844. My thanks to Jeni King, a descendant of James Newton, for pointing me towards this case. James Newton served his sentence and stayed in Australia becoming the farmer that it

seemed he desired to be and which was probably only possible in Australia. He died in 1905 aged eighty-five, with ten acres of land and a stone cottage, never having been in trouble again and therefore redeeming himself in the eyes of his relatives in Wales, regaining their respect lost with his early wrongdoings. See also Shakesheff, *Rural Conflict*, p. 43, who found crime figures were heaviest in winter due to the seasonal nature of agricultural work.

15. For example, see B. Lemire, 'Shifting Currency: The Culture and Economy of the Second Hand Trade in England, c. 1600–1850', in A. Palmer and H. Clark (eds), *Old Clothes, New Looks, Second Hand Fashion* (Oxford: Berg, 2006), pp. 29–47. Also P. Johnson, 'Credit and Thrift and the British Working Class, 1870–1939', in J. Winter (ed.), *The Working Class in Modern British History: Essays in Honour of Henry Pelling* (Cambridge: Cambridge University Press, 1983), pp. 156–7; Charpy, 'The Scope and Structure of the Nineteenth-Century Second-Hand Trade', p. 140.

16. Tomkins, *The Experience of Urban Poverty*, pp. 204–29, 240. Also E. C. Sanderson, *Women and Work in Eighteenth Century Edinburgh* (Basingstoke: Macmillan, 1996), pp. 150–1, who suggests clothing was kept for the specific purpose of pawning, to get cash when needed.

17. M. Ginsberg, 'Rags to Riches: The Second-Hand Clothes Trade 1700–1978', *Costume*, 14 (1980), pp. 123–4.

18. Worcestershire Quarter Session Papers, 1818, WRO, 632/147–150, and Quarter Session Order Book, Vol. 10, p. 206b, WRO.

19. Gregson and Crewe, *Second-Hand Cultures*, pp. 2–4, 112. See also D. Miller, 'Introduction, The Birth of Value', in P. Jackson, M. Lowe, D. Miller and F. Mort (eds), *Commercial Cultures: Economies, Practices, Spaces* (Oxford: Berg, 2000), pp. 80, 82.

20. Gregson and Crewe, *Second-Hand Cultures*, pp. 44, 49.

21. Ibid., pp. 52, 56, 58–60. See also J. Stobart, 'Clothes, Cabinets and Carriages: Second-hand Dealing in Eighteenth Century England', in Blondé *et al.*, *Buyers and Sellers*, p. 233.

22. A. Toplis, 'A Stolen Garment or a Reasonable Purchase? The Male Consumer and the Illicit Second-Hand Clothing Market in the First Half of the Nineteenth Century', in Stobart and Van Damme (eds), *Modernity and the Second-Hand Trade*, pp. 65–7.

23. R. E. Ommer and N. J. Turner, 'Informal Rural Economies in History', *Labour/Le Travail*, 53 (Spring 2004), pp. 128–31.

24. Ommer and Turner, 'Informal Rural Economies', p. 137.

25. Stobart, 'Clothes, Cabinets and Carriages', pp. 238 and 242. Also Stobart, 'In and Out of Fashion?', p. 142, who suggests that fashion was not paramount in the second-hand markets, but other concerns, utility, quality and value, were.

26. Lemire, 'Plebeian Commercial Circuits', p. 260.

27. See also Stobart, 'In and Out of Fashion?', p. 134, who warns about overplaying the divisions between the first and second-hand markets.

28. In 1815, it was estimated that the pauper population of Herefordshire was 10.5 per cent of the county population, a proportion which had increased further by the mid century. Shakesheff, *Rural Conflict*, p. 38. The total working-class population was around 80–90 per cent. See Introduction, p. 3.

29. S. King, 'Reclothing the English Poor, 1750–1840', *Textile History*, 33:1 (2002), pp. 37–47; P. Jones, 'Clothing of the Poor in Early-Nineteenth-Century England', *Textile History*, 37:1 (2006), pp. 17–37; Richmond, 'No Finery'.

30. King, 'Reclothing the English Poor', pp. 46–7.
31. B. Lemire, *Fashion's Favourite*, p. 107. See also King, 'The Clothing of the Poor', p. 370, who discusses if it is possible to judge what was a 'normal' standard of dress.
32. R. Dryburgh, 'Not granted until you appear leaner': Administrative Corruption and the Payment of Rent by the Old Poor Law in Bolton', at http://www.ehs.org.uk/othercontent /dryburgh.htm, pp. 1–5 [accessed 23 November 2010].
33. Castlemorton Parish Records, Select Vestry Book, 1824–68, 3 August 1832, WRO, 9581/20.
34. Bromyard Parish, Linton Township Overseers' Accounts, Disbursements, Weekly and Occasional Pay, 1815–20, 31 July 1818, HRO, E38/20.
35. S. King, '"I Fear You Will Think Me Too Presumtuous in My Demands but Necessity Has No Law": Clothing in English Pauper Letters. 1800–1834', *International Review of Social History*, 54:2 (2009), pp. 224–5, 227.
36. Hope under Dinmore Parish, Complaints Book, 1825–7, 12 March 1826, HRO, N31/163.
37. King, 'I Fear You Will Think Me Too Presumtuous', p. 221.
38. P. Sharpe, 'The Bowels of Compation': A Labouring Family and the Law, *c.* 1790–1834' in T. Hitchcock, P. King and P. Sharpe (eds), *Chronicling Poverty, The Voices and Strategies of the English Poor, 1640–1840* (Basingstoke: Macmillan, 1997), pp. 87, 100–3. She notes that families were often treated collectively in an application for relief, especially where there was some sort of moral wrongdoing. See p. 101. See also King, 'I Fear You Will Think Me Too Presumtuous', pp. 211, 220.
39. T. Sokoll, 'Old Age in Poverty: The Record of Essex Pauper Letters 1780–1834', in Hitchcock, King, and Sharpe (eds), *Chronicling Poverty*, p. 159.
40. Droitwich, St Peter's Parish, Parish Correspondence, 13 June 1812, WRO, 5476/17.
41. D. R. Green, 'Pauper Protests: Power and Resistance in early Nineteenth Century London Workhouses', *Social History*, 31:2 (2006), p. 159.
42. T. Sokoll, 'Negotiating a Living: Essex Pauper Letters from London 1800–1834', in Fontaine and Schlumbohm (eds), *Household Strategies*, p. 43.
43. R. Jütte, *Poverty and Deviance in Early Modern Europe* (Cambridge: Cambridge University Press, 1994), p. 17.
44. See, for example, the case of Maria Fudger above, p. 93.
45. Droitwich, St Peter's Parish, Overseers' Correspondence, Letter, 6 January 1833, WRO, 5476/17.
46. Droitwich, St Peter's Parish, Overseers' Correspondence, Letter, 9 February 1833, WRO, 5476/17.
47. Droitwich, St Peter's Parish, Overseers' Correspondence, Bill to Overseers from John Pumfrey, 7 May 1833, WRO, 5476/12.
48. St John in Bedwardine, Worcester, Parish Correspondence, Letter from Mary Bodel, Deptford, to the Overseers, 3 May 1825, WRO, 1671/21.
49. See Chapter 1, pp. 31–2.
50. McCulloch, 'Some Aspects of Victorian Bromyard from the 1851 Census', p. 135.
51. In a survey of directories of the period, Bromyard had a similar number of tailors and drapers to towns of a comparable size, such as Tenbury and Kington. However, it had three times as many clothes dealers as Kington, neither having a pawnbroker. Tenbury had only one 'clothes shop', run by a pawnbroker.
52. Bromyard Parish, Linton Township, Overseers' Accounts, Disbursements, Weekly and Occasional Pay, 1800–3, 1808–9, 1815–20, Bill from James Amiss, Bromyard to Mr

Page for 7 May and 4 July 1816, settled 11 November 1816, HRO, E38/20. Amiss was a victualler, draper and grocer who went bankrupt in 1823. See *Hereford Journal*, 1 May and 15 May 1823.

53. Bromyard Parish, Winslow Overseers' Accounts, 14 March 1812, HRO, E38/62, and Herefordshire Quarter Sessions Minute Books, Vol. 25, Epiphany 1843, no page number, HRO.

54. *Robson's Commercial Directory*, 1838.

55. Bromyard Parish, Winslow Overseers' Accounts, 17 August 1833, HRO, E38/62.

56. Bromyard Parish, Linton Township, Overseers' Accounts, Disbursements, Weekly and Occasional Pay, 1800–3, 1808–9, 1815–20, 5 June 1817 and 24 June 1818, HRO, E38/20.

57. Bromyard Parish, Winslow Overseers' Accounts, 7 December 1833, HRO, E38/63.

58. Bromyard Parish, Linton Township, Overseers' Accounts, Disbursements, Weekly and Occasional Pay, 1800–3, 1808–9, 1815–20, 24 October 1820 and 21 May 1820, HRO, E38/20.

59. Bromyard Parish, Linton Township, Overseers' Accounts, Disbursements, Weekly and Occasional Pay, 1800–3, 1808–9, 1815–20, 18 August 1820, HRO, E38/20.

60. See S. King, 'The Dress of the Poor', pp. 380–1.

61. Bromyard Parish, Winslow Parish Correspondence for Relief, 21 July 1833, HRO, E38/74.

62. Bromyard Parish, Winslow Overseers' Accounts, Birmingham Tea Company Bill, 3 October 1833, HRO, E38/62.

63. See pp. 31–2.

64. Snell, *Annals of the Labouring Poor*, pp. 174–7.

65. Castlemorton Parish Records, Overseers' Accounts, 1836, WRO, 9581/22.

66. Castlemorton Parish Records, Overseers' Accounts, WRO, 9581/22. In the listings for the quarter ending on 25 March 1836 and the quarter ending on midsummer 1836 combined, reasons for seeking relief were detailed: 36 per cent were old age or 'past work'; around 20 per cent were 'bastard' children; around 20 per cent had a 'weak intellect'; around 10 per cent were widows with children; and around 14 per cent were injured including lameness and 'rupture'. The injury figure was the one with most variation, with two claimants in the winter rising to four in the spring quarter, possibly reflecting seasonal working patterns.

67. Castlemorton Parish Records, Select Vestry Book, 1824–68, WRO, 9581/20, and Castlemorton Parish Records, Overseers' Accounts, 1836, WRO, 9581/22.

68. Snell, *Annals of the Labouring Poor*, p. 28, who states were worst periods of rural poverty were when a man was about thirty-four years old with a family of three or more children not yet able to work, and also in old age. The same would be equally true for women. See also, Tomkins, *The Experience of Urban Poverty*, p. 13, for a summary of recent work about this subject.

69. S. King, '"Meer Pennies for my Baskitt will be Enough", Women, Work and Welfare, 1770–1830', in P. Lane, N. Raven and K. D. M. Snell (eds), *Women, Work and Wages in England 1600–1850* (Woodbridge: Boydell, 2004), pp. 138–9.

70. King, 'Meer Pennies for my Baskitt', p. 139. See also King and Tomkins, 'Conclusion', in King and Tomkins (eds), *The Poor in England*, pp. 268–9, n. 27, and Snell, *Annals of the Labouring Poor*, pp. 51–66.

71. Castlemorton Parish Records, Select Vestry Book, 1824–68, 1825, WRO, 9581/20.

72. See Sharpe, *Adapting to Capitalism*, p. 69, for examples in Essex.

73. For example, 'Blind William Lewis' in 1801, 'old Ann Jackson' in 1802 and also the familiar 'Blind Dick' in the same year. Abbey Dore Parish Records, Parish Book, 1790–1849, HRO, AC16/26.

74. Abbey Dore Parish Records, Parish Book, 1790–1849, 1808, HRO, AC16/26.

75. J. Styles, 'Involuntary Consumers? Servants and their Clothes in Eighteenth Century England', *Textile History*, 33:1 (2002), pp. 9–21, on p. 18.

76. Traditionally a new article of dress, however small, was bought for Easter Sunday, it being unlucky to forget. See E. M. Leather, *The Folklore of Herefordshire* (Hereford: Lapridge Publications, 1991), p. 99.

77. Abbey Dore Parish Records, Parish Book, 1790–1849, 2 April 1804, HRO, AC16/26. In contrast, £1 was allowed for apprentices' clothes in Castlemorton. Castlemorton Parish Records, Overseers' Accounts, 1831–36, WRO, 9581/20.

78. Crompton has found that this idea became more pronounced when children were in workhouses and there was a danger of institutionalization. Up until the age of ten, children were not thought to be responsible for their own destitution and clothing was not marked with the union name. Some guardians ordered that their apprentice clothing not be identifiable as 'pauper' by any markings, so they had less stigma attached to them. See F. Crompton, *Workhouse Children* (Stroud: Sutton Publishing Ltd, 1997), pp. 213–14.

79. Abbey Dore Parish Records, Parish Book, 1790–1849, 21 April 1805, 26 March 1804, 8 March 1807, HRO, AC16/26.

80. Abbey Dore Parish Records, Parish Book, 1790–1849, 8 June 1806, HRO, AC16/26.

81. Sharpe, *Adapting to Capitalism*, pp. 109–10.

82. Abbey Dore Parish Records, Parish Book, 1790–1849, 29 January and 17 February 1807 HRO, AC16/26.

83. Abbey Dore Parish Records, Parish Book, 1790–1849, 1 February and 22 February 1807, HRO, AC16/26.

84. Abbey Dore Parish Records, Parish Book, 1790–1849, HRO, AC16/26. Dean presented a bill for £6 16s 11d on 3 May 1802. James 'Deen' of Wyebridge Street, Hereford, was noted as a tailor and salesman in Pigot and Co.'s *National and Commercial Directory and Topography ... for Herefordshire, 1822* (London: James Pigot and Co., 1822).

85. Herefordshire Census, 1841, HRO. A tailor was noted in the village by 1851. See Directory and *Gazetteer of Herefordshire* (Birmingham: Lascelles & Co., 1851).

86. Herefordshire Census, 1841, HRO, and Abbey Dore Parish Records, Parish Book, 1790–1849, 1813–31, HRO, AC16/26.

87. For example, Abbey Dore Parish Records, Parish Book, 1790–1849, 3 February 1806, HRO, AC16/26; Ann Morgan was allowed half a stone of hurds costing 3s 6d, to make her husband a frock.

88. King, 'I Fear You Will Think Me Too Presumtuous', pp. 221, 223.

89. The Droitwich population was 2,176 in 1821; Abbey Dore's was 523.

90. See Chapter 1, p. 24–6.

91. Droitwich, St Peter's Parish, Day Book, 1797–1801, 1800, WRO, 5476/19.

92. Droitwich, St Peter's Parish, Parish Book, 1808–17, 1808, WRO, 5476/19.

93. Droitwich, St Peter's Parish, Day Book, 1797–1801, 1800, WRO, 5476/19.

94. Droitwich, St Peter's Parish, Parish Book, 1808–17, WRO, 5476/19. For example, 14 June 1808, 'Paid for cleaning Mary Pemberton from Lise [sic] and making bedgound [sic], 4s'.

95. Droitwich, St Peter's Parish: Day Book, 1797–1801, WRO, 5476/19, Parish Book, 1802–6, WRO, 5476/19, and Parish Book, 1808–17, WRO, 5476/19.

96. Droitwich, St Peter's Parish, Parish Book, 1808–17, 1816–17, WRO, 5476/19.

97. Droitwich, St Peter's Parish, miscellaneous bills and receipts, 1816 and 1817, WRO, 5476/12. See Baumgarten, *What Clothes Reveal*, p. 114, for another example of the similar use of grogram and see glossary, p. 158, for a definition.

98. Abbey Dore Parish Records, Parish Book, 1790–1849, 1816–17, HRO, AC16/26.

99. See Toplis, 'The Non-Elite Consumer', pp. 248–55, for full listings.

100. Worcestershire Census, 1841, WRO.

101. She was noted living in the Droitwich Union Workhouse aged forty-five in 1841 and again, in 1851, although then aged sixty-three. Worcestershire Census, 1841 and 1851, WRO.

102. Castlemorton had an annual budget of between £500 and 550 for relief in the early 1830s, just under half of which was for casual relief which included clothing. Castlemorton Parish, Overseers' Accounts, WRO, 9581/22.

103. See Appendix, p. 157.

104. Droitwich, St Peter's Parish, miscellaneous bills and receipts, bill from Heming & Taylor, Droitwich, to the Overseers of the Parish of St Peter, Droitwich, July 1807 – February 1808, WRO, 5476/12.

105. See L. D. Smith, *Carpet Weavers and Carpet Makers. The Hand Loom Carpet Weavers of Kidderminster 1780–1850* (Middle Habberley, Kidderminster: Kenneth Tomkinson Ltd, 1986), pp. 90, 110, 140.

106. Kidderminster, St Mary's Parish, Churchwarden's Accounts, 1833–6, 1834, WRO, 4766/14/ii. Both men were noted as clothes dealers in Pigot and Co.'s *National and Commercial Directory and Topography ... for Worcestershire ... 1835* (London: James Pigot and Co.).

107. See Chapter 1, p. 22, for trade directory impressions.

108. A. Richards, *Bygone Bromsgrove: An Illustrated Story of the Town in Days Gone By* (Bromsgrove: Bromsgrove Society, 1996), p. 60.

109. See Chapter 1, p. 32, and the Bromyard drapers.

110. *Berrow's Worcester Journal*, 9 March 1837.

111. Ibid., 3 September 1840.

112. Ibid., 14 September 1837.

113. Ibid., 17 August 1837.

114. Ibid., 8 December 1836.

115. Ibid., 19 January 1837.

116. Papers of the Parish Officers of Ombersley, 'Rules and Regulations Obser. & Practis'd for the year 1805 to 1811', Ombersley House of Industry, WRO, 3572/15.

117. Richmond, 'No Finery', pp. 182–3.

118. King, 'Reclothing the English Poor', pp. 46–7. See also Tomkins, *The Experience of Poverty*, p. 71, who also agrees that the poor in this period were relatively well-clothed and clothing the poor was a basic task of parish relief.

119. Stoke Edith Parish Records, Clothing Account Bills, bill from James Symonds, draper, Hereford, 18 August 1825, HRO, G53/8.

120. King, 'I Fear you will Think me too Presumtuous', pp. 235–6.

121. Ibid., p. 234.

5 Clothing the Poor: Charity

1. C. Jones, 'Some Recent Trends in the History of Charity', in M. Daunton (ed.), *Charity, Self Interest and Welfare in the English Past* (London: UCL Press, 1996), p. 55.

2. See Chapter 4, p. 93, for pauper letters which demanded relief. See also A. Kidd, *State, Society and the Poor in Nineteenth-Century England* (Basingstoke: Macmillan, 1999), pp. 3–4 and 65.

3. For example, the Dorcas Society in Worcester was established in 1819. See below, p. 121.

4. E. Rowley, *Fruits of Righteousness in the Life of Susannah Knapp* (Worcester: Hamilton, Adams & Co., F. Osborn, 1866), p. 88.

5. Tomkins, *The Experience of Urban Poverty*, pp. 83–5.

6. See *The Reports of the Commissioners appointed in Pursuance of Various Acts of Parliament to Enquire Concerning Charities in England and Wales Relating to the County of Hereford-shire 1819–1839* (London: Henry Gray, *circa* 1841), p. 346.

7. *Reports ... Herefordshire*, p. 122.

8. S. Sweetinburgh, 'Clothing the Naked in Late Medieval East Kent', in C. Richardson (ed.), *Clothing Culture, 1350–1650* (Aldershot: Ashgate, 2004), p. 112.

9. *Reports ... Herefordshire*, p. 265.

10. Ibid., p. 60, relating to William Brydges Charity, Bosbury.

11. Ibid., p. 12.

12. Ibid., p. 109. See also Tomkins, *The Experience of Urban Poverty*, pp. 79–83, for contemporary concerns about charity.

13. *The Reports of the Commissioners to Enquire Concerning Charities in England and Wales Relating to the County of Worcester 1819–1837* (London: Henry Gray, *circa* 1840), pp. 414–416, Worcestershire Record Office, [hereafter WRO], 5306/1.

14. Styles, 'Clothing the North', p. 147.

15. Styles, 'Involuntary Consumers?', p. 21.

16. Mr Brecknell's Charity, Accounts of Distributions, 1834–57, WRO, 12326/1.

17. *Reports ... Herefordshire*, p. 330.

18. *Reports ... Worcestershire*, pp. 312–313.

19. See below, pp. 114–18.

20. Bromsgrove Charity Book, 1812, No. 1, WRO, 302/1.

21. Cartwright Charity, Trustees Minutes and Clothing Accounts, 1822–1955, Dudley Record Office, Acc. 8531.

22. Cartwright Charity, Trustees Minutes and Clothing Accounts, 1822–1955, p. 23, Dudley Record Office, Acc. 8531. By 1824, the colour of the clothing was noted as blue, see p. 32.

23. Cartwright Charity, Trustees Minutes and Clothing Accounts, 1822–1955, p. 25, Dudley Record Office, Acc. 8531.

24. St Andrew's, Worcester, Parish Correspondence, WRO, 4426/12.

25. *Berrow's Worcester Journal,* 14 July 1831.

26. *Holden's Triennial Directory* (1811).

27. *Worcestershire ... Directory for 1820* (Lewis) and see pp. 18, 48.

28. Parish Correspondence of St Andrew's, Worcester, William Spriggs Bill, 1820, WRO, 4426/12.

29. Bill from James Walter, Worcester, 1833, to the parish of Hindlip, Hindlip Parish Records, WRO, 8669/6i–39.

30. See Powick Parish Records, bill from S. Burden to the Overseers of Powick, 18 November 1818, WRO, 3802/10. There were over 170 items of clothing noted, a third of which were smock frocks or jackets, with no coats mentioned.
31. *Berrow's Worcester Journal*, 20 August 1835.
32. *Hereford Journal*, 16 November 1831.
33. R. Pantall, *George Jarvis (1704–1793) and his Notorious Charity* (Leominster: Orphans Press Ltd, 1993), ch. 1.
34. Ibid., pp. 33–4. Interest on £11,000 was allocated to Staunton, £13,000 to Bredwardine and £6,000 to Letton.
35. Ibid., pp. 37–9.
36. Ibid., *George Jarvis*, p. 40.
37. *Reports ... Herefordshire*, pp. 144–5.
38. Castlemorton had an annual budget of between £500–550 for relief in the early 1830s, Castlemorton Parish, Overseers' Accounts, WRO, 9581/22 and see above chapter 4, pp. 97–8. The total Staunton poor rate was around £225 per year itself, see Pantall, *George Jarvis*, p. 43.
39. Pantall, *George Jarvis*, p. 43.
40. *Reports ... Herefordshire*, p. 140.
41. This was still substantial in comparison to the 30 shillings spent on clothing women in Worcester, see above, p. 113.
42. See above, pp. 103–4. The exception to this was 1821 when Thomas Poney was given just over £2 (equivalent to 40 shillings) worth of clothing.
43. *Reports ... Herefordshire*, p. 144.
44. Pantall, *George Jarvis*, p. 46. The first advertisement for tender for clothing for the Jarvis Charity has been found in the *Hereford Journal* on 11 October 1837. Items asked for included: drab wool cloth, calicoes, Russia Duck for frocks, hats, hose, flannel, dark printed cottons, skirt stuff, linsey woolsey, checks, ginghams, fustians, handkerchiefs.
45. Pantall, *George Jarvis*, p. 44. For example in Staunton the school was established in 1815 and taught sixty to eighty children. The girls were taught knitting and sewing.
46. Both tailors were mentioned in a list of tradesmen supplying articles for the charity. See 'A list of Persons of whom Articles are bought of, for the use of Mr Jarvis's Charity, being freeholders in, and for the County of Hereford. April 6th 1811', Herefordshire Record Office, [hereafter HRO], BA89/2/9.
47. Craik, *Uniforms Exposed*, pp. 4–5.
48. *Reports ... Herefordshire*, p. 140.
49. Cited in Pantall, *George Jarvis*, p. 43.
50. King, 'Reclothing the English Poor', pp. 46–7.
51. Staunton upon Wye Overseers' Accounts, 1820–1, HRO, AA2/24.
52. Letton Parish Church, Churchwardens' Accounts, 1769–1887, HRO, AA1/7.
53. See Chapter 4, pp. 98–100. In comparison, in Bromyard there were approximately twelve items of clothing in total available per year from various charities. *Reports...Herefordshire*, pp. 8, 20, 12, 16.
54. See Herefordshire Census, 1841 and 1851, HRO.
55. Tomkins, *The Experience of Urban Poverty*, p. 85.
56. Tomkins, *The Experience of Urban Poverty*, pp. 80–3.
57. *Hereford Journal*, 2 November 1842. Bredwardine – £271 1s 5¾d; Staunton – £268 17s 11½d; Letton – £127 5s 1½d.
58. *Hereford Journal*, 30 November 1842, 21 December 1842, 9 November 1843.

59. Pantall, *George Jarvis*, pp. 51–6.
60. G. Griffith, *The Free Schools of Worcestershire and their Fulfilment* (London: Charles Gilpin, 1852).
61. Ibid., Preface, p. xi.
62. Tomkins, *The Experience of Urban Poverty*, pp. 165–6.
63. *Reports ... Herefordshire*, p. 40.
64. Craik, *Uniforms Exposed*, pp. 82–3. See also, Tomkins, *The Experience of Urban Poverty*, p 163.
65. *Reports ... Herefordshire*, p. 42.
66. *Reports ... Worcestershire*, pp. 250–1. Fees without receiving clothing were ¼d or 1d. Each of the 100 boys would receive approximately £1 13s for clothing, equivalent to 33 shillings per year. If they paid fees of 2d for fifty-two weeks, this would amount to around 8 shillings, or about quarter of the cost of their clothing.
67. This compares favourably to the 16 shillings cost of a suit of charity school clothes as calculated by the SPCK (Society for Promotion of Christian Knowledge), see Tomkins, *The Experience of Urban Poverty*, p. 177.
68. Tomkins, *The Experience of Urban Poverty*, pp. 177–8, 184.
69. M. Southall, *A Description of Malvern, including a Guide to the Drives, Rides, Walks and Excursions ...* (Stourport: G. Nicholson, 1825), p. 103.
70. Southall, *A Description of Malvern*, p. 105.
71. Tomkins, *The Experience of Urban Poverty*, p. 84.
72. *Berrow's Worcester Journal*, 2 January 1845.
73. Ibid., 10 January 1850.
74. Ibid., 10 January 1850.
75. Ibid., 2 January 1845.
76. Mingay (ed.), *The Agrarian History of England and Wales*, pp. 906–7, 912–13.
77. *Hereford Journal*, 11 December 1832, 18 December 1832, 25 December 1832.
78. Ibid., 9 October 1839, comment on Ross Clothing Society.
79. Aymestrey Parish Records, letter from Aymestrey Vicarage, *circa* 16 January 1844, HRO, F71/153.
80. The Bromsgrove Dorcas Society held its ninth annual meeting in 1850. The previous year it had distributed 400 garments. *Berrow's Worcester Journal*, 24 January 1850.
81. *New Testament*, Acts, ix, v. 36–43.
82. L. S. Garrad, 'Dorcas Society', p. 1, at http://www.isle-of-man.com/manxnotebook/history/ poor /dorcas.htm [accessed 23 November 2010].
83. *Guide and Directory to the City and Suburbs of Worcester for 1837 ...* (Worcester: T. Stratford, 1837), p. 94.
84. *Berrow's Worcester Journal*, 24 February 1825.
85. *Berrow's Worcester Journal*, 26 November 1840.
86. Ibid., 24 April 1845.
87. Ibid., 22 February 1832.
88. Ibid., 28 November 1832.
89. Ibid., 27 November 1839.
90. Ibid., 7 December 1842
91. Ibid., 6 December 1843.
92. Ibid., 13 January 1841.
93. Anon., *The Workwoman's Guide, Containing Instructions ... in Cutting Out and Completing those Articles of Wearing Apparel, &c. which are Usually Made at Home ... By a Lady*

(London: Simpkin, Marshall and Co.,1838); see also E. E. Perkins, *A Treatise on Haberdashery &c.* (London: T. Hurst, 1834).

94. Burman and J. White, 'Fanny's Pockets' pp. 37, 42–3.

95. See Zakim, *Ready-Made Democracy*, pp. 180–1, 184, for clothing charity organizations in America and the problem of competition with existing businesses and workers.

96. *Hereford Journal*, 17 December 1845.

97. Unfortunately, there is a lack of useful poor law records for Ross for comparison.

98. *Hereford Journal*, 29 November 1848.

99. Ibid., 8 April 1835, and 2 April 1845.

100. Ibid., 29 March 1837.

101. Ibid., 15 April 1835.

102. Ibid., 29 March 1843.

103. See Chapter 2, p. 63, for comment about cheap ready-made clothing.

104. See *Reports ... Worcestershire*, p. 186.

105. Richmond, 'No Finery', p. 227. See also V. Richmond, 'Indiscriminate liberality subverts the Morals and depraves the habits of the Poor': A Contribution to the Debate on the Poor Law, Parish Clothing Relief and Clothing Societies in Early Nineteenth-Century England', *Textile History*, 40:1 (2009), pp. 56–9.

106. See Jones, 'Clothing of the Poor', pp. 29–31.

107. M. Hanly, 'The Economy of Makeshifts and the Role of the Poor Law: a Game of Chance?', in S. King and A. Tomkins (eds), *The Poor in England 1700–1850: An Economy of Makeshifts* (Manchester: Manchester University Press, 2003), p. 94.

108. See Finn, *The Character of Credit*, pp. 81–2. See also Richmond, 'Indiscriminate Liberality', pp. 58–9.

109. Kidd, *State, Society and the Poor*, pp. 67–70.

110. Tomkins, *The Experience of Urban Poverty*, pp. 110–11, 241.

111. See for example, provision in Edvin Ralph, p. 111 above, and chapter 4 for parish relief.

112. See Richmond, 'No Finery', pp. 226–7, who links the spread of clothing societies to an attack on poor relief from the 1820s onwards.

113. See F. K. Prochaska, *Women and Philanthropy in Nineteenth Century England* (Oxford: Clarendon, 1980), pp. vii–viii and 42, for general informal working-class charity.

114. Kidd, *State, Society and the Poor*, pp. 153–4, notes that working-class social obligations were the expectation of a similar service if needed at a future date, even inter-generationally.

115. S. Barrett, 'Kinship, Poor Relief and the Welfare Process in Early Modern England', in King and Tomkins (eds), *The Poor in England*, p. 218.

6 Fashion and the Working-Class Consumer

1. L. Svendsen, *Fashion: A Philosophy* (London: Reaktion Books, 2006), pp. 12–13.

2. See Stobart, 'In and Out of Fashion?', p. 133, for a discussion of 'fashion' in a broader context. Also Riello, *A Foot in the Past*, pp. 58–9.

3. H. Berry, 'Promoting Taste in the Provincial Press: National and Local Culture in Eighteenth-century Newcastle upon Tyne', *British Journal for Eighteenth-Century Studies*, 25 (2002), p. 2.

4. B. Lemire, 'Second hand Beaux and 'red armed belles'; Conflict and the Creation of Fashion in England, *circa* 1660–1800', *Continuity and Change*, 15:3 (2000), pp. 391–417; C. Fairchilds, 'The Production and Marketing of Populuxe Goods in Eighteenth-Century

Paris', in J. Brewer and R. Porter (eds), *Consumption and the World of Goods* (London: Routledge, 1994), pp. 228–48. See also de Vries, *The Industrious Revolution*, p. 149.

5. B. Lemire, *The Business of Everyday Life,* pp. 114, 120–2, and *idem.*, 'Second hand Beaux'; pp. 391–412. M. Thale (ed.), *The Autobiography of Francis Place* (London: Cambridge University Press, 1972), p. 63.

6. D. A. Frey Jr, 'Industrious Households: Survival Strategies of Artisans in a Southwest German Town during the Eighteenth and Early Nineteenth Centuries', in Fontaine and Schlumbohm (eds), *Household Strategies*, pp. 132–5.

7. Johnson, 'Credit and Thrift and the British Working Class', p. 156.

8. Finn, *The Character of Credit*, pp. 9–10, 21. See also Sanderson, *Women and Work in Eighteenth Century Edinburgh*, p. 24, for a similar point.

9. See *Pigot and Co.'s, National and Commercial Directory and Topography ... for Herefordshire* (London: James Pigot and Co., 1835) for entry for Thomas Ward, p. 98. He was listed in all trade directories published for Ledbury during the 1830s, but not in 1822 or 1844. See *Pigot and Co.'s... Directory ... for Herefordshire 1822, 1830, 1844*. See also R. Palmer, 'Herefordshire Street Ballads', *Transactions of the Woolhope Naturalists Field Club*, 47:1 (1991), p. 68.

10. Dyck, *William Cobbett and Rural Popular Culture* (Cambridge: Cambridge University Press, 1992), p. 149.

11. Jones, 'Clothing the Poor', pp. 32–3, who suggests that the 'poor' actively desired to be clothed in such 'decent' garments. See also Styles, *The Dress of the People*, pp. 199–202, who sees this type of plain dress as a 'customary, oppositional identity, worn in defiance of enclosing landlords, opulent farmers and oppressive vestrymen'.

12. An idea propounded in New York in 1853, see Zakim, 'Sartorial Ideologies', p. 1572.

13. See Ibid., p. 1562, for the similar 'Homespun' movement in America. Plain clothing was equated with the values of democracy and equality in the relatively new Republic. This entailed the elite loosing their silks and finery as a patriotic act and a symbol of civic membership.

14. Shakesheff has found that literacy rates were less than 50 per cent in the Herefordshire prison population by the mid-nineteenth century. Shakesheff, *Rural Conflict*, p. 26. See also Reay, *Microhistories*, pp. 235–53, for a discussion about literacy during this period.

15. See also Y. Kawamura, *Fashion-ology, An Introduction to Fashion Studies* (Oxford: Berg, 2005), p. 14.

16. *Berrow's Worcester Journal*, 28 June 1804.

17. Baumgarten, *What Clothes Reveal*, p. 114.

18. Snell, *Annals of the Labouring Poor*, pp. 254–60.

19. *Hereford Journal,* 19 February 1812.

20. *Berrow's Worcester Journal,* 24 February 1814.

21. Such spots had been fashionable since the last quarter of the eighteenth century. See N. Rothstein, *The Victoria and Albert Museum's Textile Collection, Woven Textile Design in Britain from 1750–1850* (London: Victoria and Albert Museum, 1994), particularly catalogue numbers 112, 123, 131.

22. *Hereford Journal*, 24 July 1805.

23. Ibid., 11 September 1805.

24. *Berrow's Worcester Journal,* 20 August 1801.

25. Ibid., 25 June 1801.

26. Verey (ed.), *The Diary of a Cotswold Parson*, pp. 135–6.

27. B. Fine and E. Leopold, 'Consumerism and the Industrial Revolution', *Social History*, 15:1 (1990), pp. 168–71.
28. Northwick Park Records, Servants' Wage Receipts, 1 August 1818, Worcester Record Office [hereafter WRO], 4221/35.
29. Nott Family Records, Household Accounts, William Spriggs bill, 5 May 1835, WRO, 3164/20.
30. By the 1830s, apprenticeship was treated as regular waged work. Premiums were not paid and lodgings, food and other necessaries were not provided. Instead wages and hours were agreed from the outset. For example, William Edwards was apprenticed to Joseph Welden, a tailor, in Worcester in 1837. In lieu of meat, drink and other necessities he would be paid weekly, in the first year 2 shillings per week, up to 8 shillings in the final seventh year. Worcester City Library Collection, Indenture, 1837, WRO, 8782/27/E73/4. The first mention of wages found by Butcher researching Worcestershire apprenticeship indentures was in 1811 for a brazier's apprentice. From 1826 he noted that hours of work were recorded. V. Butcher, 'Worcester Apprentices, 1700–1850' (unpublished pamphlet, Worcester Record Office, 1986), pp. 12–13.
31. *Berrow's Worcester Journal*, 20 November 1800. Another example of 'broad striped velveteen breeches' was also noted in the newspaper on 20 August 1801, and another similar from 1 October 1801.
32. *Berrow's Worcester Journal*, 14 March 1805.
33. Ibid., 26 May 1803.
34. 'A bunch of st[r]ings at the knees and about a dozen of buttons close together with white cotton or silk stocking shewed [*sic*] a lad who was especially knowing. The stockings were usually white with broad stripes. Afterwards patent stockings became the fashion, these were woven the length way and had a bright red or blue stripe, made very narrow – and put at from a quarter of an inch to two inches apart'. Thale (ed.), *The Autobiography of Francis Place*, p. 63.
35. *Hereford Journal*, 12 January 1831.
36. For example, see V. Foster, *A Visual History of Costume, The Nineteenth Century* (London: Batsford, 1992), pp. 64–5, number 58, 'Two Dandies, 1843'. Also, 'Winter Fashions for 1837 & 38 ...', illustrated in C. Fox (ed.), *London – World City 1800–1840* (London: Yale University Press, Exhibition Catalogue, Museum of London, 1992), p. 600, number 682b.
37. A. Ribeiro, *Dress and Morality* (London: Batsford, 1986), pp. 111–13. See also Breward, *The Hidden Consumer*, p. 203, who notes that 'cockney' fashions were well established in the first half of the nineteenth century, espoused by characters such as Sam Weller in the *Pickwick Papers* of 1837. This way of dressing used tight, bright clothing, an urban 'flashness', to mock the priggishness and vanity of the elite.
38. Hereford Museum holds the majority of these, with sixteen drawings and watercolours, with further works in other collections including the Dyer Collection and New Art Gallery, Walsall.
39. Burke, *Eyewitnessing*, pp. 184–8, for a summary of the problems and solutions for interpreting images.
40. J. Tisdall, *Joshua Cristall 1768–1847: In Search of Arcadia* (Hereford: Lapridge Publications, 1996), pp. 48 and 61–3.
41. J. Barrell, *The Dark Side of the Landscape: The Rural Poor in English Painting, 1730–1840* (Cambridge: Cambridge University Press, 1980), pp. 173–4, n. 99. Also, Burke, *Eyewitnessing*, p. 119.

42. Mitchell, *The Wye Tour and its Artists*, p. 95.
43. C. Payne, *Toil and Plenty, Images of the Agricultural Landscape in England 1780–1890* (London: Yale University Press, 1993), chapter 2, especially pp. 35–6.
44. Burke, *Eyewitnessing*, p. 122.
45. Ibid., pp. 10, 15–16, 19, 115.
46. Ibid., p. 19. R. Worth, 'Developing a Method for the Study of the Clothing of the "Poor"; Some Themes in the Visual Representation of Rural Working-Class Dress, 1850–1900', *Textile History*, 40:1 (2009), p. 82.
47. Burke, *Eyewitnessing*, p. 97, 117. See also Worth, 'Developing a Method', pp. 82, 88–90, for a discussion of methodology.
48. Mitchell, *The Wye Tour*, p. 95.
49. B. Taylor, *Joshua Cristall (1768–1847), Exhibition, February-April 1975, Victoria & Albert Museum* (London: HMSO, London, 1975), pp. 21–3.
50. Burke, *Eyewitnessing*, pp. 81, 92.
51. Deed of William Dew of Copped [sic] Wood, 28 March 1791, Herefordshire Record Office [hereafter HRO], O68/III/11. William Dew, labourer, was given rights to timber and quarries on his land from the Lord of the Manor, for a ninety-nine year term, with a rent of 2s 6d every six months.
52. Cited by L. Pitman, *Pigsties and Paradise, Lady Diarists and the Tour of Wales 1795–1860* (Llanrwst: Gwasg Carreg Gwalch, 2009), p. 31.
53. Along with James, the only named sitters noted by Tidsdall. See Tisdall, *Joshua Cristall*, p. 71. Herefordshire Census, 1841, HRO.
54. Goodrich Overseers' Accounts, 1806–26, 7 June 1815 and 1 March 1816 HRO, BF16/57.
55. Goodrich Overseers' Accounts, 1806–26, 11 October 1817, HRO, BF16/57. See also, chapter 4, pp. 000.
56. J. Tisdall, *The Settlement of Coppett Hill, The Story of a Herefordshire Common* (Goodrich: The Friends of Coppett Hill, 1998), p. 3.
57. See, for example, 'Elizabeth Rachel and David Dew, Coppet Hill, July 1825, Herefordshire, J. Cristall', drawing, Hereford Museum, catalogue number 1791 (2).
58. There are versions of this watercolour in the Dyer Collection and also the New Art Gallery, Walsall. Reproduced Mitchell, *The Wye Tour*, p. 97, plate 17, with another sketch of the girl in the same clothes, sitting down, from the Dyer Collection, plate 16.
59. For example, see 'J. Cristall, 1826 – Coppet Hill', drawing, Hereford Museum, catalogue number 6394.
60. 'Coppet Hill Goodrich J. Cristall 1826', drawing, Hereford Museum, catalogue number 783. See, for comparison, from the same date, 'Woman in a day dress, 1824–7', who wears a 'Marie Stuart' cap and ruff, a self-consciously Elizabethan look, in Foster, *A Visual History of Costume*, p. 46, number 35. See also number 32, p. 44, for another similar outfit.
61. See pp. 30–1 above.
62. Sharpe, *Adapting to Capitalism*, p. 103, notes Francis Place employed servants when a jobbing tailor, and similarly other small tradesmen.
63. Parish of Ombersley, parish correspondence, letter from Sarah Brown, undated, WRO, 3572/13.
64. Sharpe, *Adapting to Capitalism,* p. 108.
65. Northwick Park Records, Servants' Wages Book, WRO, 4221/24/1.

66. See also Styles, *The Dress of the People*, p. 279, who comments that it was a normal expectation for female servants to acquire their own clothes, with no formal livery for female domestics.
67. Diary of Thomas Wheeler, 7 October 1828, WRO, 5044/7.
68. See for example, Finn, *The Character of Credit*, p. 83, and Styles, 'Involuntary Consumers?', particularly pp. 9–10 and 18–19.
69. *Hereford Journal*, 15 April 1835.
70. See above, p. 124.
71. Johnson, 'Credit and Thrift', p. 159.
72. Cotton wedding dress, Hereford Museum, accession number 2728.
73. Foster, *A Visual History of Costume*, p. 12, for comments about contemporary dress construction.
74. Cotton wedding dress, Hereford Museum, accession number 1048. For comparable textile samples see Sotheby's auction catalogue, *Important Costumes, Textiles and Fabric Swatch Books* (London: Sotheby's, 4 and 5 March 1998), particularly illustrated lots 9 and 17, dated 1820s and 1830s, part of the Calico Printers' Association Archive.
75. Silk wedding dress, Hereford Museum, accession number 4209.
76. Edward Francis is listed in *Pigot and Co.'s, National and Commercial Directory and Topography ... for Herefordshire,* 1830 (London: James Pigot and Co.), trading from New Street. Powell Indenture, 1822, HRO, O17/1.
77. Powell Indenture, 1843, HRO, O17/2.
78. 1841 Census, HRO.
79. Cotton wedding dress, Hereford Museum, accession number 1999–22.
80. Johnson, 'Credit and Thrift', pp. 159, 169–70.
81. See C. Richardson, 'Havying nothing upon hym saving onely his sherte'. Event, Narrative and Material Culture in Early Modern England', in C. Richardson (ed.), *Clothing Culture, 1350–1650* (Aldershot: Ashgate, 2004), pp. 217–20. Also Richardson, C., 'Introduction', in *idem.*, p. 9.
82. de Vries, *The Industrious Revolution*, pp. 15–17.
83. Kingsland Parish Records, Settlement Examination of Sarah Boulton, 11 April 1822, HRO, F17/30. For general discussion see also J. S. Taylor, *Poverty, Migration, and Settlement, Sojourners' Narratives* (Palo Alto, CA: The Society for the Promotion of Science and Scholarship, 1989), ch. 3. See also Sharpe, *Adapting to Capitalism*, pp. 104–10, for examples from Essex.
84. W. Exell and N. M. Marshall (eds), *Autobiography of Richard Boswell Belcher of Banbury and Blockley – 1898, and The Riot at Blockley in 1878* (Blockley: Blockley Antiquarian Society, 1976).
85. Sharpe, *Adapting to Capitalism*, p. 128.
86. Lemire, *The Business of Everyday Life*, p. 104.
87. R. W. Malcolmson, *Popular Recreations in English Society 1700–1850* (Cambridge: Cambridge University Press, 1973), p. 87.
88. J. Styles, 'Custom or Consumption? Plebeian Fashion in Eighteenth-Century England', in M. Berg and E. Eger (eds), *Luxury in the Eighteenth Century: Debates, Desires and Delectable Goods* (Basingstoke: Palgrave Macmillan, 2003), pp. 103–15, on pp. 111–12.
89. Johnson, 'Credit and Thrift', p. 157. See also Lemire, 'Shifting Currency', pp. 46–7.
90. *Hereford Journal*, 29 April 1835 and see above p. 1.
91. *Berrow's Worcester Journal*, 24 April 1845.
92. de Vries, *The Industrious Revolution*, pp. 178–9.

93. Sharpe, *Adapting to Capitalism,* p. 52.
94. Zakim, *Ready-Made Democracy*, p. 196.
95. Fowler, 'Robert Mansbridge', p. 36, citing the example of Sam Cordery, aged twenty-two, a liveried servant.
96. See also Styles, *The Dress of the People,* pp. 304 and 324.
97. Ibid., p. 160
98. See above pp. 122.
99. Lemire, *The Business of Everyday Life,* p. 2

Conclusion

1. See Deceulaer, 'Entrepreneurs in the Guilds', pp. 139–40, for the importance of the rural market in clothing for an earlier period in the Low Countries.
2. See Smart Martin, 'Ribbons of Desire', pp. 179–200, for a female perspective.
3. Lambert, '"Cast-off Wearing Apparell"', pp. 22–3.
4. *Berrow's Worcester Journal,* 4 December 1800.
5. A scarlet cloak or 'cardinal' survives in Worcestershire County Museum, associated with Betty Keelay, a donkey woman at Malvern, accession number 1967/2252. See A. Buck, 'Variations in English Women's Dress in the Eighteenth Century', *Folk Life,* 9 (1971), p. 16, for a full description of this cloak. Ablett, *Reminiscences of an Old Draper,* p. 54, states how drapers would make up cloaks themselves.
6. Lemire, '"In the Hands of Work Women"', p. 27.
7. *Hereford Journal,* 23 November 1825.
8. *Hereford Journal,* 29 September 1830.
9. Toplis, 'The Manufacture and Provision of Rural Garments', pp. 152–69, for further discussion of the urban manufacture of smock frocks.
10. See Honeyman, *Well Suited,* pp. 2, 33, 45, who notes that John Barran was first a retail tailor before becoming a manufacturer of men's ready-made suits.
11. Edward Meates, Worcester, previously a draper, a 'Ready-Made Clothes and Smock Frock Warehouse', bill to overseers, 8 December 1832, Ombersley Parish Accounts, Worcestershire Record Office, 3572/16.
12. See Buck, 'Buying Clothes in Bedfordshire', p. 218, for a provincial eighteenth century example.
13. St John in Bedwardine, Worcester, Parish Correspondence, Letter from Amelia Cook to the Overseers, 9 April 1834, Worcester Record Office, 1671/21.
14. *Berrow's Worcester Journal,* 7 March 1833. They paid with a stolen £5 Kidderminster bank note, this leading partly to their capture and subsequent execution, along with the blood stains on their old frocks.
15. For debate about the role of more elite male shoppers see, D. Hussey, 'Guns, Horses and Stylish Waistcoats? Male Consumer Activity and Domestic Shopping in Late-Eighteenth and Early-Nineteenth-Century England', in D. Hussey and M. Ponsonby (eds), *Buying for the Home, Shopping for the Domestic from the Seventeenth Century to the Present* (Aldershot: Ashgate, 2008), pp. 47–69; also M. Finn, 'Men's Things: Masculine Possession in the Consumer Revolution', *Social History,* 25:2 (2000), pp. 133–55; and Walsh, 'Shops, Shopping and the Art of Decision Making in Eighteenth Century England', p. 167.
16. See I. Van Damme, 'The Lure of the New: Urban Retailing in the Surroundings of Antwerp (Late Seventeenth – Early Eighteenth Centuries)', in B. Blondé, N. Coquery, J.

Stobart and I. Van Damme (eds), *Fashioning Old and New: Changing Consumer Preferences in Europe (Seventeenth – Nineteenth Centuries)*, (Turnhout: Brepols, Studies in Urban History, 1100–1800, 18, 2009), pp. 97–120, for an interesting discussion about the competition between rural and urban retailers in an earlier period and the importance of rural demand in over-coming urban decline.

17. See above, p. 69.
18. See above pp. 107–8.
19. See above, p. 63.
20. See above pp. 144–5.

WORKS CITED

Primary Sources – Archival

Worcestershire Record Office

Account Book of Joseph Blewitt, 1816–29, 9600/9iii.

Mr Brecknell's Charity, Accounts of Distributions, 1834–57, 12326/1.

Broadway Parish Records, 1800–42, 4869/6/iv.

Bromsgrove Charity Book, 1812, 302/1, No. 1.

Castlemorton Parish Records, Select Vestry Book, 1824–68, 9581/20.

Castlemorton Parish Records, Overseers' Accounts, 1835–50, 9581/22.

Droitwich, St. Peter's Parish Records, Papers and Accounts, 1800–50, 5476/12.

Droitwich, St Peter's Parish Records, Bills 1804–31, 5476/13.

Droitwich, St. Peter's Parish, Parish Correspondence, 1800–50, 5476/17.

Droitwich, St. Peter's Parish, Day Book, 1797–1801, 5476/19, Parish Book, 1802–6, 5476/19, and Parish Book, 1808–17, 5476/19,

Hindlip Parish Records, 1800–50, 8669/6i–iii.

Kidderminster Market Minute and Order Book, 1822–6, 10470/365.

Kidderminster, St. Mary's Parish, Churchwarden's Accounts, 1833–6, 4766/14/ii.

Collection of George Marshall's Bills, 1800–50, 9937/2.

Nott Family Records,1800–50, 3164/20.

Northwick Park Records, Servants' Wage Receipts, 1817–18, 4221/35.

Northwick Park Records, Servants' Wages Book, 1835–54, 4221/24/1.

Ombersley, Parish Correspondence, 1800–30, 3572/13.

Ombersley, Papers of the Parish Officers, 1800–30, 3572/15.

Ombersley Parish Accounts, 1800–32, 3572/16.

Powick Parish Records, 1800–30, 3802/10.

St Andrew's, Worcester, Parish Correspondence, 1800–50, 4426/12.

St Andrew's, Worcester, Parish Bills from Parish of St. Helen's, 1800–50, 4426/17.

St John in Bedwardine, Worcester, Parish Correspondence, 1800–50, 1671/21.

St Martins, Worcester, Parish Accounts, Bill to Parish 1798, 5234/14.

St Nicholas, Worcester, Parish Receipts, Accounts and Financial Papers relating to the Churchwardens, Overseers and Officials, Bills from John Sanders, 10 June 1778 and 22 November 1778, 3696/9.

Richard Sanders, Bills and Receipts, 1829–37, 2193/77 iv.

Thomas Wheeler's Diary, 1828–39, 5044/7.

Worcestershire Census, 1841 and 1851.

Worcester City Records, Minutes of the Company of Master Tailors, 1800–41, C9, Shelf 647, Box 1.

Worcester City Records, Market Accounts, 1823–35, B7, box 2.

Worcester City Library Collection, Apprenticeship Indenture, 1837, 8782/27/E73/4.

Worcestershire Quarter Sessions Order Books, Volumes 10 (1815–21) and 11 (1821–9).

Worcestershire Quarter Session Papers, Summary Sheets and Indexes, 1800–24, 1825–49, 1/559–778.

Herefordshire Record Office

Abbey Dore Parish Records, Parish Book, 1790–1849, AC16/26.

Aymestrey Parish Records, Miscellaneous Items, Letter from the Vicar of Aymestrey, *circa* 16 January 1844, F71/153.

Bromyard Parish, Linton Township, Overseers' Accounts, Disbursements, Weekly and Occasional Pay, 1800–3, 1808–9, 1815–20, E38/20.

Bromyard Parish, Winslow Overseers' Accounts, 1800–35, E38/62–63.

Bromyard Parish, Winslow Parish Correspondence for Relief, 1800–34, E38/74.

The Minute Book of the Bromyard Union, 1836–8, K42/1.

'Calendar of the Prisoners to be tried at the Michelmas … Sessions', 1845.

Deed of William Dew of Copped [sic] Wood, 28 March 1791, O68/III/11.

Goodrich Overseers' Accounts, 1806–26, BF16/57.

Hereford Assizes Calendar, Lent 1844.

Hereford City Market Account Books, Volumes 1–2, 1810–35, BG11/13.

Hereford City Quarter Session Papers, Mayors Court, 12 November 1804 and 24 February 1812[?].

St. Peter's, Hereford, Overseers' Accounts, 1808–27, 1827–48, AR77/19.

Herefordshire Census, 1841 and 1851.

Herefordshire Quarter Session Minute Books, Volumes 17 (1802–5), 20 (1812–17), 22 [labelled 23 though should be 22] (1819–25), 23 (1825–33), 24 (1833–42), 25 (1842–4), 26 (1844–9).

Herefordshire Quarter Session Order Books, Volumes 17 (1825–39) and 18 (1839–47).

Hope under Dinmore Parish, Complaints Book, 1825–7, N31/163.

'A list of Persons of whom Articles are bought of, for the use of Mr Jarvis's Charity, being freeholders in, and for the County of Hereford. April 6th 1811', BA89/2/9.

Kingsland Parish Records, Settlement Examination, 1822, F17/30.

Letton Parish Church, Churchwardens' Accounts, 1769–1887, AA1/7.

Bills of Captain Patershall, 1822–36, F60.

Powell Indentures, 1822 and 1843, O17/1–2.

Staunton upon Wye Overseers' Accounts, 1820–1, AA2/24.

Stoke Edith Parish Records, Clothing Account Bills, 1800–35, G53/8.

Tailors Account Books, Brampton Bryan, 1834–50, E61/2/1–2.

National Archives, Kew

Minute Books of the Hackney Coach Commissioners, 1807–12, IR51/2.

Treasury Letter Books of the Hackney Coach Commissioners, 1820–6, IR51/3.

Entry Book of Letters between the Treasury and Board of Stamps, 1831–4, IR51/5.

Board of Stamps, and Board of Stamps and Taxes Out-Letter Book concerning Hackney Carriage and Hawkers and Pedlars Licences, 1831–6, IR51/6.

Entry Book of Deputations to Distributors of Stamps, 1832–60, IR51/7.

British Library

British Library, Manuscript Collection, Francis Place Papers, Volume XXXIX, 'Manners, Morals, Improvement of the People and its Causes ...', 1646–1836', Volume III, Add. 27827.

Bodleian Library

Account Book of William Baker, 59 Parsons Street, Banbury, 1813–22, MS.Top.Oxon.c.453.

Dudley Record Office

Cartwright Charity, Trustees Minutes and Clothing Accounts, 1822–1955, Acc. 8531.

Greater Manchester County Record Office

'Day Book of 'G', a Manchester firm ... 1773–79', GB127.MS ff 657 D43.

Primary Sources – Publications

Anonymous, *A Concise History of the City and Suburbs of Worcester* (Worcester: T. Eaton, 1816).

Anonymous, *The Workwoman's Guide, Containing Instructions ... in Cutting Out and Completing those Articles of Wearing Apparel, &c. which are Usually Made at Home ... By a Lady* (London: Simpkin, Marshall and Co., 1838).

Ablett, W., *Reminiscences of an Old Draper* (London: Sampson Low, Marston, Searle and Rivington, 1876).

Aylesbury News, 1836–50.

Bentley's History and Guide and Alphabetical and Classified Directory of Worcester ..., Evesham ..., Dudley ..., Stourbridge ..., and Bentley's History, Gazetteer, Directory and Statistics of Worcestershire (Birmingham: Bull & Turner, 1840–2), 3 vols.

Berridge, E. (ed.), *The Barrett's at Hope End, The Early Diary of Elizabeth Barrett Browning* (London: J. Murray, 1974).

Berrow's Worcester Journal, weekly, 1800–50.

The Bucks Herald, 1840.

Coburn, K. (ed.), *The Letters of Sara Hutchinson from 1800 to 1835* (London: Routledge & Kegan Paul, 1954).

Directory and Gazetteer of Herefordshire (Birmingham: Lascelles & Co., 1851).

Eden, F. M., *The State of the Poor. A History of the Labouring Classes in England with Parochial Reports,* ed. A. G. L. Rogers (London: George Routledge & Sons Ltd, 1928).

Elson, G., *The Last of the Climbing Boys* (London: John Long, 1900).

Engels, F., *The Condition of the Working Class in England* (London: Penguin, 1987).

Exell, A. W., and Marshall, N. M. (eds), *Autobiography of Richard Boswell Belcher of Banbury and Blockley – 1898, and The Riot at Blockley in 1878* (Blockley: Blockley Antiquarian Society, 1976).

Griffith, G., *The Free Schools of Worcestershire and their Fulfilment* (London: Charles Gilpin, 1852).

Guide and Directory to the City and Suburbs of Worcester for 1837... (Worcester: T. Stratford, 1837).

Hayward's Directory of the City and Borough of Worcester (Worcester: R. Haywood, 1840).

Hereford Journal, weekly, 1800–50.

Holden's Triennial Directory (Fifth Edition) for 1809, 1810, 1811, 2nd Volume (London: John Davenport [printer], 1811).

Holden's Annual Directory, 1st Edition for the Years 1816 & 1817 (London: Thomas Underhill, 1817).

Hunt & Co.'s Commercial Directory; for the Cities of Gloucester, Hereford, and Worcester ... (London: E. Hunt and Co., 1847).

Hurle, P., *Castlemorton Farmer, John Rayner Lane 1798–1871* (Storridge: P. Hurle, 1996).

Kingsley, C., 'Cheap Clothes and Nasty', in *Novels, Poems & Letters of Charles Kingsley, Alton Locke* (1898; London: Kessinger Publishing, 2003).

Laird, F. C., *Worcestershire or Original Delineations, Topographical, Historical and Descriptive of that County, The Result of Personal Survey* (London: J. Hams, 1818).

Mayhew, H., *Mayhew's London, being selections from 'London Labour and the London Poor'* (1851; London: Spring Books, undated modern reprint, n.d.).

Perkins, E. E., *A Treatise on Haberdashery &c.* (London: T. Hurst, 1834).

Pigot and Co.'s, National and Commercial Directory and Topography ... for Herefordshire 1822, 1830, 1835, 1842, 1844, 1850, *for Worcestershire ...* 1828, 1835, 1842 (London: James Pigot and Co.).

Pigot and Son's General Directory of Manchester, Salford &c. (Manchester: J. Pigot and Sons, 1830).

Pitt, W., *A General View of the Agriculture of the County of Worcester, a Reprint of the Work Drawn up for the Consideration of the Board of Agriculture and Internal Improvement* (1813; Newton Abbot: David and Charles, 1969).

The Reports of the Commissioners appointed in Pursuance of Various Acts of Parliament to Enquire Concerning Charities in England and Wales Relating to the County of Herefordshire 1819–1839 (London: Henry Gray, *circa* 1841).

The Reports of the Commissioners to Enquire Concerning Charities in England and Wales Relating to the County of Worcester 1819–1837 (London: Henry Gray, *circa* 1840).

Robson's Commercial Directory of the Western Counties, viz. ... Hereford ... Worcester (London: William Robson, 1838).

Rowley, E., *Fruits of Righteousness in the Life of Susanna Knapp* (Worcester: Hamilton, Adams & Co., F. Osborn, 1866).

Smith, A., *The Natural History of the Gent* (London: D. Bogue, 1847).

Spevack, M. (ed.), *A Victorian Chronicle, The Diary of Henrietta Halliwell-Phillipps* (Hildesheim: Georg Olms Verlag AG, 1999).

Southall, M., *A Description of Malvern, including a Guide to the Drives, Rides, Walks and Excursions...* (Stourport: G. Nicholson, 1825).

Thale, M. (ed.), *The Autobiography of Francis Place* (London: Cambridge University Press, 1972).

Turberville, T. C., *Worcestershire in the Nineteenth Century, A Complete Digest of the Facts Occurring in the County since the Commencement of the Year 1800* (London: Longman, Brown, Green and Longmans, 1852).

Verey, D. (ed.), *The Diary of a Cotswold Parson, Reverend F. E. Witts, 1783–1854* (Stroud: Sutton, 1978).

Wood, Mrs H., *Mrs Halliburton's Troubles* (London and Glasgow: Collins Clear-Type Press, undated, original 1862).

Wood, Mrs H., *Johnny Ludlow,* 3rd series (London: Macmillan, 1898).

Wood, Mrs H., *Johnny Ludlow,* 6th series (London: Macmillan, 1901).

Woodforde, The Rev. J., *The Diary of a Country Parson, Volume V: 1797–1802*, J. Beresford (ed.), (Oxford: Oxford University Press, 1981).

The Worcester Royal Directory (Worcester: J. Grundy, 1790).

Worcester Royal Directory for the Year 1794 (Worcester: J. Grundy, 1794).

Worcestershire General and Commercial Directory for 1820 (Worcester: S. Lewis, 1820).

Secondary Sources

Adburgham, A., *Shops and Shopping 1800–1914* (London: George Allen and Unwin Ltd, 1981).

Alexander, D., *Retailing in England during the Industrial Revolution* (London: Athlone, 1970).

Arnold, J., 'Smocks, Shirts, Falling Bands and Mantuas: Evidence of Loosely-Fitting Garments and Neckwear produced for the Ready-to Wear Market, *c.* 1560–1700', in *Per Una Storia della Moda Pronta, Problemi e Richerchi, Atti del v Convegno Internazionale del CISST, Milano, 26–28 Febbraio 1990* (Florence: Edifir Edizioni, 1991), pp. 17–27.

Asquith, I., 'The Structure, Ownership and Control of the Press, 1780–1855', in G. Boyce, J. Curran and P. Wingate (eds), *Newspaper History from the Seventeenth Century to the Present Day* (London: Constable (etc.) for the Press Group of the Acton Society, 1978), pp. 98–116.

Attfield, J., *Wild Things: The Material Culture of Everyday Life* (Oxford: Berg, 2000).

Backhouse, A., *The Worm-Eaten Waistcoat* (York: A R Backhouse, 2003).

Barker, H., 'Catering for Provincial Tastes? Newspapers, Readers and Profit in Late Eighteenth-Century England', *Historical Research,* 69:168 (1996), pp. 42–61.

—, *Newspapers, Politics and English Society, 1695–1855* (Harlow: Longman, 2000).

—, *Business of Women: Female Enterprise and Urban Development in Northern England 1760–1830* (Oxford: Oxford University Press, 2006).

Barrell, J., *The Dark Side of the Landscape, The Rural Poor in English Painting, 1730–1840* (Cambridge: Cambridge University Press, 1980).

Barrett, S., 'Kinship, Poor Relief and the Welfare Process in Early Modern England', in S. King and A. Tomkins (eds), *The Poor in England 1700–1850. An Economy of Makeshifts* (Manchester: Manchester University Press, 2003), pp. 199–227.

Baumgarten, L., *What Clothes Reveal, The Language of Clothing in Colonial and Federal America* (Williamsburg, VA: The Colonial Williamsburg Foundation and Yale Press, 2002).

Becker, M. J., 'Match Coats and the Military: Mass-Produced Clothing for Native Americans as Parallel Markets in the Seventeenth Century', *Textile History*, 41:1 Supplement (2010), pp. 153–81.

Benson, J., *The Penny Capitalists, A Study of Nineteenth-Century Working-Class Entrepreneurs* (Dublin: Gill and Macmillan, 1983).

—, *The Working Class in Britain 1850–1939* (Harlow: Longman, 1989).

—, *The Rise of Consumer Society in Britain, 1880–1980* (London: Longman, 1994).

—, 'Retailing', in J. Benson and G. Shaw (eds), *The Retailing Industry, Volume 2, The Coming of the Mass Market, 1800–1945* (London: IB Tauris, 1999), pp. 132–62.

Benson, J., and L. Ugolini, 'Introduction: Historians and the Nation of Shopkeepers', in J. Benson and L. Ugolini (eds), *A Nation of Shopkeepers: Retailing in Britain, 1550–2000* (London: IB Tauris, 2003), pp. 1–21.

—, 'Beyond the Shop: Problems and Possibilities', *Journal of Historical Marketing*, 2:3 (2010), pp. 256–69.

— (eds), 'Retailing Beyond the Shop: Britain *c*. 1400–1900', *Journal of Historical Research in Marketing, Special Issue*, 2:3 (2010) pp. 256–69

Berg, M., *Luxury and Pleasure in Eighteenth Century Britain* (Oxford: Oxford University Press, 2005).

Berridge, V., 'Content Analysis and Historical Research on Newspapers', in M. Harris and A. Lee (eds), *The Press in English Society from the Seventeenth to the Nineteenth Centuries* (London: Rutherford, 1986), pp. 201–18.

Berry, H., 'Promoting Taste in the Provincial Press: National and Local Culture in Eighteenth-century Newcastle upon Tyne', *British Journal for Eighteenth-Century Studies*, 25 (2002), pp. 1–17.

Blondé, B., P. Stabel, I. Van Damme and J. Stobart, 'Retail Circuits and Practices in Medieval and Early Modern Europe: An Introduction', in B. Blondé, P. Stabel, I. Van Damme and J. Stobart (eds), *Buyers and Sellers: Retail Circuits and Practices in Medieval and Early Modern Europe* (Turnhout: Brepols, Studies in European Urban History, 1100–1800, 9, 2006), pp. 7–22.

—, Coquery, N., Stobart, J., and Van Damme, I. (eds), *Fashioning Old and New: Changing Consumer Preferences in Europe (Seventeenth – Nineteenth Centuries)*, (Turnhout: Brepols, Studies in Urban History, 1100–1800, 18, 2009).

Borsay, P., *The English Urban Renaissance, Culture and Society in the Provincial Town 1660–1770* (Oxford: Clarendon, 1989).

Breward, C., *The Hidden Consumer, Masculinities, Fashion and City Life 1860–1914* (Manchester: Manchester University Press, 1999).

Bridges, T., and C. Mundy, *Worcester, A Pictorial History* (Chichester: Phillimore & Co. Ltd, 1996).

Brown, D., '"Persons of Infamous Character" or "an Honest, Industrious and Useful Description of People"? The Textile Pedlars of Alstonfield and the Role of Peddling in Industrialization', *Textile History,* 31:1 (2000), pp. 1–26.

Buck, A., 'The Countryman's Smock', *Folk Life*, 1 (1963), pp. 16–34.

—, 'Variations in English Women's Dress in the Eighteenth Century', *Folk Life*, 9 (1971), pp. 5–28.

—, *Dress in Eighteenth-Century England* (London: Batsford, London, 1979).

—, 'Buying Clothes in Bedfordshire: Customers and Tradesmen, 1700–1800', *Textile History*, 22:2 (1991), pp. 211–37.

Burke, P., *Eyewitnessing: The Uses of Images as Historical Evidence* (London: Reaktion Books, London, 2001).

Burman, B., and C. Turbin, 'Introduction: Material Strategies Engendered', *Gender and History*, 14:3 (2002), pp. 371–81.

Burman, B., and J. White, 'Fanny's Pockets: Cotton, Consumption and Domestic Economy, 1780–1850', in J. Batchelor and C. Kaplan (eds), *Women and Material Culture, 1660–1830* (Basingstoke: Palgrave Macmillan, 2007), pp. 31–51.

Burnett, J., *A History of the Cost of Living* (Harmondsworth: Pelican, 1969).

Butcher, V., 'Worcester Apprentices, 1700–1850' (unpublished pamphlet, Worcester Record Office, 1986).

Chapman, S., 'The Innovating Entrepreneurs in the British Ready-made Clothing Industry', *Textile History*, 24:1 (1993), pp. 5–25.

—, *Merchant Enterprise in Britain, From the Industrial Revolution to World War I* (Cambridge: Cambridge University Press, 1999).

—, 'The "Revolution" in the Manufacture of Ready-made Clothing 1840–1860', *London Journal*, 29:1 (2004), pp. 44–61.

Charpy, M., 'The Scope and Structure of the Nineteenth-Century Second-Hand Trade in the Parisian Clothes Market', in L. Fontaine (ed.), *Alternative Exchanges, Second-hand Circulations from the Sixteenth Century to the Present* (Oxford: Berghahn Books, 2008), pp. 127–51.

Clapham, J. H., 'The Organisation of Commerce', in J. Benson and G. Shaw (eds), *The Retailing Industry, Volume 2, The Coming of the Mass Market, 1800–1945* (London: IB Tauris, 1999), pp. 39–45.

Clark, A., *The Struggle for the Breeches. Gender and the Making of the British Working Class* (London: University of California Press, 1997).

Clark, P., *The English Ale House, A Social History, 1200–1830* (Harlow: Longman, 1983).

Corfield, P. J., *The Impact of English Towns 1700–1800* (Oxford: Oxford University Press, 1982).

Cox, N., *The Complete Tradesman, A Study of Retailing, 1550–1820* (Aldershot: Ashgate, 2000).

Craik, J., *Uniforms Exposed, From Conformity to Transgression* (Oxford: Berg, 2005).

Crompton, F., *Workhouse Children* (Stroud: Sutton Publishing Ltd, 1997).

Cunnington, C. W. and P. E., and Beard, C., *A Dictionary of English Costume 900–1900* (London: A. and C. Black, 1960).

Davidoff, L., and Hall, C., *Family Fortunes, Men and Women of the English Middle Class, 1780–1850* (London: Routledge, 1992).

Deceulaer, H., 'Entrepreneurs in the Guilds: Ready-to-wear Clothing and Subcontracting in late Sixteenth and early Seventeenth-century Antwerp', *Textile History*, 31:2 (2000), pp. 133–49.

—, 'Dealing with Diversity: Pedlars in the Southern Netherlands in the Eighteenth Century', in B. Blondé, P. Stabel, I. Van Damme and J. Stobart (eds), *Buyers and Sellers: Retail Circuits and Practices in Medieval and Early Modern Europe* (Turnhout: Brepols, Studies in European Urban History, 1100–1800, 9, 2006), pp. 171– 98.

—, 'Second-Hand Dealers in the Early Modern Low Countries, Institutions, Markets and Practices', in L. Fontaine (ed.), *Alternative Exchanges, Second-hand Circulations from the Sixteenth Century to the Present* (Oxford: Berghahn Books, 2008), pp. 13–42.

de Vries, J., *The Industrious Revolution, Consumer Behaviour and the Household Economy, 1650 to the Present* (Cambridge: Cambridge University Press, 2008).

Didsbury, B., 'Cheshire Saltworkers', in R. Samuel (ed.), *Miners, Quarrymen and Saltworkers* (London: Routledge and Kegan Paul, 1977), pp. 137–203.

Dryburgh, R., 'Not granted until you appear leaner': Administrative Corruption and the Payment of Rent by the Old Poor Law in Bolton', at http://www.ehs.org.uk /othercontent/ dryburgh.htm, pp. 1–5 [accessed 23 November 2010].

Dyck, I., *William Cobbett and Rural Popular Culture* (Cambridge: Cambridge University Press, 1992).

Ewing, E., *Everyday Dress 1650–1900* (London: Batsford, 1984).

Fairchilds, C., 'The Production and Marketing of Populuxe Goods in Eighteenth-Century Paris', in J. Brewer and R. Porter (eds), *Consumption and the World of Goods* (London: Routledge, 1994), pp. 228–48.

Fawcett, T., 'Bath's Georgian Warehouses', *Costume*, 26 (1992), pp. 32–9.

Fine, B., and E. Leopold, 'Consumerism and the Industrial Revolution', *Social History*, 15:1 (1990), pp. 151–79.

—, and Leopold, E., *The World of Consumption* (London: Routledge, 1993).

Finn, M., 'Men's Things: Masculine Possession in the Consumer Revolution', *Social History*, 25:2 (2000), pp. 133–55.

—, 'Scotch Drapers and the Politics of Modernity: Gender, Class and National Identity in the Victorian Tally Trade', in M. Daunton and M. Hilton (eds), *The Politics of Consumption, Material Culture and Citizenship in Europe and America* (Oxford: Berg, 2001), pp. 89–107.

—, *The Character of Credit, Personal Debt in English Culture 1740–1914* (Cambridge: Cambridge University Press, 2003).

Fontaine, L., *History of Pedlars in Europe* (Cambridge: Polity, 1996).

Fontaine, L., and J. Schlumbohm, (ed.), *Alternative Exchanges, Second-hand Circulations from the Sixteenth Century to the Present* (Oxford: Berghahn Books, 2008).

—, 'Household Strategies for Survival: An Introduction', in L. Fontaine and J. Schlumbohm (eds), *Household Strategies for Survival 1600–2000: Fission, Faction and Cooperation* (Cambridge: Cambridge University Press, International Review of Social History supplement, 2000), pp. 1–18.

Foster, V., *A Visual History of Costume, The Nineteenth Century* (London: Batsford, 1992).

Fowler, C., 'Robert Mansbridge, A Rural Tailor and his Customers 1811–15', *Textile History*, 28:1 (1997), pp. 29–38.

—, 'Satisfying Popular Consumer Demand 1775–1815 with Specific Reference to the Dress Trades in Hampshire' (PhD dissertation, University of Portsmouth, 1998).

Fox, C. (ed.), *London – World City 1800–1840* (London: Yale University Press, Exhibition Catalogue, Museum of London, 1992).

French, H. R., *The Middle Sort of People in Provincial England, 1600–1750* (Oxford: Oxford University Press, 2007).

Frey, D. A., Jr, 'Industrious Households: Survival Strategies of Artisans in a Southwest German Town during the Eighteenth and Early Nineteenth Centuries', in L. Fontaine and J. Schlumbohm (eds), *Household Strategies for Survival 1600–2000: Fission, Faction and Cooperation* (Cambridge: Cambridge University Press, International Review of Social History supplement, 2000), pp. 115–36.

Garrad, L. S., 'Dorcas Society', at http://www.isle-of-man.com/manxnotebook/ history/ poor/dorcas.htm p. 1 [accessed 23 November 2010].

Gaut, R. C., *A History of Worcestershire Agriculture and Rural Evolution* (Worcester: Littlebury, 1939).

Gillet, M., 'Supply of Shopkeepers in Besançon in the First Part of the Nineteenth Century: Novelties between 'Old' and 'New'', in B. Blondé, N. Coquery, J. Stobart and I. Van Damme (eds), *Fashioning Old and New: Changing Consumer Preferences in Europe (Seventeenth – Nineteenth Centuries)* (Turnhout: Brepols, Studies in Urban History, 1100–1800, 18, 2009), pp. 145–65.

Ginsberg, M., 'The Tailoring and Dressmaking Trades, 1700–1850', *Costume*, 6 (1972), pp. 64–71.

—, 'Rags to Riches: The Second-Hand Clothes Trade 1700–1978', *Costume,* 14 (1980), pp. 121–35.

Godley, A., 'Singer in Britain: the Diffusion of Sewing Machine Technology and its Impact of the Clothing Industry in the United Kingdom, 1860–1905', *Textile History*, 27:1 (1996), pp. 59–76.

Green, D. R., 'Street Trading in London: A Case Study of Casual Labour, 1830–60', in J. Benson and G. Shaw (eds), *The Retailing Industry, Volume 2, The Coming of the Mass Market, 1800–1945* (London: IB Tauris, 1999), pp. 115–31.

—, 'Pauper Protests: Power and Resistance in Early Nineteenth Century London Workhouses', *Social History*, 31:2 (2006), pp. 137–59.

Gregson, N., and L. Crewe, *Second-Hand Cultures* (Oxford: Berg, 2003).

Gwilliam, B., *Old Worcester: People and Places* (Bromsgrove: Halfshire Books, 1993).

Hall, M., *Smocks* (Princes Risborough: Shire Publications, 1979).

Hamilton, P., 'Haberdashery for Use in Dress 1550–1800' (PhD dissertation, University of Wolverhampton, 2007).

Hamish Fraser, W., *The Coming of the Mass Market* (Basingstoke: Macmillan, 1981).

Hanly, M., 'The Economy of Makeshifts and the Role of the Poor Law: a Game of Chance?', in S. King and A. Tomkins (eds), *The Poor in England 1700–1850. An Economy of Make-shifts* (Manchester: Manchester University Press, 2003), pp. 76–99.

Hann, A., 'Industrialisation and the Service Economy', in J. Stobart and N. Raven (eds), *Towns, Regions and Industries, Urban and Industrial Change in the Midlands, c. 1700–1840* (Manchester: Manchester University Press, 2005), pp. 42–61.

Hey, D., *Packmen, Carriers and Packhorse Roads, Trade and Communications in North Derbyshire and South Yorkshire* (Leicester: Leicester University Press, 1980).

Hodson, D., '"The Municipal Store", Adaptation and Development in the Retail Markets of Nineteenth Century Urban Lancashire', *Business History*, 40:4 (1998), pp. 94–114.

Honeyman, K., *Well Suited, A History of the Leeds Clothing Industry, 1850–1990* (Oxford: Oxford University Press, Pasold Research Fund, 2000).

Hood, A. D., 'Material Culture and Textiles: An Overview', *Material History Bulletin*, 31 (1990), pp. 5–10.

Hopkins, E., *Birmingham: The First Manufacturing Town in the World, 1760–1840* (London: Weidenfeld & Nicolson, 1989).

Hosgood, C. P., 'The 'Knights of the Road': Commercial Travellers and the Culture of the Commercial Room in Late-Victorian and Edwardian England', *Victorian Studies*, 37:4 (1994), pp. 519–47.

Hudson, P., 'Proto-Industrialisation: the Case of the West Riding Wool Textile Industry in the Eighteenth and Early Nineteenth Centuries', *History Workshop Journal*, 12 (1981), pp. 34–61.

Hussey, D., 'Guns, Horses and Stylish Waistcoats? Male Consumer Activity and Domestic Shopping in Late-Eighteenth and Early-Nineteenth-Century England', in D. Hussey and M. Ponsonby (eds), *Buying for the Home, Shopping for the Domestic from the Seventeenth Century to the Present* (Aldershot: Ashgate, 2008), pp. 47–69.

Jaumain, S., 'Un Métier Oublié: Le Colporteur dans La Belgique du XIXe Siècle', *Belgisch Tijdschrift voor Nieuwste Geschiedemis*, 16: =3–4 (1985), pp. 307–56.

Johnson, P., 'Credit and Thrift and the British Working Class, 1870–1939', in J. Winter (ed.), *The Working Class in Modern British History: Essays in Honour of Henry Pelling* (Cambridge: Cambridge University Press, 1983), pp. 147–70.

Jones, C., 'Some Recent Trends in the History of Charity', in M. Daunton (ed.), *Charity, Self Interest and Welfare in the English Past* (London: UCL Press, 1996), pp. 51–63.

Jones, P., 'Clothing of the Poor in Early-Nineteenth-Century England', *Textile History*, 37:1 (2006), pp. 17–37.

Jütte, R., *Poverty and Deviance in Early Modern Europe* (Cambridge: Cambridge University Press, 1994).

Kawamura, Y., *Fashion-ology, An Introduction to Fashion Studies* (Oxford: Berg, 2005).

Kershen, A. J., *Uniting the Tailors, Trade Unionism Amongst the Tailors of London and Leeds, 1870–1939* (Ilford: Frank Cass & Co. Ltd, 1995).

—, 'Morris Cohen and the Origins of the Women's Wholesale Clothing Industry in the East End', *Textile History*, 28:1 (1999), pp. 39–46.

Kidd, A., *State, Society and the Poor in Nineteenth-Century England* (Basingstoke: Macmillan, 1999).

Kidwell, C. B., *Suiting Everyone, The Democratization of Clothing in America* (Washington D. C.: Smithsonian Institution Press, 1974).

King, S., *Poverty and Welfare in England, 1700–1850, A Regional Perspective* (Manchester: Manchester University Press, 2000).

—, 'Reclothing the English Poor, 1750–1840', *Textile History*, 33:1 (2002), pp. 37–47.

—, 'Meer Pennies for my Baskitt will be Enough': Women, Work and Welfare, 1770–1830', in P. Lane, N. Raven and K. D. M. Snell (eds), *Women, Work and Wages in England 1600–1850* (Woodbridge: Boydell, 2004), pp. 119–40.

—, 'The Clothing of the Poor: A Matter of Pride or Shame?', in A. Gestrich, S. King and L. Raphael (eds), *Being Poor in Modern Europe: Historical Perspectives 1800–1940* (Oxford: Peter Lang, 2006), pp. 365–87.

—, 'I Fear You Will Think Me Too Presumtuous in My Demands but Necessity Has No Law': Clothing in English Pauper Letters. 1800–1834', *International Review of Social History*, 54:2 (2009), pp. 207–36.

King, S., and A. Tomkins, (eds), *The Poor in England 1700–1850. An Economy of Makeshifts* (Manchester: Manchester University Press, 2003).

King, S., and C. Muldrew, 'Cash, Wages and the Economy of Makeshifts in England, 1650–1800', in P. Scholliers and L. Schwarz (eds), *Experiencing Wages: Social and Cultural Aspects of Wage Forms in Europe since 1500* (Oxford: Berghahn Books, 2003), pp. 155–80.

Lambert, J. A., *A Nation of Shopkeepers, Trade Ephemera from 1654 to the 1860s in the John Johnson Collection* (Oxford: Bodleian Library, Exhibition Catalogue, 2001).

Lambert, M., '"Cast-off Wearing Apparel": The Consumption and Distribution of Second-hand Clothing in Northern England during the Long Eighteenth Century', *Textile History*, 35:1 (2004), pp. 1–26.

Lane, P., 'Work on the Margins: Poor Women and the Informal Economy of Eighteenth and Early Nineteenth-Century Leicestershire', *Midland History*, 22 (1997), pp. 85–99.

Large, P., 'Urban Growth and Agricultural Change in the West Midlands during the Seventeenth and Eighteenth Centuries', in P. Clark (ed.), *The Transformation of English Provincial Towns 1600–1800* (London: Hutchinson, 1984), pp. 169–89.

Leather, E. M., *The Folklore of Herefordshire* (Hereford: Lapridge Publications, 1991).

Lemire, B., 'Developing Consumerism and the Ready-made Clothing Trade in Britain, 1750–1800', *Textile History*, 15:1 (1984), pp. 21–44.

—, 'Consumerism in Pre-Industrial and Early Industrial England, The Trade in Second Hand Clothes', *Journal of British Studies*, 27:1 (1988), pp. 1–24.

—, 'A Good Stock of Cloathes': The Changing Market for Cotton Clothing in Britain 1750–1800', *Textile History*, 22:2 (1991), pp. 311–28.

—, *Fashion's Favourite, The Cotton Trade and the Consumer in Britain, 1660–1800* (Oxford, Oxford University Press, Pasold Research Fund, 1991).

—, 'Redressing the History of the Clothing Trade in England: Ready-made Clothing, Guilds, and Women Workers, 1650–1800', *Dress*, 21 (1994), pp. 61–74.

—, *Dress, Culture and Commerce, The English Clothing Trade before the Factory, 1660–1800* (Basingstoke: Macmillan, 1997).

—, 'In the Hands of Work Women'. English Markets, Cheap Clothing and Female Labour, 1650–1800', *Costume*, 33 (1999), pp. 23–35.

—, 'Second hand Beaux and 'red armed belles'; Conflict and the Creation of Fashion in England, *circa* 1660–1800', *Continuity and Change*, 15:3 (2000), pp. 391–417.

—, *The Business of Everyday Life, Gender, Practice and Social Politics in England, c. 1600–1900* (Manchester: Manchester University Press, 2006).

—, 'Shifting Currency: The Culture and Economy of the Second Hand Trade in England, c. 1600–1850', in A. Palmer and H. Clark (eds), *Old Clothes, New Looks, Second Hand Fashion* (Oxford: Berg, 2006), pp. 29–47.

—, 'Plebeian Commercial Circuits and Everyday Material Exchange in England, *circa* 1600–1900', in B. Blondé, P. Stabel, I. Van Damme and J. Stobart (eds), *Buyers and Sellers: Retail Circuits and Practices in Medieval and Early Modern Europe* (Turnhout: Brepols, Studies in European Urban History, 1100–1800, 9, 2006), pp. 245–66.

Leopold, E., 'The Manufacture of the Fashion System', in J. Ash and E. Wilson (eds), *Chic Thrills, A Fashion Reader* (London: Pandora, 1992), pp. 101–17.

Levitt, S., 'Cheap Mass-Produced Men's Clothing in the Nineteenth and Early Twentieth Centuries', *Textile History*, 22:2 (1991), pp. 179–92.

—, 'Bristol Clothing Trades and Exports in the Georgian Period', in *Per Una Storia della Moda Pronta, Problemi e Richerchi, Atti del v Convegno Internazionale del CISST, Milano, 26–28 Febbraio 1990* (Florence: Edifir Edizioni, 1991), pp. 29–41.

Malcolmson, R. W., *Popular Recreations in English Society 1700–1850* (Cambridge: Cambridge University Press, 1973).

Mann, J. de L., *The Cloth Industry in the West of England from 1640 to 1880* (Oxford: Clarendon, 1971).

McCulloch, J., 'Some Aspects of Victorian Bromyard from the 1851 Census', in J. G. Hillaby and E. D. Pearson (eds), *Bromyard: A Local History* (Worcester: Bromyard and District Local History Society, 1970), pp. 134–47.

McKendrick, N., Brewer, J., and Plumb, J. H., *The Birth of a Consumer Society: The Commercialization of Eighteenth Century England* (London: Europa, 1982).

Miller, A., *Dressed to Kill, British Naval Uniform, Masculinity and Contemporary Fashions, 1748–1857* (London: National Maritime Museum, 2007).

Miller, D., 'Introduction, The Birth of Value', in P. Jackson, M. Lowe, D. Miller, and F. Mort (eds), *Commercial Cultures: Economies, Practices, Spaces* (Oxford: Berg, 2000), pp. 77–83.

Mingay, G. E. (ed.), *The Agrarian History of England and Wales, Vol. VI, 1750–1850* (Cambridge: Cambridge University Press, 1989).

Mitchell, I., 'The Development of Urban Retailing 1700–1815', in P. Clark (ed), *The Transformation of English Provincial Towns 1600–1800* (London: Hutchinson, 1984), pp. 259–83.

—, 'Retailing Innovation and Urban Markets, c. 1800–1850', *Journal of Historical Marketing*, 2:3 (2010), pp. 287–99.

Mitchell, J., *The Wye Tour and its Artists* (Almeley: Logaston, 2010).

Morgan, V., 'Producing Consumer Space in Eighteenth-Century England: Shops, Shopping and the Provincial Town' (PhD dissertation, Coventry University, 2003).

—, 'Beyond the Boundary of the Shop: Retail Advertising Spaces in Eighteenth Century Provincial England', in J. Benson and L. Ugolini (eds), *Cultures of Selling: Perspectives on Consumption and Society since 1700* (Aldershot: Ashgate, 2006), pp. 59–79.

Mui, H. C., and L. H. Mui, *Shops and Shopkeeping in Eighteenth Century England* (London: Routledge, 1989).

Nevett, T., 'Advertising and Editorial Integrity in the Nineteenth Century', in M. Harris and A. Lee (eds), *The Press in English Society from the Seventeenth to the Nineteenth Centuries* (London: Rutherford, 1986), pp. 149–67.

Norton, J. E., *Guide to the National and Provincial Directories of England and Wales* (London: Offices of the Royal Historical Society, 1984).

Ommer, R. E., and Turner, N. J., 'Informal Rural Economies in History', *Labour/Le Travail*, 53: Spring (2004), pp. 127–57.

Page, D., 'Commercial Directories and Market Towns', *Local Historian*, 11:2 (1974), pp. 85–8.

Page, W., and J. W. Willis-Bund, (eds), *The Victoria History of the County of Worcester* (Folkestone: Dawsons, 1971).

Palmer, R. E., 'The Funny Rigs of Good and Tender-hearted Masters in the Happy Town of Kidderminster. Anno 1828', *Transactions of the Worcestershire Archaeological Society*, 3 (1970–72), pp. 105–13.

—, 'Herefordshire Street Ballads', *Transactions of the Woolhope Naturalists Field Club*, 47:1 (1991), pp. 67–81.

Pantall, R., *George Jarvis (1704–1793) and his Notorious Charity* (Leominster: Orphans Press Ltd, 1993).

Pawson, E., *Transport and Economy: The Turnpike Roads of Eighteenth Century Britain* (London: Academic Press, 1977).

Payne, C., *Toil and Plenty, Images of the Agricultural Landscape in England 1780–1890* (London: Yale University Press, 1993).

Payne, S., *The Gurteens of Haverhill, Two Hundred Years of Suffolk Textiles* (Cambridge: Woodhead-Faulkner, 1984).

Perrot, P., *Fashioning the Bourgeoisie, A History of Clothing in the Nineteenth Century* (Chichester: Princeton University Press, 1994).

Pickering, P., 'Class without Words; Symbolic Communication in the Chartist Movement', *Past and Present*, 112 (1986), pp. 144–62.

Pitman, L., *Pigsties and Paradise, Lady Diarists and the Tour of Wales 1795–1860* (Llanrwst: Gwasg Carreg Gwalch, 2009).

Prochaska, F. K., *Women and Philanthropy in Nineteenth Century England* (Oxford: Clarendon, 1980).

Prown, J. D., *Art as Evidence, Writings on Art and Material Culture* (London: Yale University Press, 2001).

Raven, N., 'The Trade Directory: A Source for the Study of Early Nineteenth Century Urban Economies', *Business Archives, Sources and History*, 74 (1997), pp. 13–30.

Reay, B., *Microhistories: Demography, Society and Culture in Rural England, 1800–1939* (Cambridge: Cambridge University Press, 2002).

—, *Rural Englands* (Basingstoke: Palgrave Macmillan, 2004).

Reed, M., 'Gnawing it Out': A New Look at Economic Relations in Nineteenth Century Rural England', *Rural History*, 1:1 (1990), pp. 83–94.

Reilly, V., *The Official Illustrated History, The Paisley Pattern* (Glasgow: Richard Drew Publishing Ltd, Glasgow, 1987).

Ribeiro, A., *Dress and Morality* (London: Batsford, 1986).

—, 'Provision of Ready-Made and Second-Hand Clothing in the Eighteenth Century in England', in *Per Una Storia della Moda Pronta, Problemi e Richerchi, Atti del v Convegno Internazionale del CISST, Milano, 26–28 Febbraio 1990* (Florence: Edifir Edizioni, 1991), pp. 85–94.

Richards, A., *Bygone Bromsgrove: An Illustrated Story of the Town in Days Gone By* (Bromsgrove: Bromsgrove Society, 1996).

Richardson, C., 'Introduction', in C. Richardson (ed.), *Clothing Culture, 1350–1650* (Aldershot: Ashgate, 2004), pp. 1–25.

—, 'Havying nothing upon hym saving onely his sherte'. Event, Narrative and Material Culture in Early Modern England', in C. Richardson (ed.), *Clothing Culture, 1350–1650* (Aldershot: Ashgate, 2004), pp. 209–21.

Richmond, V., '"No Finery": The Dress of the Poor in Nineteenth Century England' (PhD dissertation, Goldsmiths, University of London, 2004).

—, '"Indiscriminate Liberality Subverts the Morals and Depraves the Habits of the Poor": A Contribution to the Debate on the Poor Law, Parish Clothing Relief and Clothing Societies in Early Nineteenth-Century England', *Textile History*, 40:1 (2009), pp. 51–69.

Riello, G., *A Foot in the Past, Consumers, Producers and Footwear in the Long Eighteenth Century* (Oxford: Oxford University Press, Pasold Research Fund, 2006).

Roberts, G., *The Shaping of Modern Hereford* (Almeley: Logaston, 2001).

Roth, C., *The Rise of the Provincial Jewry. The Early History of the Jewish Communities in the English Countryside, 1740–1840* (London: The Jewish Monthly, 1950).

Rothstein, N., *The Victoria and Albert Museum's Textile Collection, Woven Textile Design in Britain from 1750–1850* (London: Victoria and Albert Museum, 1994).

Rubin, G. R., 'The County Courts and the Tally Trade, 1846–1914', in G. R. Rubin and D. Sugarman (eds), *Law, Economy and Society, Essays in the History of English Law 1750–1914* (Abingdon: Professional Books, 1984), pp. 321–48.

Sanderson, E. C., *Women and Work in Eighteenth Century Edinburgh* (Basingstoke: Macmillan, Basingstoke, 1996).

Schmiechen, J. A., *Sweated Industries and Sweated Labor, The London Clothing Trades, 1860–1914* (London: Croom Helm, 1984).

Seidel, J. Z., 'Ready-to-Wear Clothing in Germany in the Sixteenth and Seventeenth Centuries: New Ready-Made Garments and Second-Hand Clothes Trade', in *Per Una Storia della Moda Pronta, Problemi e Richerchi, Atti del v Convegno Internazionale del CISST, Milano, 26–28 Febbraio 1990* (Florence: Edifir Edizioni, 1991), pp. 9–16.

Shakesheff, T., *Rural Conflict, Crime and Protest: Herefordshire 1800–1860* (Woodbridge: Boydell, 2003).

Shammas, C., *The Pre-Industrial Consumer in England and America* (Los Angeles, CA: Figueroa Press, 2008).

Sharpe, P., '"Cheapness and Economy": Manufacturing and Retailing Ready-made Clothing in London and Essex 1830–50', *Textile History*, 26:2 (1995), pp. 203–13.

—, 'The Bowels of Compation': A Labouring Family and the Law, *c.* 1790–1834', in T. Hitchcock, P. King and P. Sharpe (eds), *Chronicling Poverty, The Voices and Strategies of the English Poor, 1640–1840* (Basingstoke: Macmillan, 1997), pp. 87–108.

—, *Adapting to Capitalism, Working Women in the English Economy, 1700–1850* (Basingstoke: Macmillan, 2000).

Shaw, G., *British Directories as Sources in Historical Geography* (Norwich: Geo Abstracts, Historical Geography Research Series, Number 8, 1982).

Sleigh-Johnson, N., 'Aspects of the Tailoring Trade in the City of London in the Late Sixteenth and Earlier Seventeenth Centuries', *Costume*, 37 (2003), pp. 24–32.

Smart Martin, A., 'Ribbons of Desire: Gendered Stories in the World of Goods', in J. Styles and A. Vickery (eds), *Gender, Taste and Material Culture in Britain and North America, 1700–1830* (London: Yale University Press, 2007), pp. 179–200.

Smith, L. D., 'Industrial Organisation in the Kidderminster Carpet Trade, 1780–1850', *Textile History*, 15:1 (1984), pp. 75–100.

—, *Carpet Weavers and Carpet Makers. The Hand Loom Carpet Weavers of Kidderminster 1780–1850* (Middle Habberley, Kidderminster: Kenneth Tomkinson Ltd, 1986).

Snell, K. D. M., *Annals of the Labouring Poor, Social Change and Agrarian England 1660–1900* (Cambridge: Cambridge University Press, 1985).

Sokoll, T., 'Old Age in Poverty: The Record of Essex Pauper Letters 1780–1834', in T. Hitchcock, P. King and P. Sharpe (eds), *Chronicling Poverty, The Voices and Strategies of the English Poor, 1640–1840* (Basingstoke: Macmillan, 1997), pp. 127–54.

—, 'Negotiating a Living: Essex Pauper Letters from London 1800–1834', in L. Fontaine and J. Schlumbohm (eds), *Household Strategies for Survival 1600–2000: Fission, Faction and Cooperation* (Cambridge: Cambridge University Press, International Review of Social History supplement, 2000), pp. 19–46.

Sotheby's auction catalogue, *Important Costumes, Textiles and Fabric Swatch Books* (London: Sotheby's, 4 and 5 March 1998).

Spufford, M., *The Great Re-clothing of Rural England; Petty Chapmen and their Wares in the Seventeenth Century* (London: Hambledon, 1984).

Stobart, J., 'Leisure and Shopping in the Small Towns of Georgian England, A Regional Approach', *Journal of Urban History*, 31:4 (2005), pp. 479–503.

—, 'Clothes, Cabinets and Carriages: Second-hand Dealing in Eighteenth Century England', in B. Blondé, P. Stabel, I. Van Damme and J. Stobart (eds), *Buyers and Sellers: Retail Circuits and Practices in Medieval and Early Modern Europe* (Turnhout: Brepols, Studies in European Urban History, 2006), pp. 225–44.

—, *Spend Spend Spend! A History of Shopping* (Stroud: The History Press, 2008).

—, 'In and Out of Fashion? Advertising Novel and Second-hand Goods in Georgian England', in B. Blondé, N. Coquery, J. Stobart and I. Van Damme (eds), *Fashioning Old and New: Changing Consumer Preferences in Europe (Seventeenth-Nineteenth Centuries)* (Turnhout: Brepols, Studies in Urban History, 2009), pp. 133–44.

Stobart, J., and Hann, A., 'Retailing Revolution in the Eighteenth Century? Evidence from North-West England', *Business History*, 46:2 (2004), pp. 171–94.

Stobart, J., and Raven, N., 'Introduction: Industrialisation and Urbanisation in a Regional Context', in J. Stobart and N. Raven (eds), *Towns, Regions and Industries, Urban and Industrial Change in the Midlands c. 1700–1840* (Manchester: Manchester University Press, 2005), pp. 1–19.

Stobart, J., and Van Damme, I. (eds.), *Modernity and the Second-Hand Trade, European Consumption Cultures and Practices, 1700–1900* (London: Palgrave Macmillan, 2010).

Styles, J., 'Clothing the North; the Supply of Non-Elite Clothing in the Eighteenth Century North of England', *Textile History*, 25:2 (1994), pp. 139–66.

—, 'Dress in History: Reflections on a Contested Terrain', *Fashion Theory, The Journal of Dress, Body and Culture, Methodology Special Issue,* 2:4 (1998), pp. 383–9.

—, 'Product Innovation in Early Modern London', *Past and Present*, 168 (2000), pp. 124–69.

—, 'Involuntary Consumers? Servants and their Clothes in Eighteenth Century England', *Textile History*, 33:1 (2002), pp. 9–21.

—, 'Custom or Consumption? Plebeian Fashion in Eighteenth-Century England', in M. Berg and E. Eger (eds), *Luxury in the Eighteenth Century: Debates, Desires and Delectable Goods* (Basingstoke: Palgrave Macmillan, 2003), pp. 103–15.

—, *The Dress of the People. Everyday Fashion in Eighteenth-Century England* (London: Yale University Press, 2007).

Svendsen, L., *Fashion: A Philosophy* (London: Reaktion Books, 2006).

Sweetinburgh, S., 'Clothing the Naked in Late Medieval East Kent', in C. Richardson (ed.), *Clothing Culture, 1350–1650* (Aldershot: Ashgate, 2004), pp. 109–22.

Taylor, B., *Joshua Cristall (1768–1847), Exhibition, February-April 1975, Victoria & Albert Museum* (London: HMSO, 1975).

Taylor, J. S., *Poverty, Migration, and Settlement, Sojourners' Narratives* (Palo Alto, CA: The Society for the Promotion of Science and Scholarship, 1989).

Taylor, L., *The Study of Dress History* (Manchester: Manchester University Press, 2002).

Tebbutt, M., *Making Ends Meet, Pawnbroking and Working-Class Credit* (London: Methuen, 1984).

Thirsk, J., *Economic Policy and Projects, The Development of a Consumer Society in Early Modern England* (Oxford: Clarendon Press, 1978).

—, 'Popular Consumption and the Mass Market in the Sixteenth to Eighteenth Centuries', in *Material History Bulletin*, 31 (1990), pp. 51–8.

Ticknell, S., 'The Prevention of Shoplifting in Eighteenth-Century London', *Journal of Historical Research in Marketing*, 2:3 (2010), pp. 300–13.

Tisdall, J., *Joshua Cristall 1768–1847: In Search of Arcadia* (Hereford: Lapridge Publications, 1996).

—, *The Settlement of Coppett Hill, The Story of a Herefordshire Common* (Goodrich: The Friends of Coppett Hill, 1998).

Tomkins, A., *The Experience of Urban Poverty, 1723–82, Parish, Charity and Credit* (Manchester: Manchester University Press, 2007).

Toplis, A., 'The Non-Elite Consumer and 'Wearing Apparel' in Herefordshire and Worcestershire, 1800–1850' (PhD dissertation, University of Wolverhampton, 2008).

—, 'Ready-Made Clothing Advertisements in Two Provincial Newspapers, 1800–1850', *International Journal of Regional and Local Studies*, Series 2, 5:1 (2009), pp. 85–103.

—, 'The Manufacture and Provision of Rural Garments, 1800–1850: a Case Study of Herefordshire and Worcestershire', *Textile History*, 40:2 (2009), pp. 152–69.

—, 'A Stolen Garment or a Reasonable Purchase? The Male Consumer and the Illicit Second-Hand Clothing Market in the First Half of the Nineteenth Century', in J. Stobart and I. Van Damme (eds), *Modernity and the Second-Hand Trade, European Consumption Cultures and Practices, 1700–1900* (London: Palgrave Macmillan, 2010), pp. 57–72.

Tozer, J., and Levitt, S., *Fabric of Society, A Century of People and their Clothes, 1770–1870* (Carno: Laura Ashley, 1983).

Trentmann, F., 'Beyond Consumerism: New Historical Perspectives on Consumption', *Journal of Contemporary History*, 39:3 (2004), pp. 373–401.

Van Damme, I., 'The Lure of the New: Urban Retailing in the Surroundings of Antwerp (Late Seventeenth – Early Eighteenth Centuries)', in B. Blondé, N. Coquery, J. Stobart and I.

Van Damme (eds), *Fashioning Old and New: Changing Consumer Preferences in Europe (Seventeenth-Nineteenth Centuries)*, (Turnhout: Brepols, Studies in Urban History, 1100–1800, 18, 2009), pp. 97–120.

Walsh, C., 'Shop Design and the Display of Goods in Eighteenth-Century London', in J. Benson and G. Shaw (eds), *The Retailing Industry Volume 1, Perspectives and the Early Modern Period* (London: IB Tauris, 1999), pp. 361–88.

—, 'Shops, Shopping and the Art of Decision Making in Eighteenth Century England', in J. Styles and A. Vickery (eds), *Gender, Taste and Material Culture in Britain and North America, 1700–1830* (London: Yale University Press, 2007), pp. 151–77.

Westerfield, R. B., *Middlemen in English Business Particularly Between 1660–1760* (New Haven: Yale University Press, 1915, reprint Newton Abbot: David and Charles, 1968).

Whitlock, T. C., *Crime, Gender and Consumer Culture in Nineteenth Century England* (Aldershot: Ashgate, 2005).

Williams, S., 'Earnings, Poor Relief and the Economy of Makeshifts: Bedfordshire in the Early Years of the New Poor Law', *Rural History*, 16:1 (2005), pp. 21–52.

Winstanley, M. J., *The Shopkeeper's World, 1830–1914* (Manchester: Manchester University Press, 1983).

Worth, R., 'Rural Working-Class Dress, 1850–1900: A Peculiarly English Tradition?', in C. Breward, B. Conekin and C. Cox (eds), *The Englishness of English Dress* (Oxford: Berg, 2002), pp. 97–112.

—, 'Developing a Method for the Study of the Clothing of the 'Poor'; Some Themes in the Visual Representation of Rural Working-Class Dress, 1850–1900', *Textile History*, 40:1 (2009), pp. 70–96.

Zakim, M., 'Sartorial Ideologies: From Homespun to Ready-Made', *American History Review*, 106:5 (2001), pp. 1553–86.

—, *Ready-Made Democracy, A History of Men's Dress in the American Republic, 1760–1860* (London: University of Chicago Press, 2003).

INDEX

For Product Safety Concerns and Information please contact our EU
representative GPSR@taylorandfrancis.com
Taylor & Francis Verlag GmbH, Kaufingerstraße 24, 80331 München, Germany

www.ingramcontent.com/pod-product-compliance
Ingram Content Group UK Ltd.
Pitfield, Milton Keynes, MK11 3LW, UK
UKHW021615240425
457818UK00018B/582